Devils and Realist
vol.12

story by Madoka Takadono
art by Utako Yukihiro

SEVEN SEAS ENTERTAINMENT PRESENTS

Devils and Realist

art by UTAKO YUKIHIRO / story by MADOKA TAKADONO   VOLUME 12

TRANSLATION
Jocelyne Allen

COPY EDITING
Danielle King

LETTERING AND RETOUCH
Roland Amago
Bambi Eloriaga-Amago

COVER DESIGN
Nicky Lim

ASSISTANT EDITOR
Jenn Grunigen

PRODUCTION ASSISTANT
CK Russell

PRODUCTION MANAGER
Lissa Pattillo

EDITOR-IN-CHIEF
Adam Arnold

PUBLISHER
Jason DeAngelis

MAKAI OUJI: DEVILS AND REALIST VOL. 12
© Utako Yukihiro/Madoka Takadono 2016
First published in Japan in 2016 by ICHIJINSHA Inc., Tokyo.
English translation rights arranged with ICHIJINSHA Inc., Tokyo, Japan.

Seven Seas books may be purchased in bulk for promotional, educational, or business use. Please contact your local bookseller or the Macmillan Corporate and Premium Sales Department at 1-800-221-7945, extension 5442, or by e-mail at MacmillanSpecialMarkets@macmillan.com.

Seven Seas and the Seven Seas logo are trademarks of Seven Seas Entertainment, LLC. All rights reserved.

ISBN: 978-1-626924-50-5

Printed in Canada

First Printing: April 2017

10 9 8 7 6 5 4 3 2 1

FOLLOW US ONLINE: www.gomanga.com

READING DIRECTIONS

This book reads from *right to left*, Japanese style. If this is your first time reading manga, you start reading from the top right panel on each page and take it from there. If you get lost, just follow the numbered diagram here. It may seem backwards at first, but you'll get the hang of it! Have fun!!

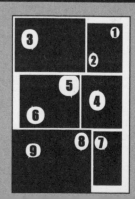

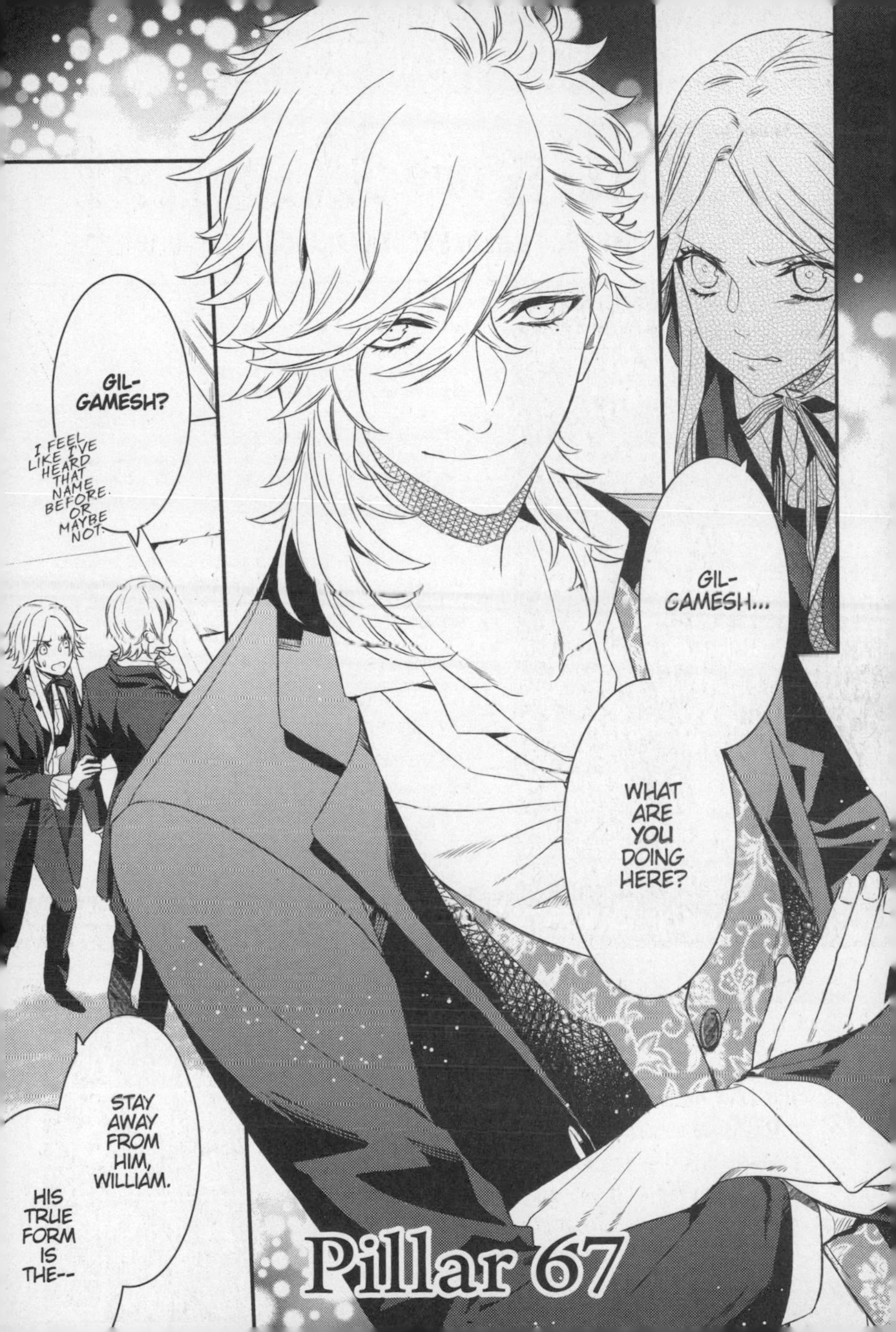
GIL-GAMESH...
WHAT ARE YOU DOING HERE?
GIL-GAMESH?
I FEEL LIKE I'VE HEARD THAT NAME BEFORE. OR MAYBE NOT.
STAY AWAY FROM HIM, WILLIAM.
HIS TRUE FORM IS THE--
Pillar 67

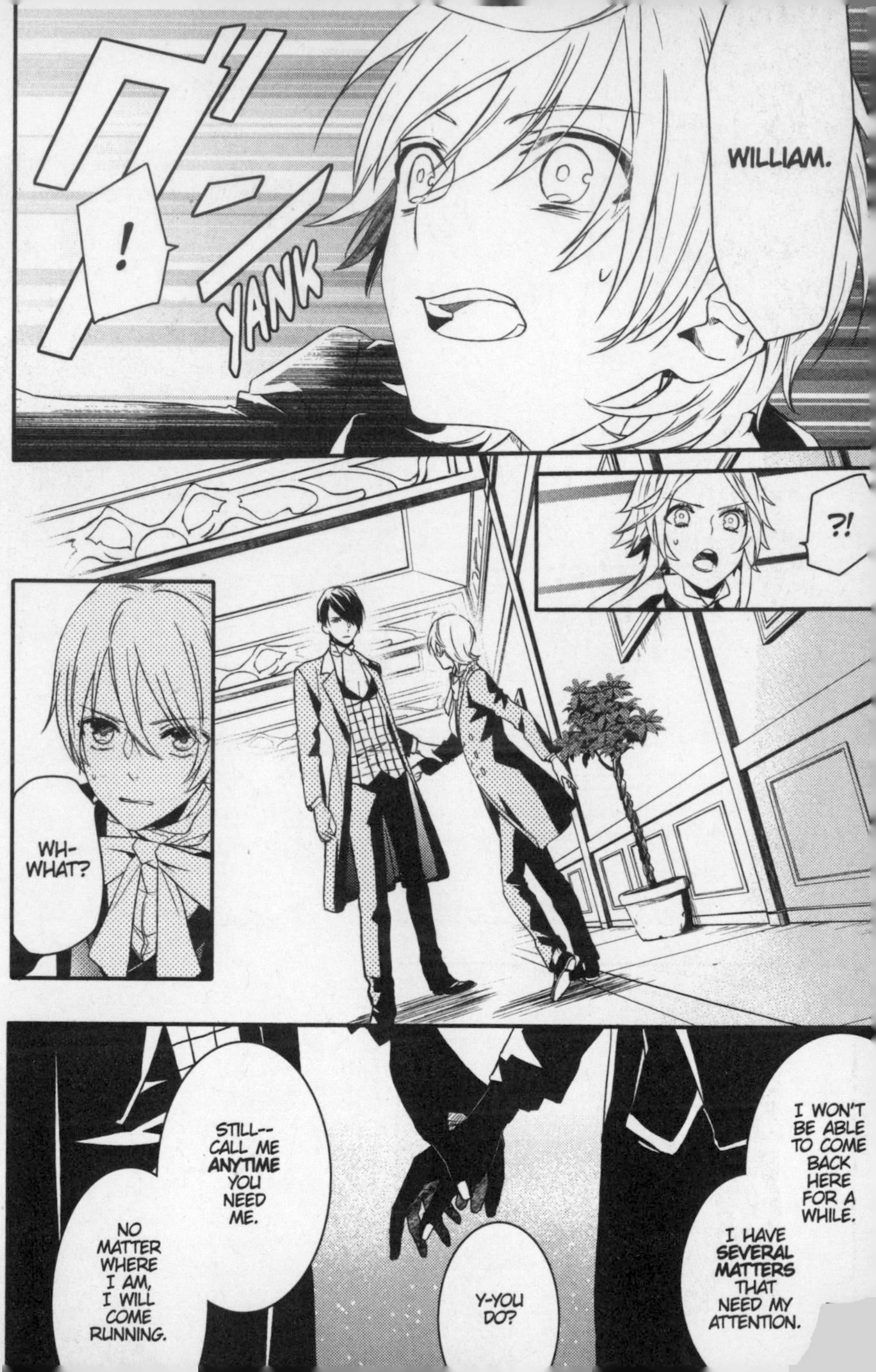
WILLIAM.
YANK
!
?!
WH- WHAT?
I WON'T BE ABLE TO COME BACK HERE FOR A WHILE.
I HAVE SEVERAL MATTERS THAT NEED MY ATTENTION.
Y-YOU DO?
STILL-- CALL ME ANYTIME YOU NEED ME.
NO MATTER WHERE I AM, I WILL COME RUNNING.

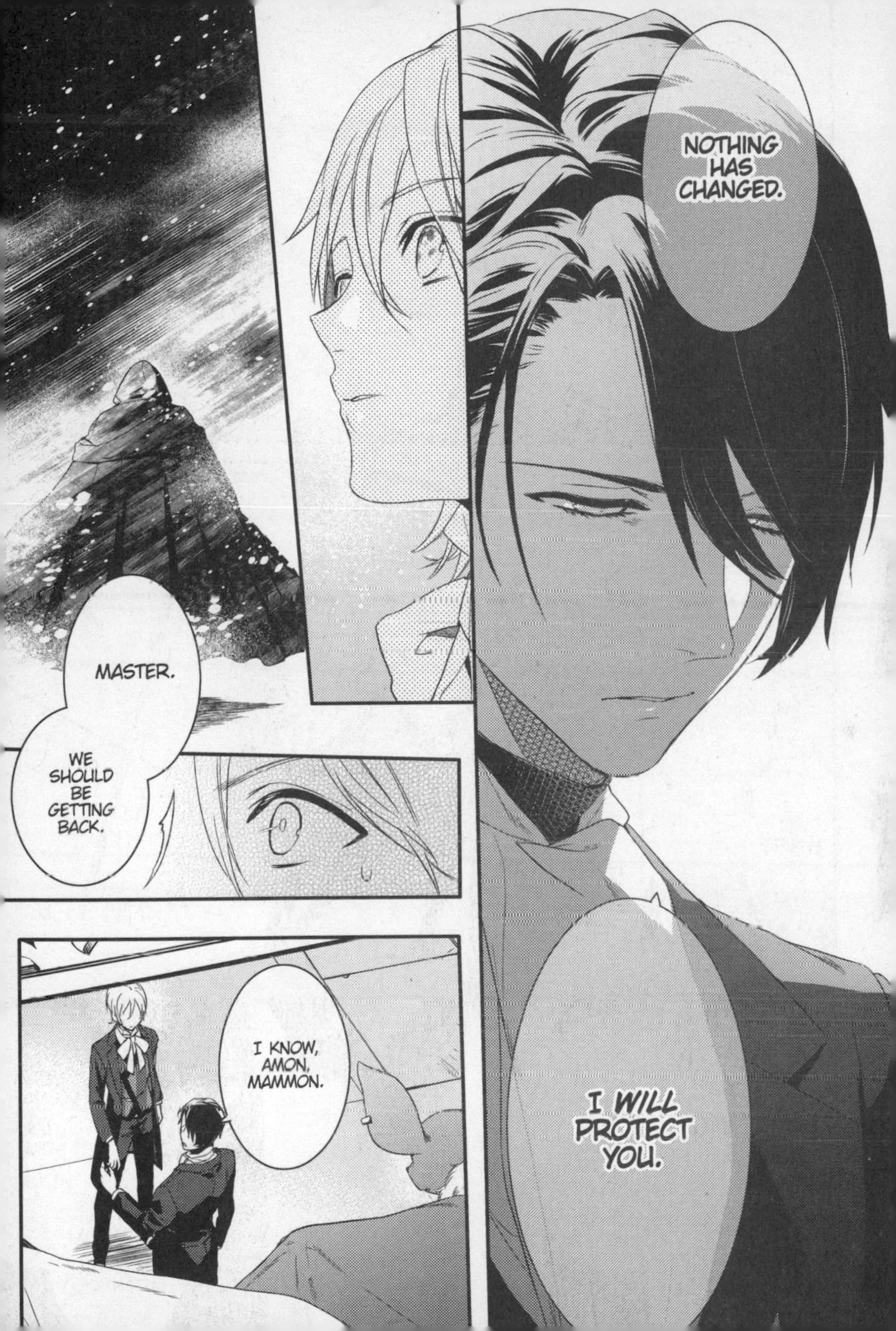
NOTHING HAS CHANGED.
I WILL PROTECT YOU.
MASTER.
WE SHOULD BE GETTING BACK.
I KNOW, AMON, MAMMON.

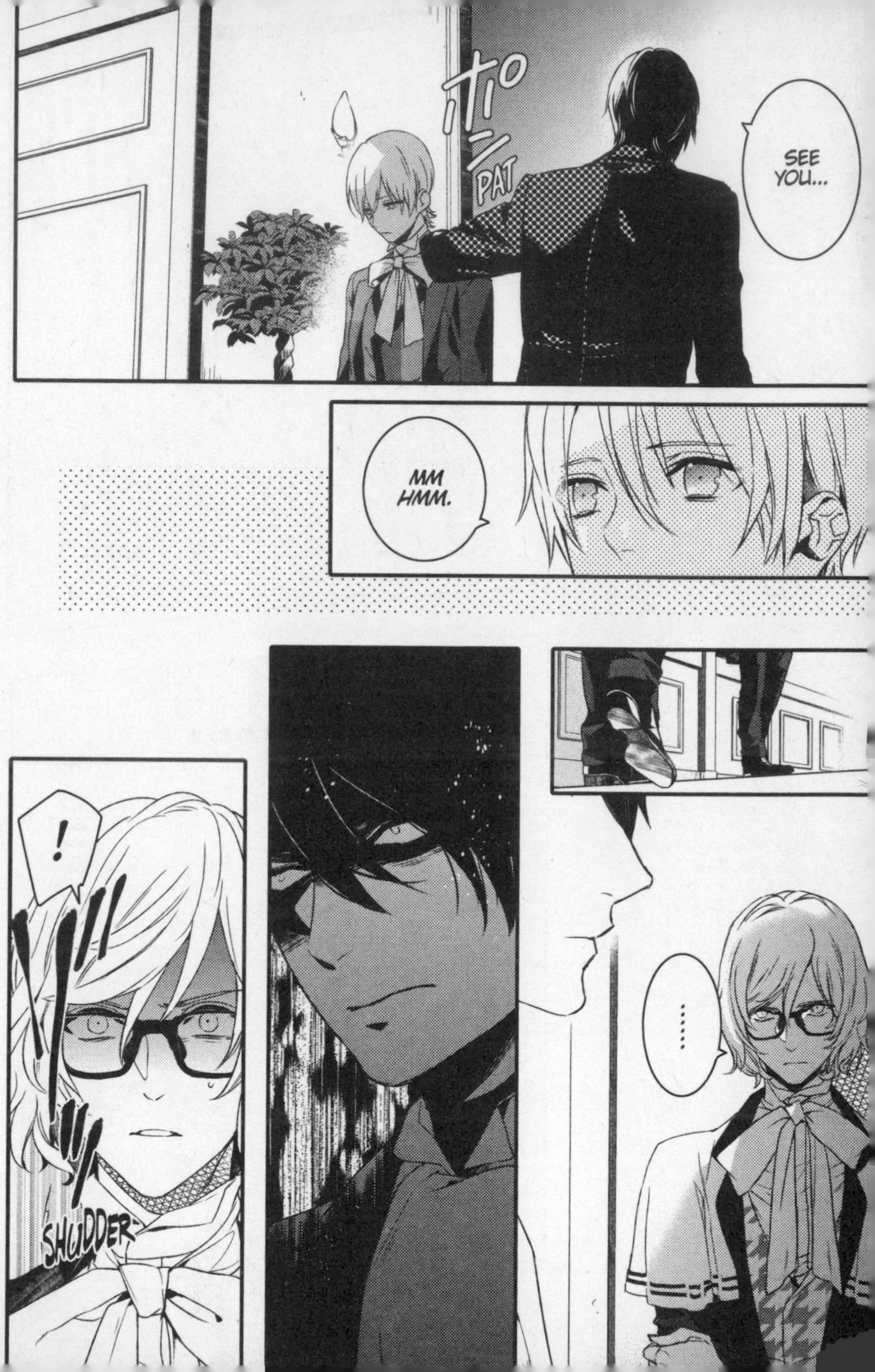
SEE YOU...
ポン
PAT
MM HMM.
......
!
SHUDDER

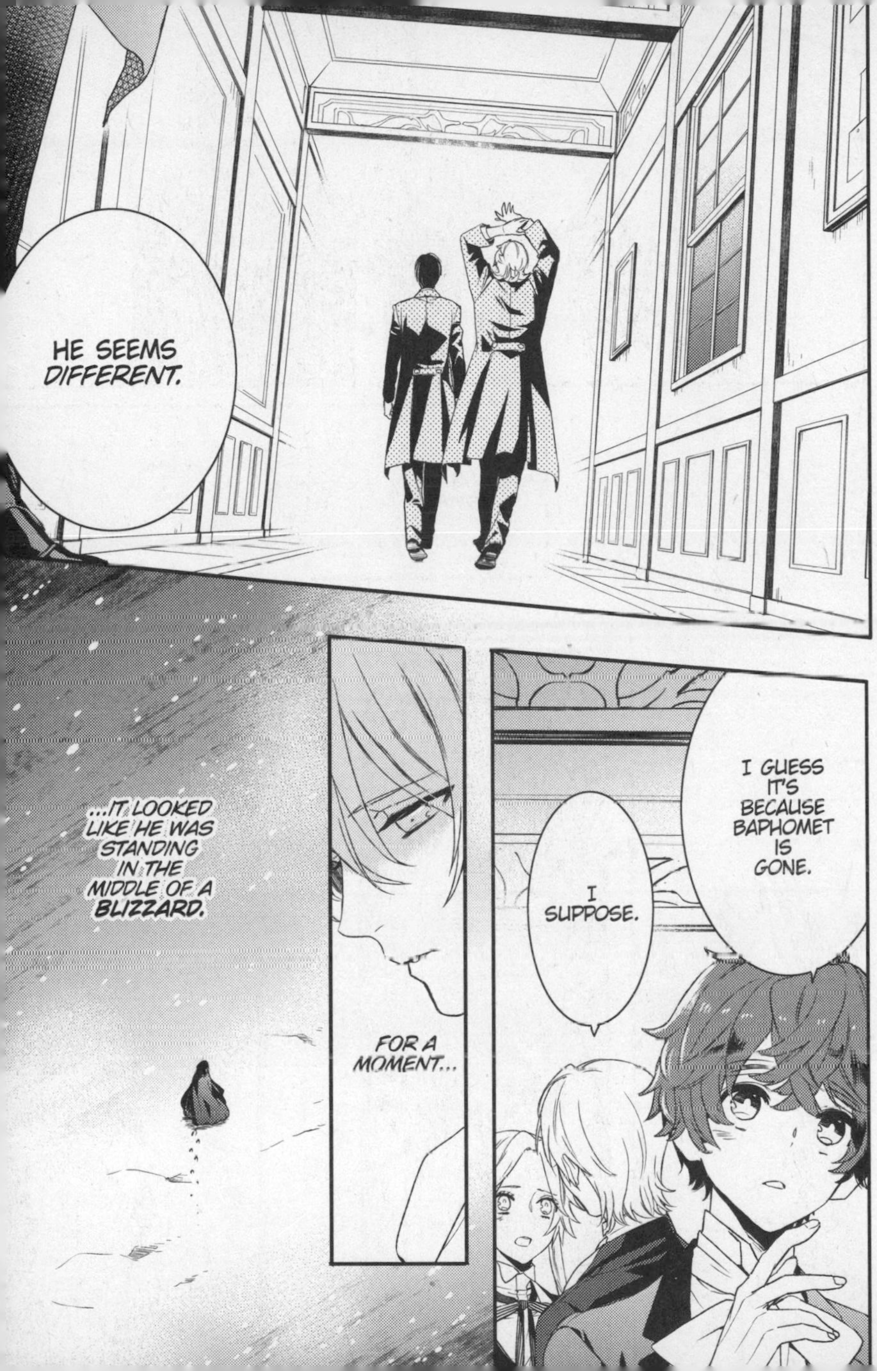
HE SEEMS DIFFERENT.
I GUESS IT'S BECAUSE BAPHOMET IS GONE.
I SUPPOSE.
FOR A MOMENT...
...IT LOOKED LIKE HE WAS STANDING IN THE MIDDLE OF A BLIZZARD.

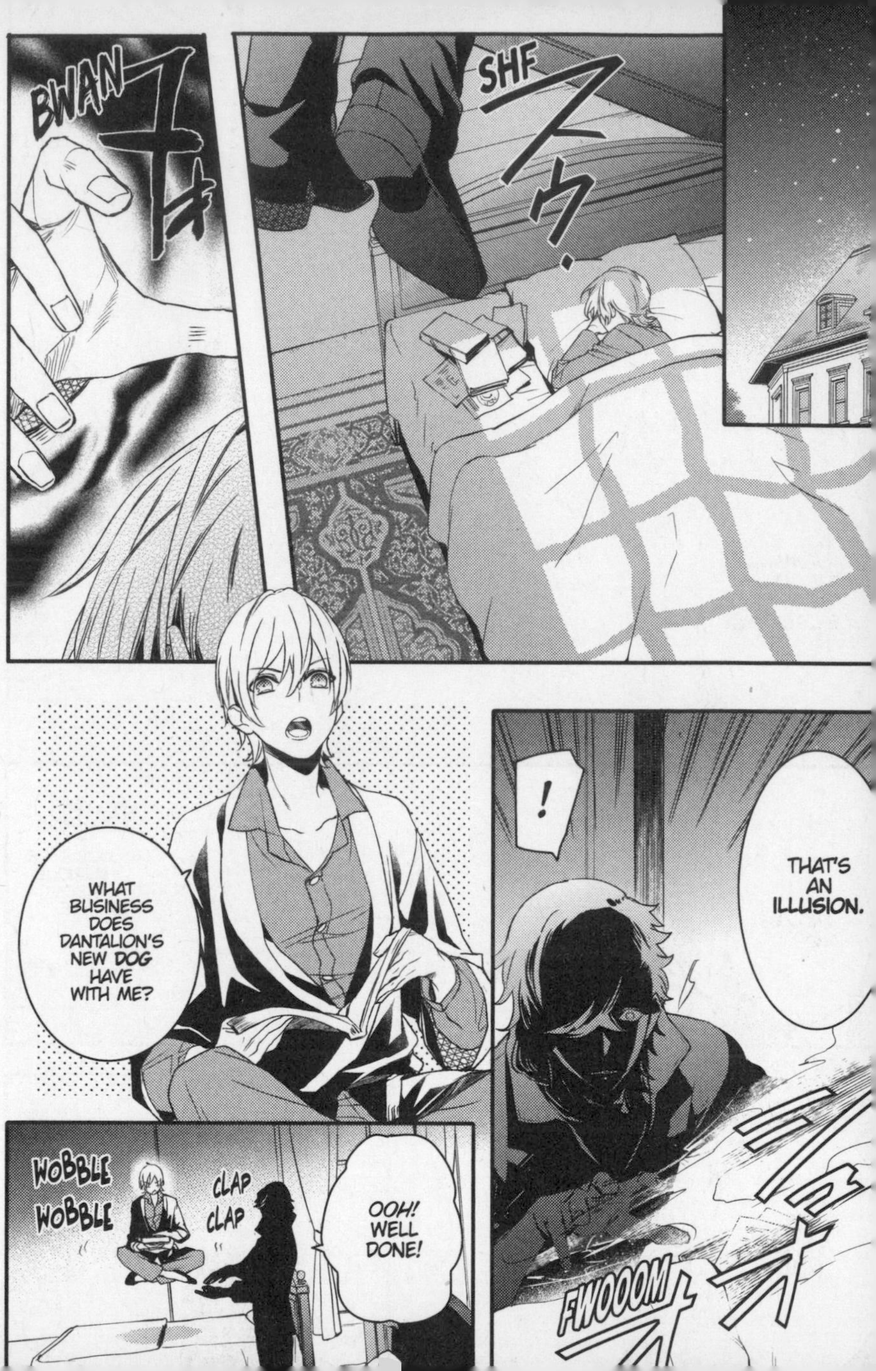
SHF
BWAN
!
THAT'S AN ILLUSION.
FWOOOM
WHAT BUSINESS DOES DANTALION'S NEW DOG HAVE WITH ME?
OOH! WELL DONE!
CLAP CLAP
WOBBLE WOBBLE

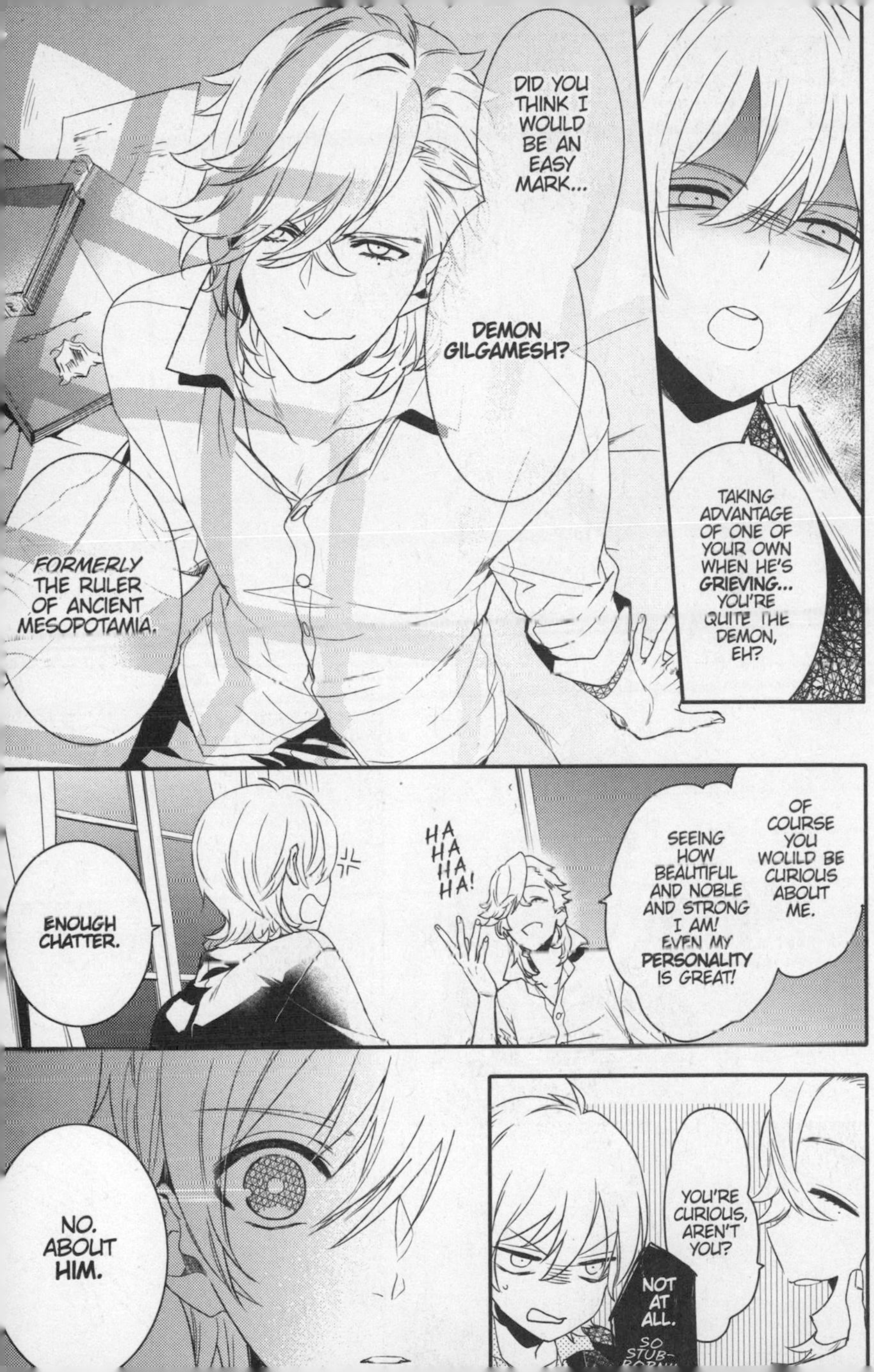
DID YOU THINK I WOULD BE AN EASY MARK...
DEMON GILGAMESH?
TAKING ADVANTAGE OF ONE OF YOUR OWN WHEN HE'S **GRIEVING**... YOU'RE QUITE THE DEMON, EH?
FORMERLY THE RULER OF ANCIENT MESOPOTAMIA.
OF COURSE YOU WOULD BE CURIOUS ABOUT ME.
SEEING HOW BEAUTIFUL AND NOBLE AND STRONG I AM! EVEN MY **PERSONALITY** IS GREAT!
HA HA HA HA!
ENOUGH CHATTER.
YOU'RE CURIOUS, AREN'T YOU?
NOT AT ALL.
SO STUB-
NO. ABOUT HIM.

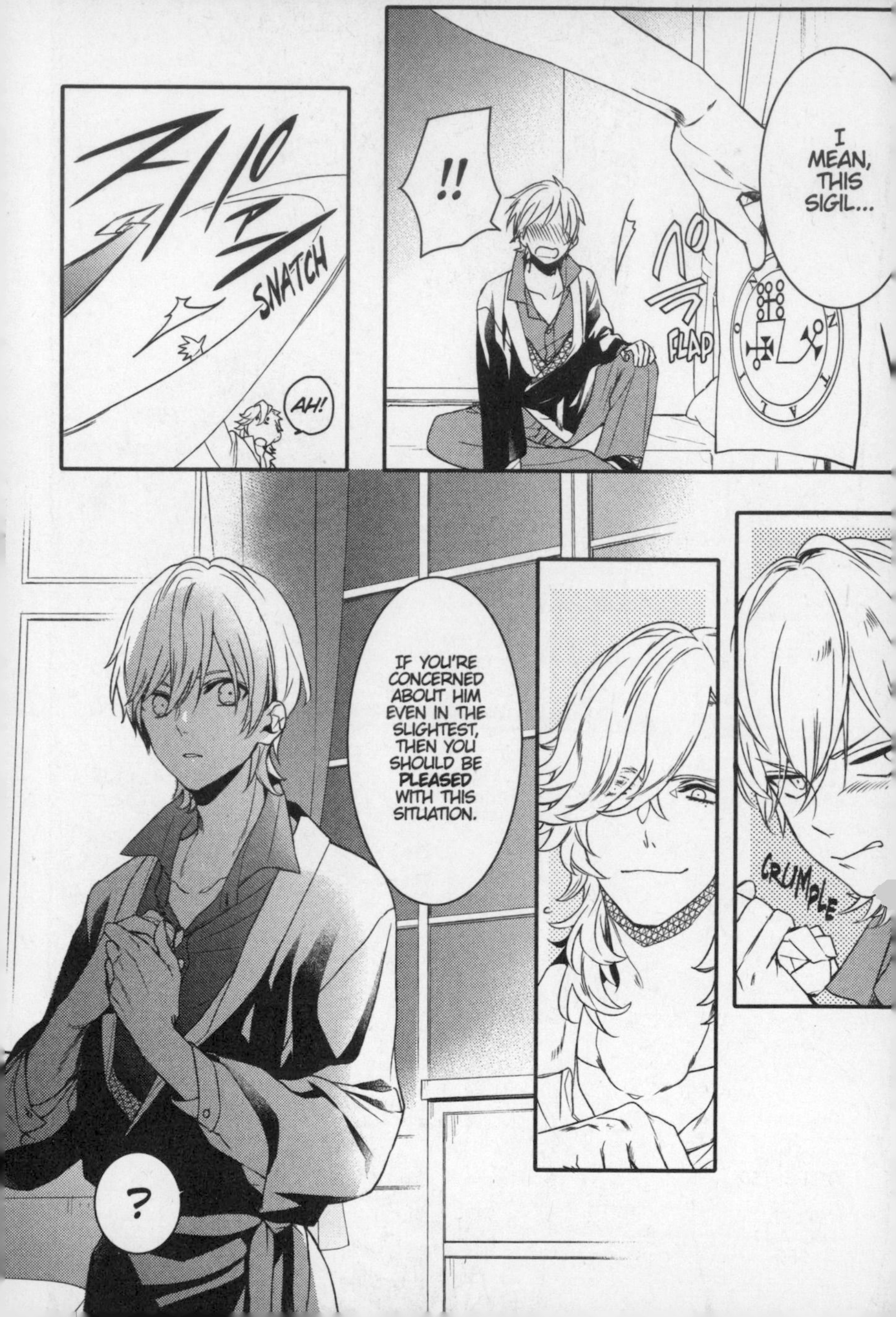
I MEAN, THIS SIGIL...
!!
FLAP
SNATCH
AH!
CRUMPLE
IF YOU'RE CONCERNED ABOUT HIM EVEN IN THE SLIGHTEST, THEN YOU SHOULD BE **PLEASED** WITH THIS SITUATION.
?

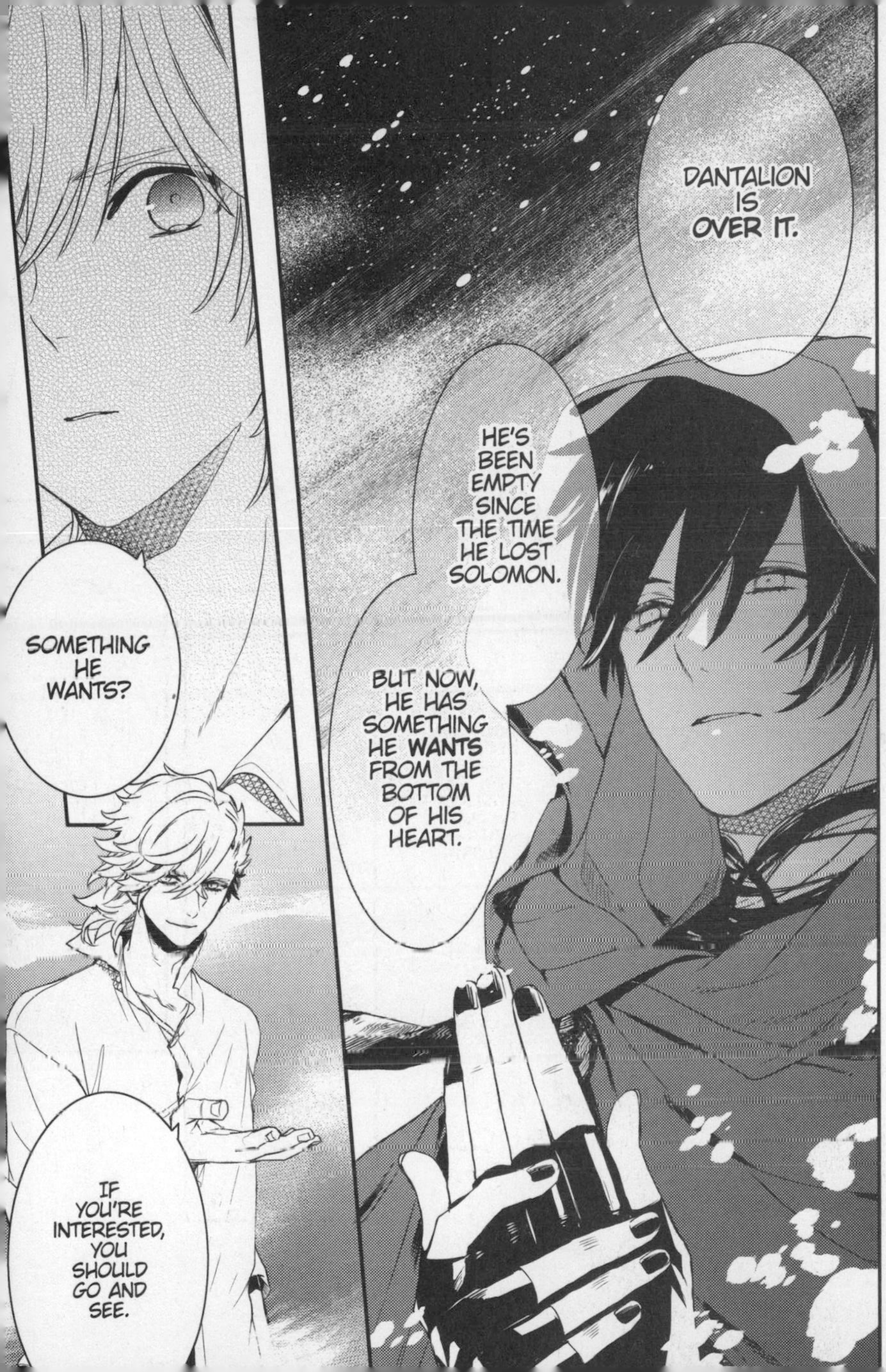
DANTALION IS OVER IT.
HE'S BEEN EMPTY SINCE THE TIME HE LOST SOLOMON.
BUT NOW, HE HAS SOMETHING HE WANTS FROM THE BOTTOM OF HIS HEART.
SOMETHING HE WANTS?
IF YOU'RE INTERESTED, YOU SHOULD GO AND SEE.

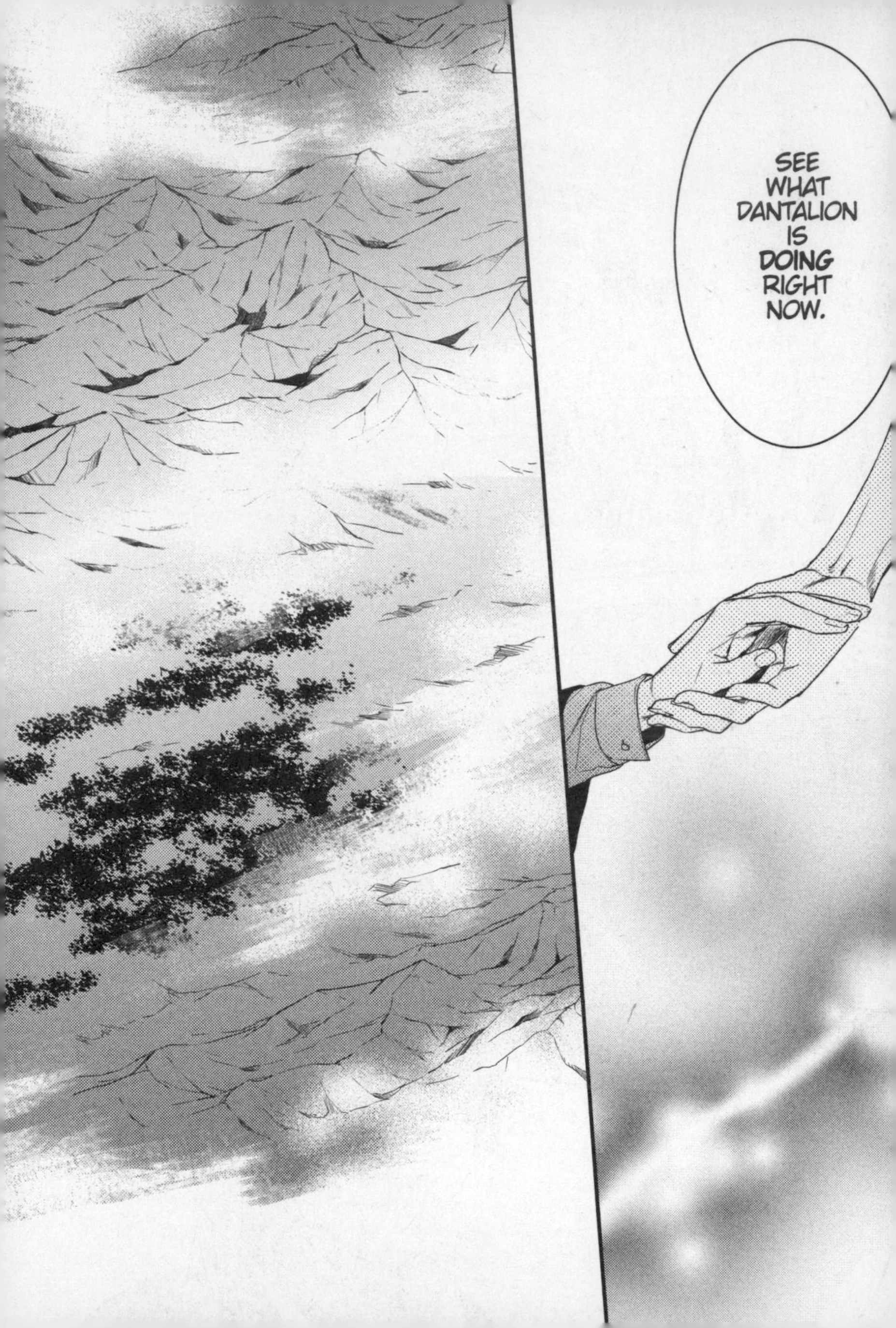
SEE WHAT DANTALION IS DOING RIGHT NOW.

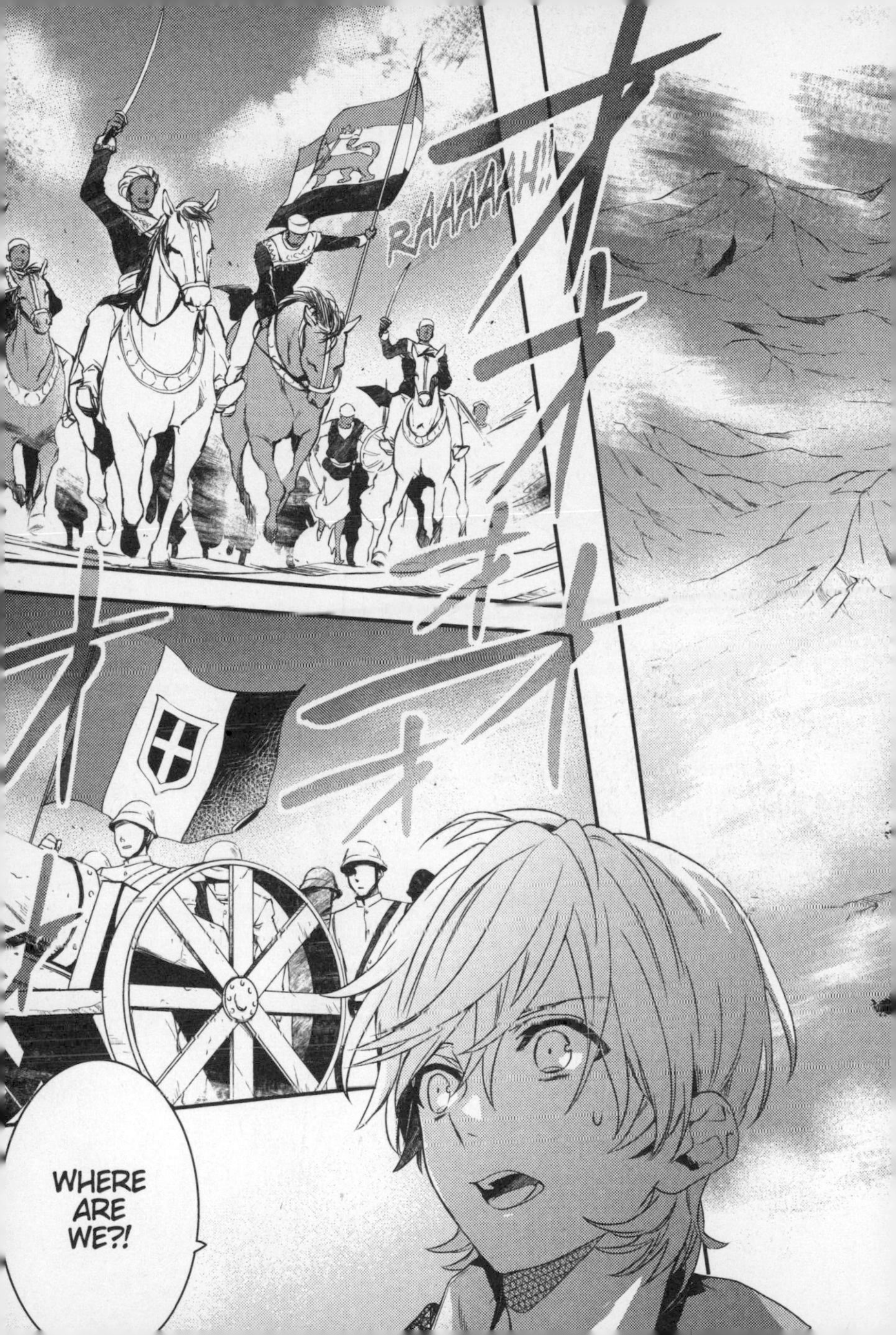
RAAAAAH!!
WHERE ARE WE?!

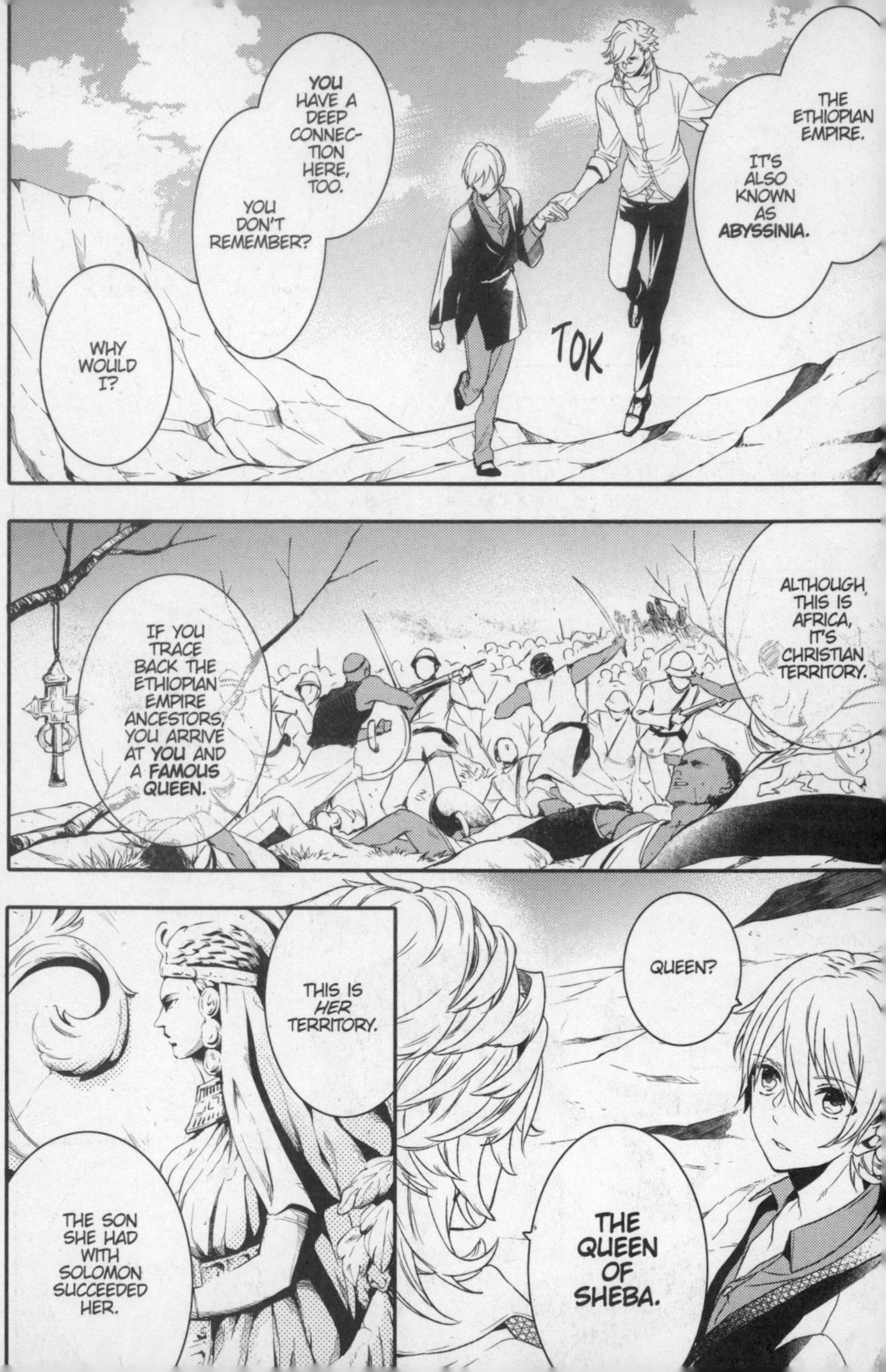
THE ETHIOPIAN EMPIRE.
IT'S ALSO KNOWN AS ABYSSINIA.
YOU HAVE A DEEP CONNECTION HERE, TOO.
YOU DON'T REMEMBER?
TOK
WHY WOULD I?
ALTHOUGH THIS IS AFRICA, IT'S CHRISTIAN TERRITORY.
IF YOU TRACE BACK THE ETHIOPIAN EMPIRE ANCESTORS, YOU ARRIVE AT YOU AND A FAMOUS QUEEN.
QUEEN?
THE QUEEN OF SHEBA.
THIS IS *HER* TERRITORY.
THE SON SHE HAD WITH SOLOMON SUCCEEDED HER.

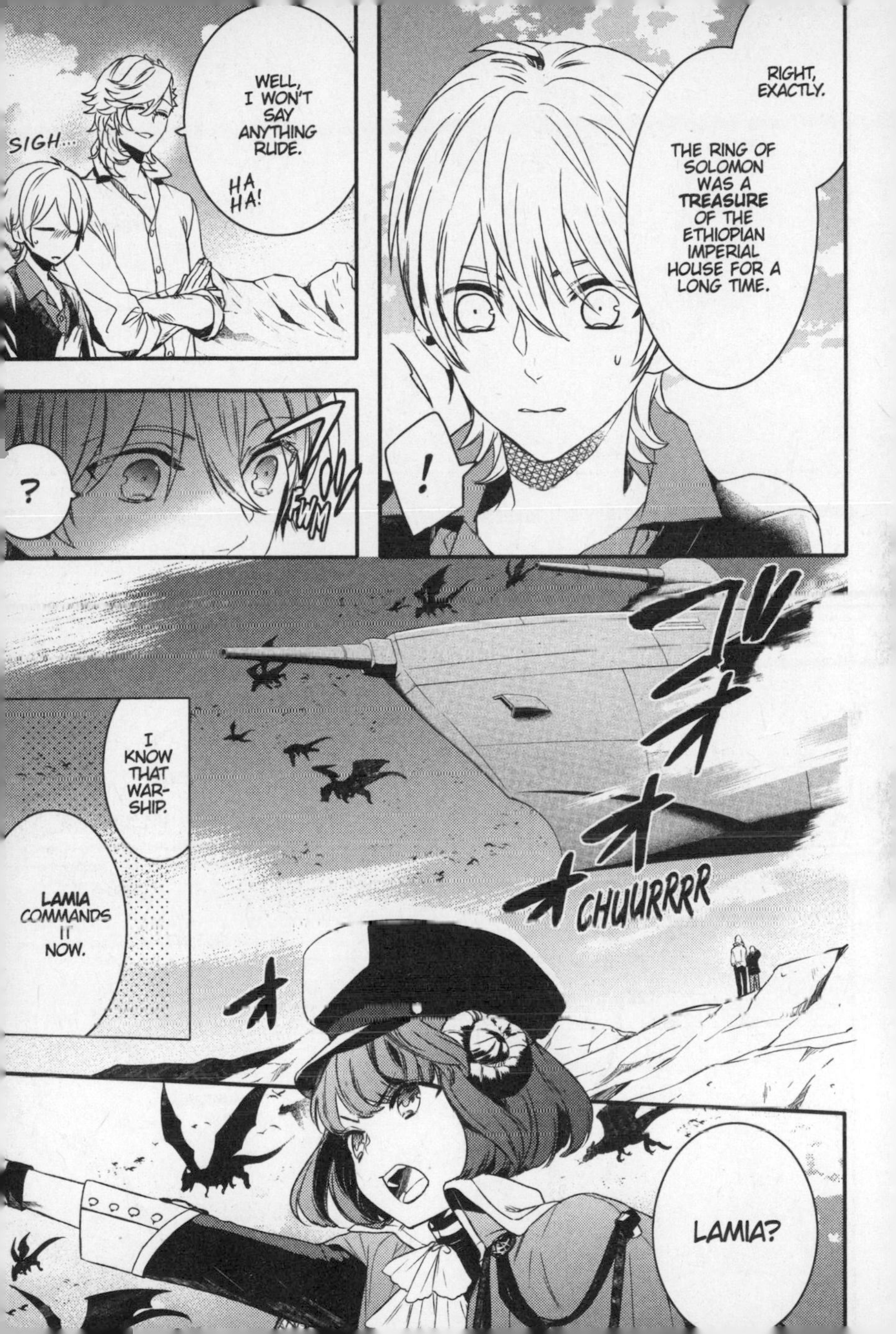
RIGHT, EXACTLY.
THE RING OF SOLOMON WAS A TREASURE OF THE ETHIOPIAN IMPERIAL HOUSE FOR A LONG TIME.
!
WELL, I WON'T SAY ANYTHING RUDE.
HA HA!
SIGH...
FWM
?
CHUURRRR
I KNOW THAT WAR-SHIP.
LAMIA COMMANDS IT NOW.
LAMIA?

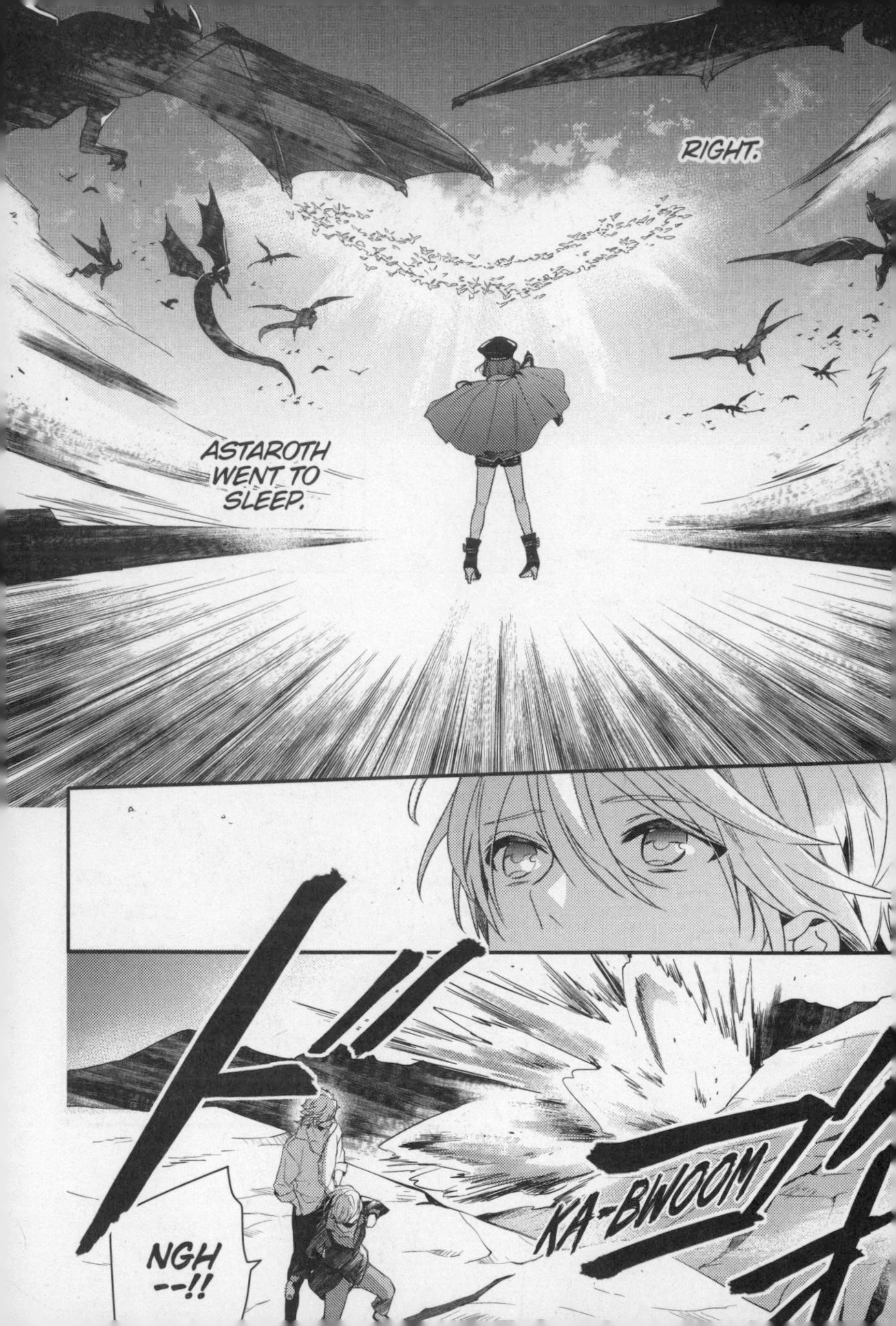
RIGHT.
ASTAROTH WENT TO SLEEP.
KA-BWOOM
NGH--!!

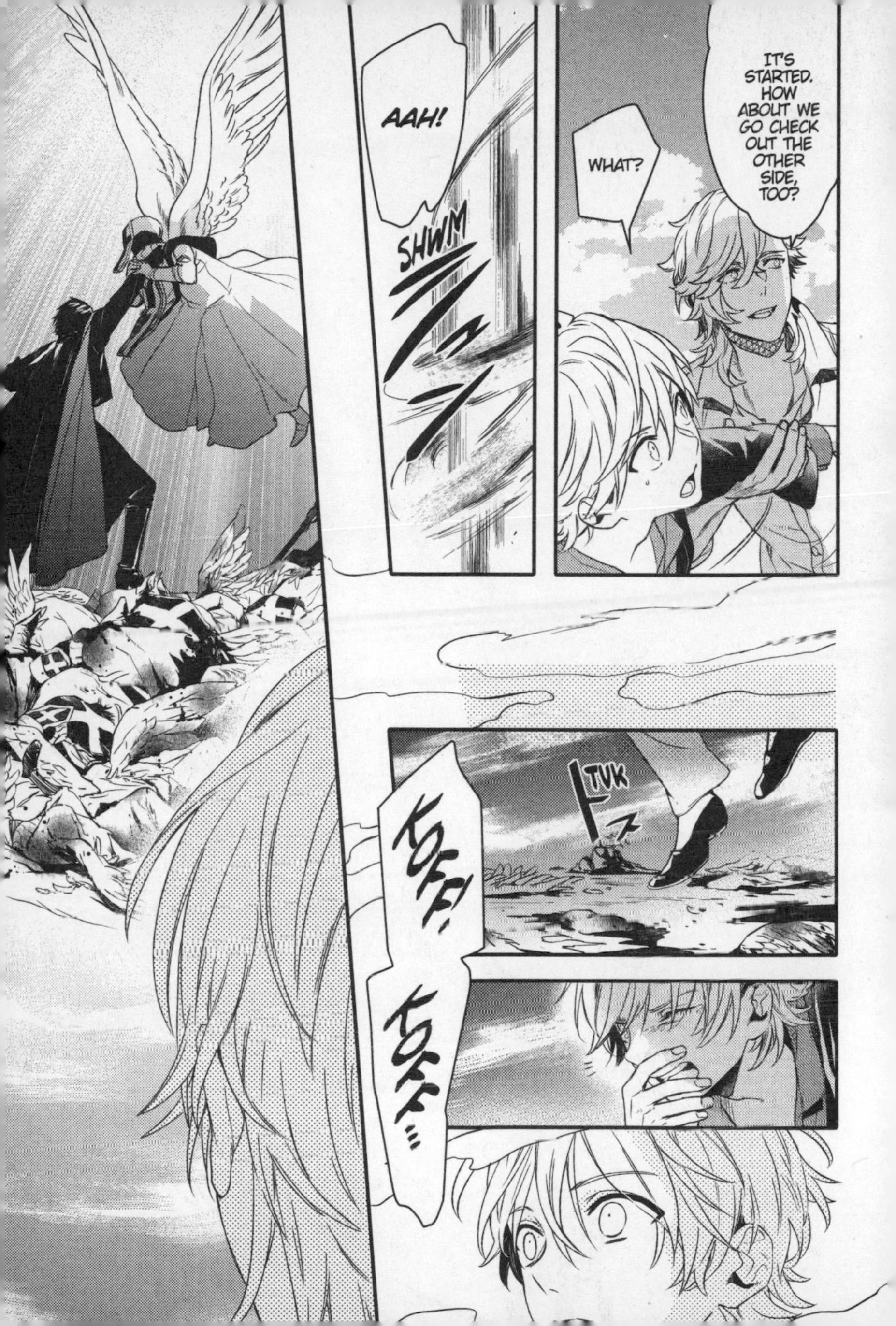
IT'S STARTED. HOW ABOUT WE GO CHECK OUT THE OTHER SIDE, TOO?
WHAT?
AAH!
SHWM
TUK
KOFF! KOFF...

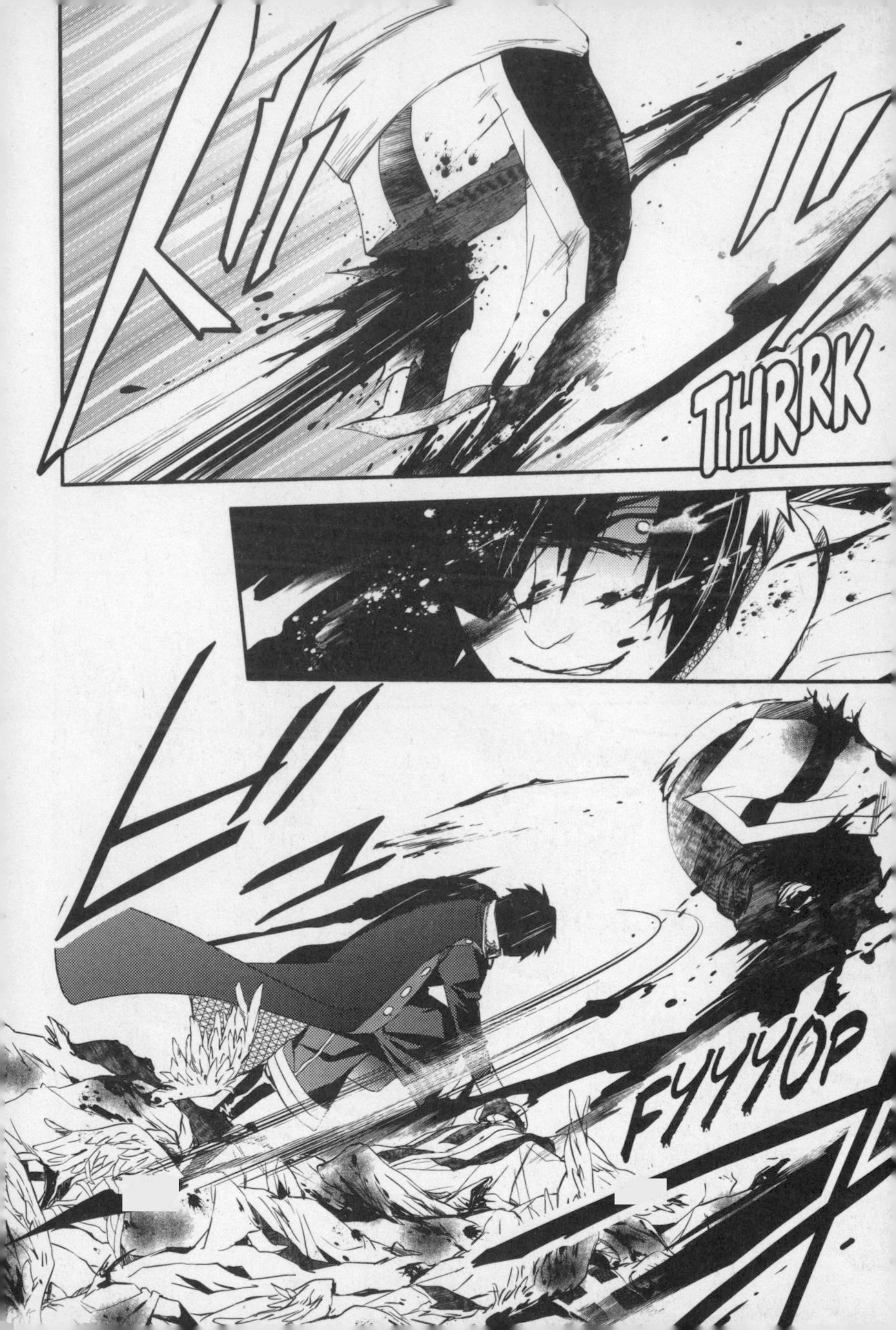
THRRK
FYYYOP

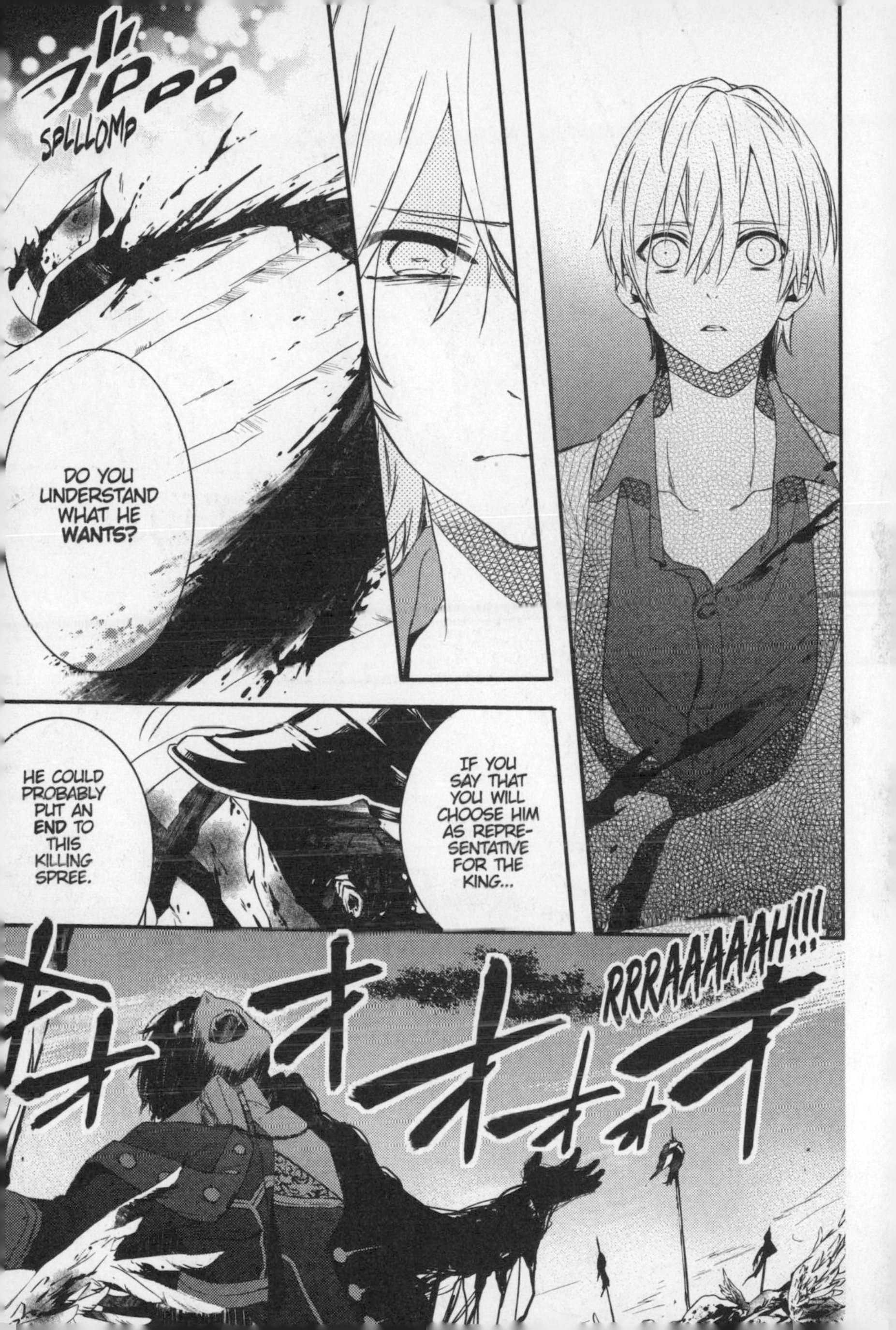
SPLLLOMP
DO YOU UNDERSTAND WHAT HE WANTS?
IF YOU SAY THAT YOU WILL CHOOSE HIM AS REPRE-SENTATIVE FOR THE KING...
HE COULD PROBABLY PUT AN END TO THIS KILLING SPREE.
RRRAAAAAH!!!

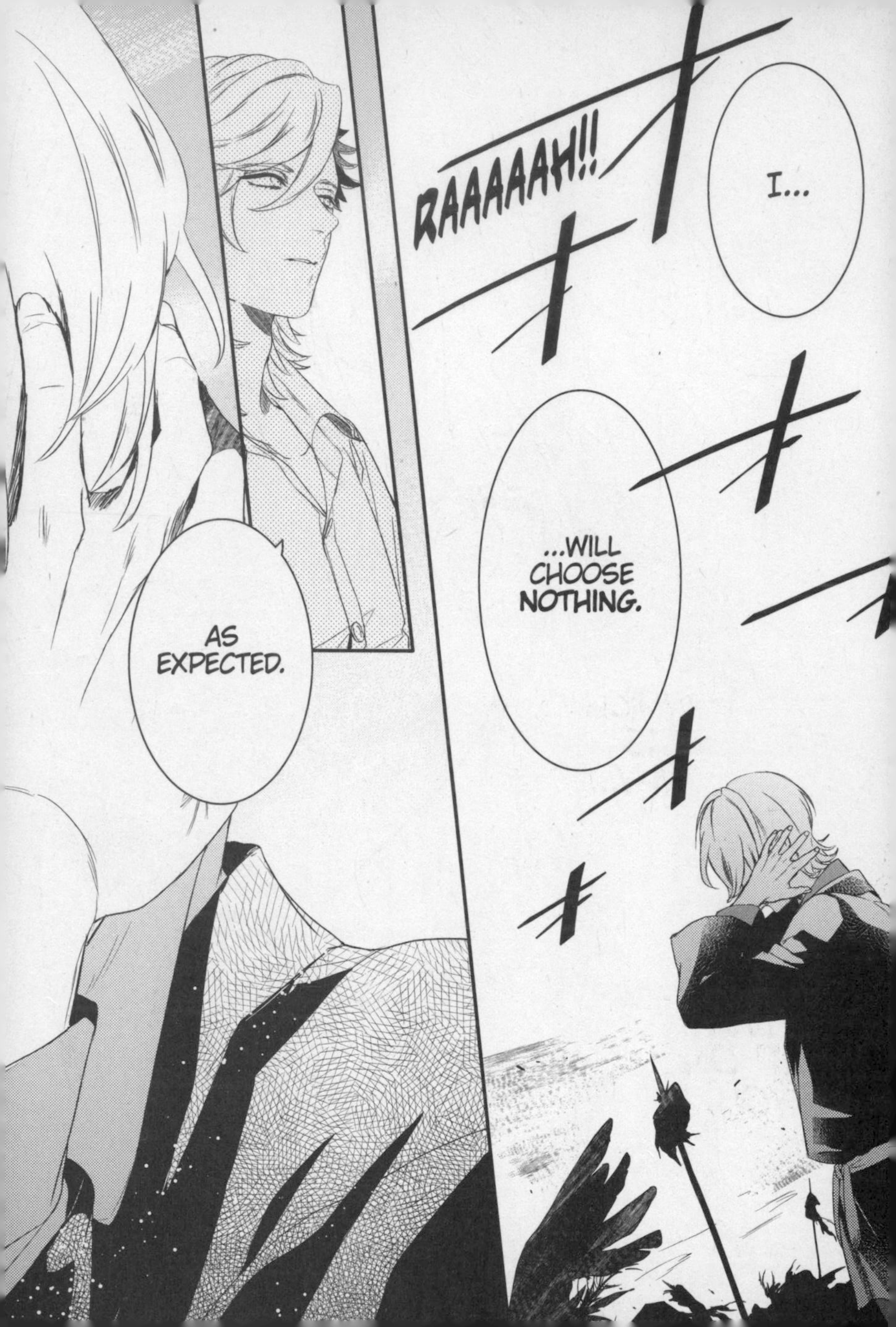
I...
RAAAAAH!!
...WILL CHOOSE NOTHING.
AS EXPECTED.

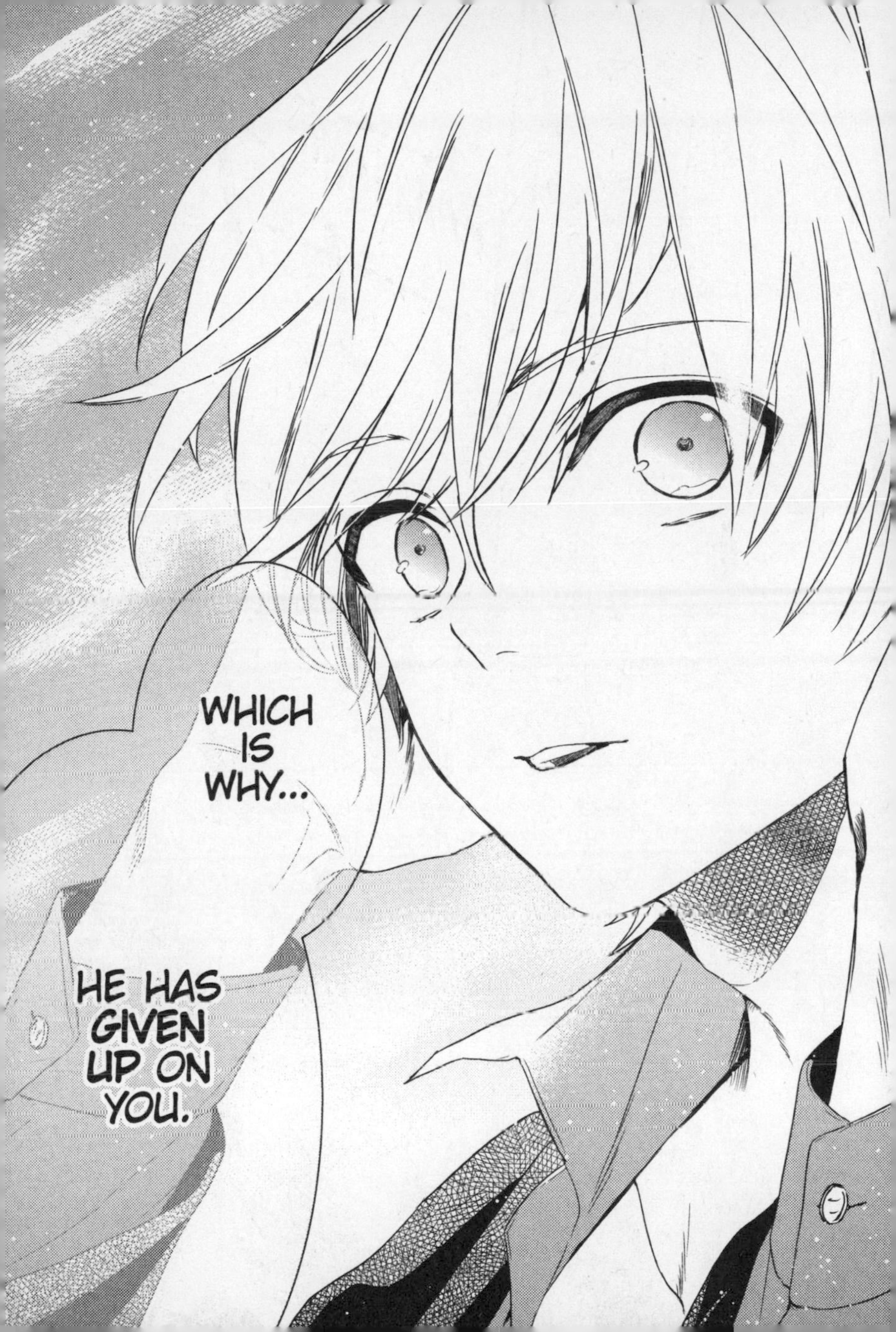
WHICH IS WHY...
HE HAS GIVEN UP ON YOU.

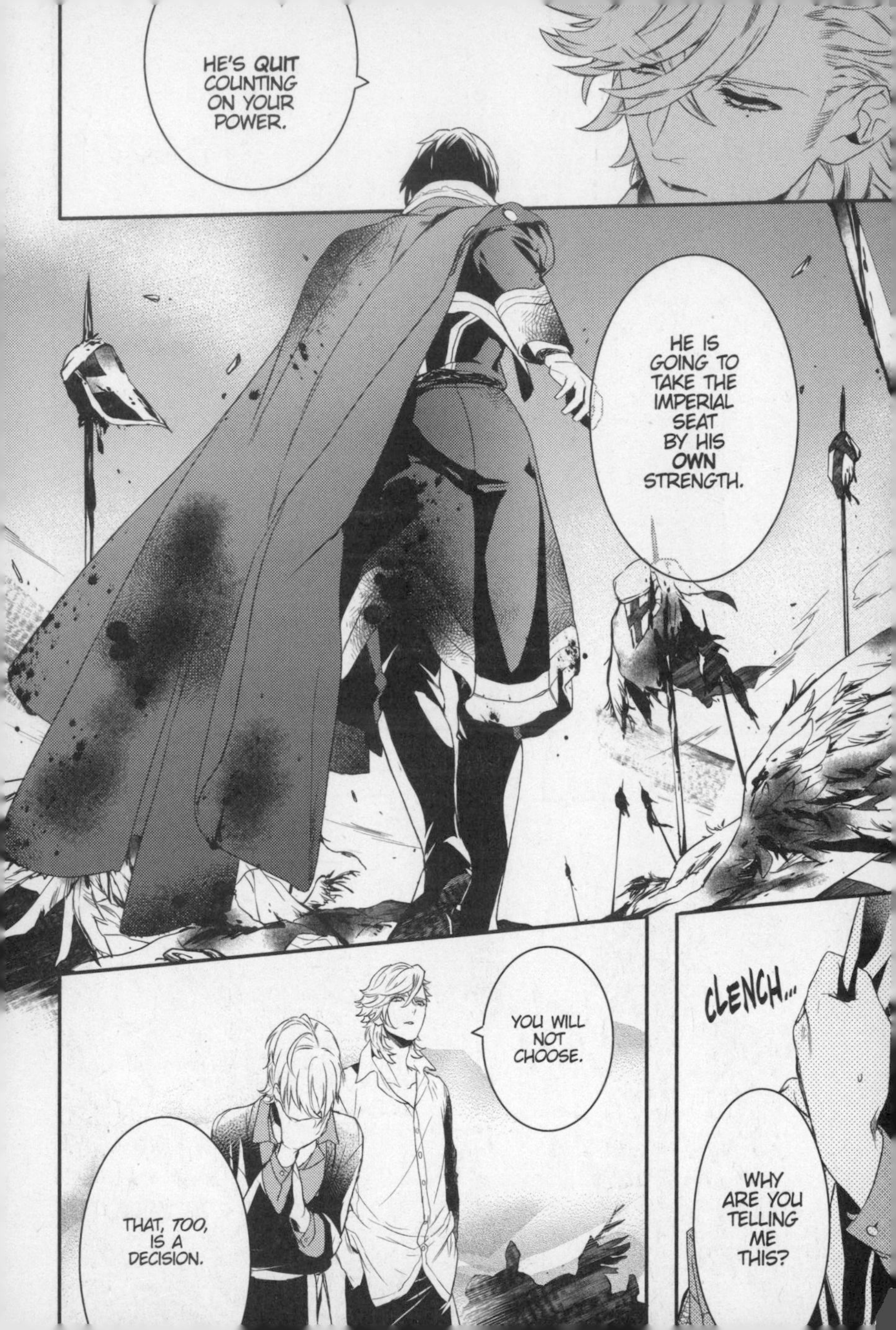
HE'S QUIT COUNTING ON YOUR POWER.
HE IS GOING TO TAKE THE IMPERIAL SEAT BY HIS OWN STRENGTH.
CLENCH...
WHY ARE YOU TELLING ME THIS?
YOU WILL NOT CHOOSE.
THAT, TOO, IS A DECISION.

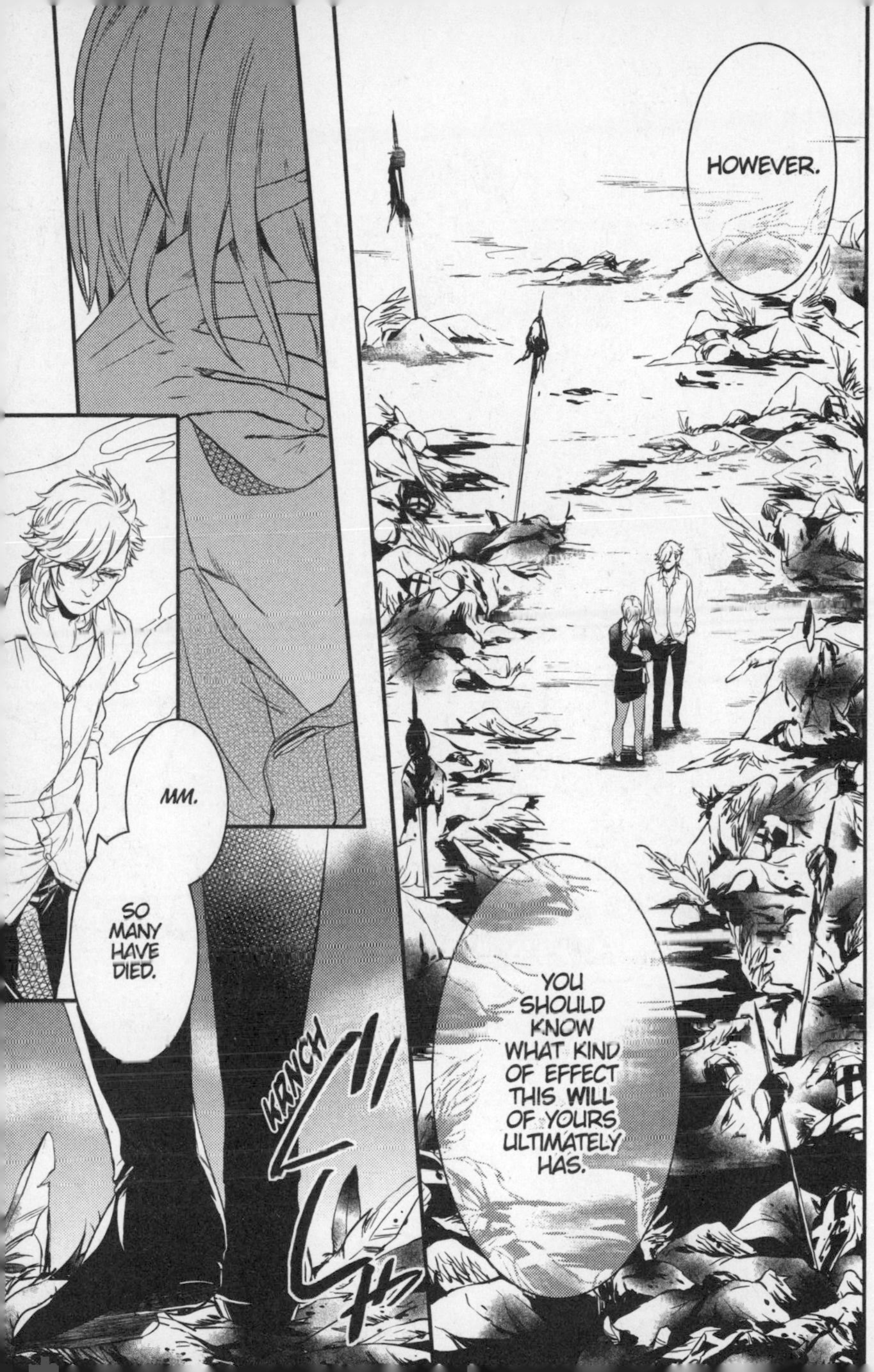
HOWEVER.
YOU SHOULD KNOW WHAT KIND OF EFFECT THIS WILL OF YOURS ULTIMATELY HAS.
MM.
SO MANY HAVE DIED.
KRNCH

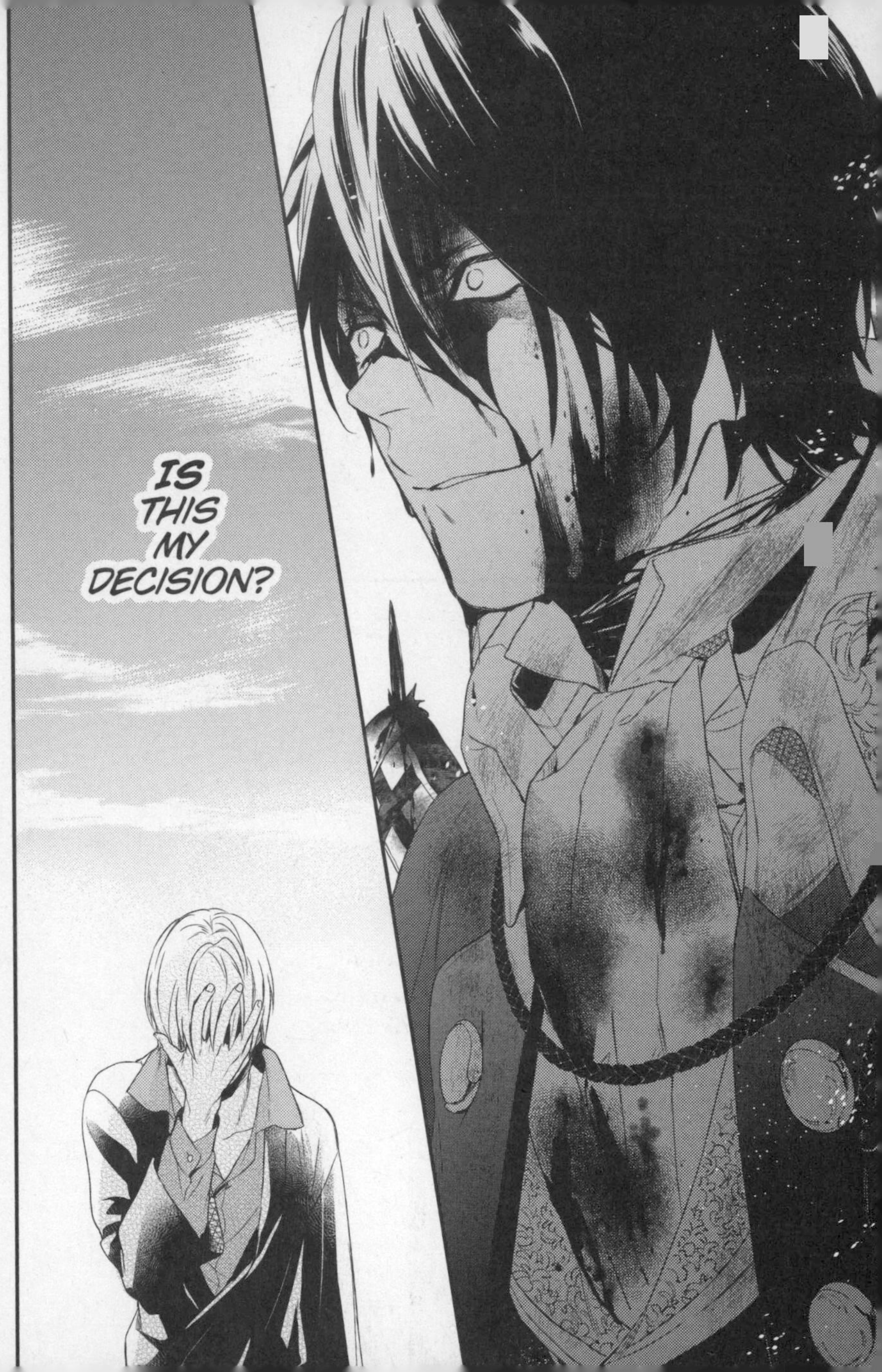
IS THIS MY DECISION?

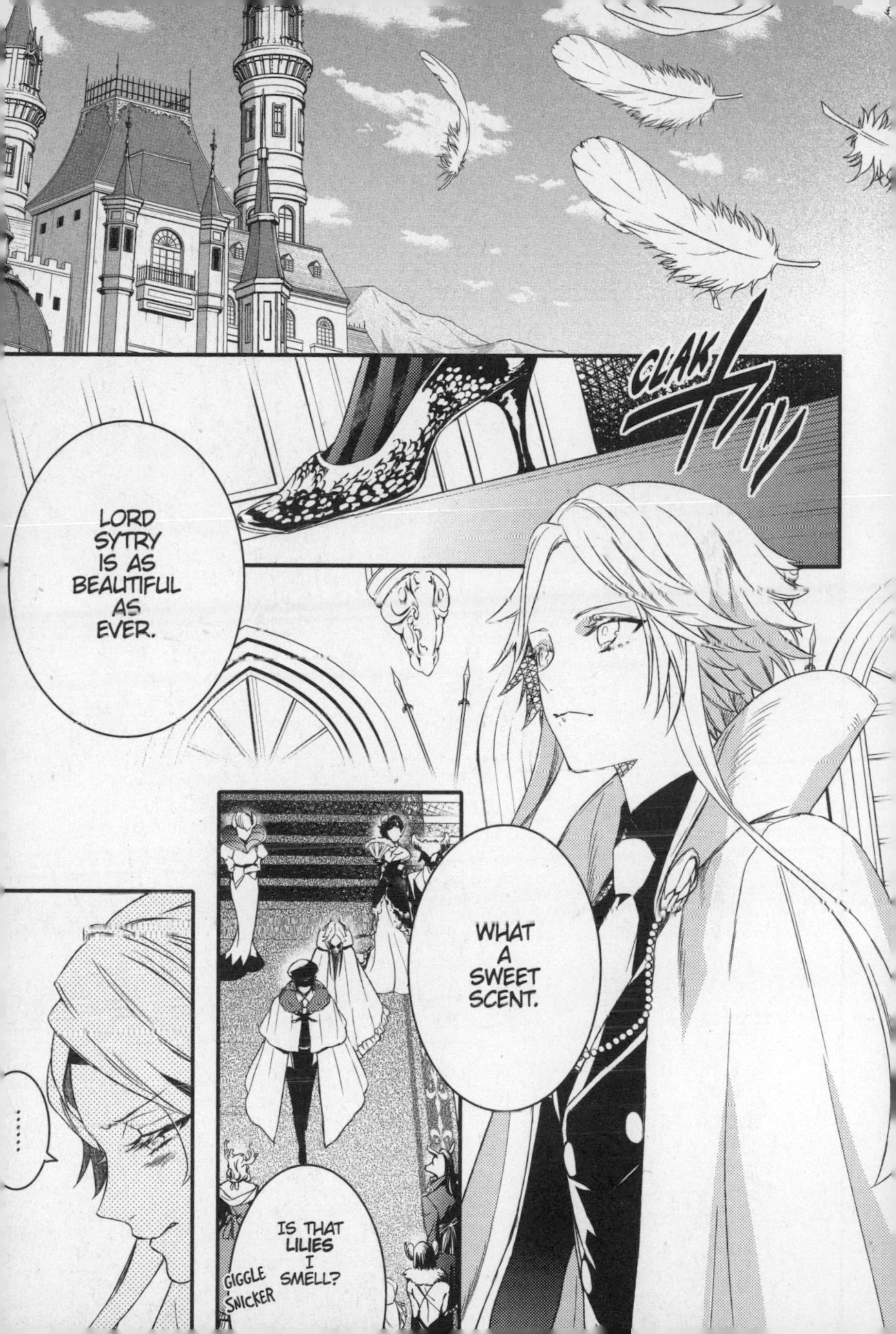
CLAK
LORD SYTRY IS AS BEAUTIFUL AS EVER.
WHAT A SWEET SCENT.
IS THAT LILIES I SMELL?
GIGGLE SNICKER
......

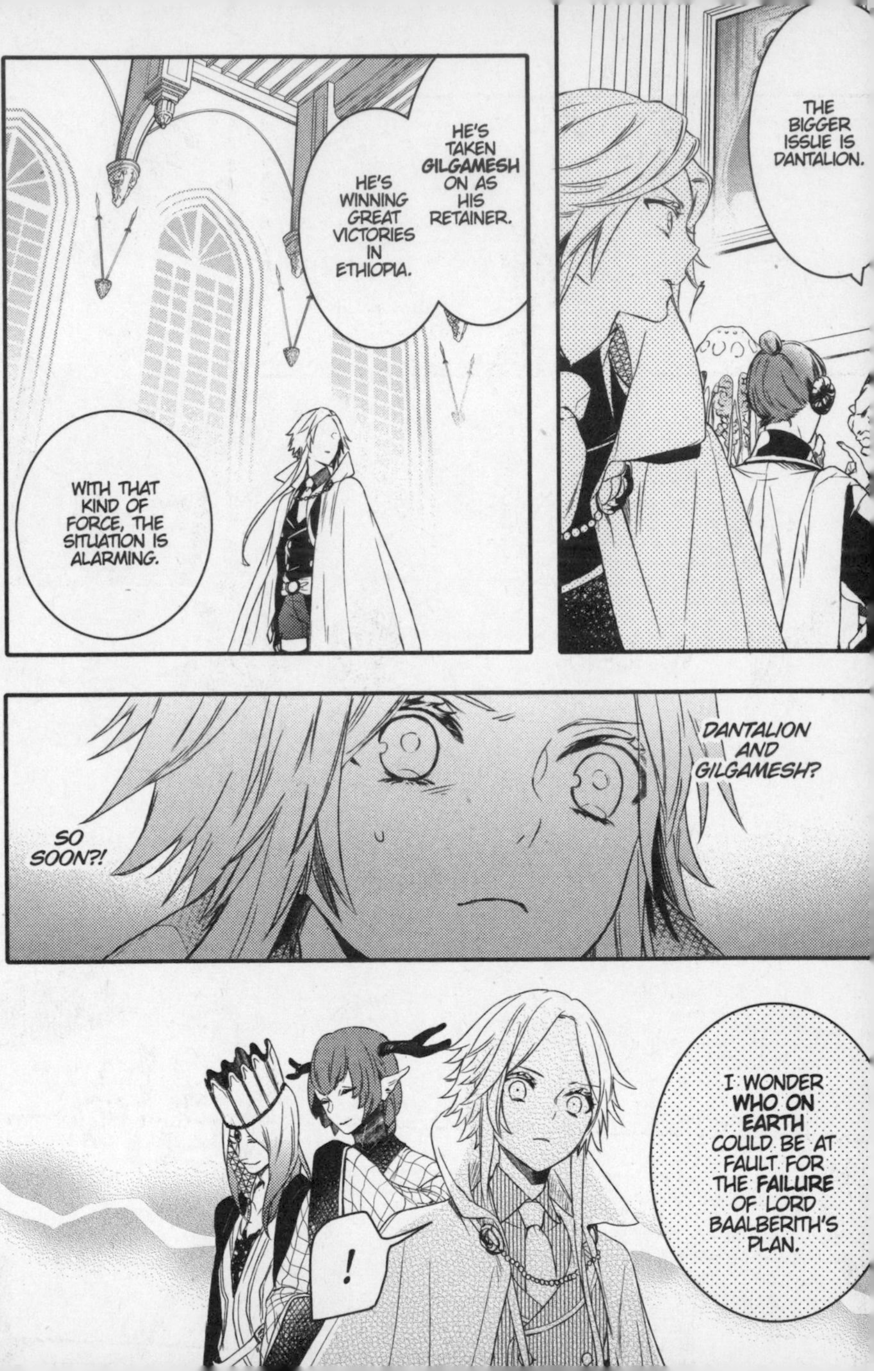
THE BIGGER ISSUE IS DANTALION.
HE'S TAKEN GILGAMESH ON AS HIS RETAINER.
HE'S WINNING GREAT VICTORIES IN ETHIOPIA.
WITH THAT KIND OF FORCE, THE SITUATION IS ALARMING.
DANTALION AND GILGAMESH?
SO SOON?!
I WONDER WHO ON EARTH COULD BE AT FAULT FOR THE FAILURE OF LORD BAALBERITH'S PLAN.
!

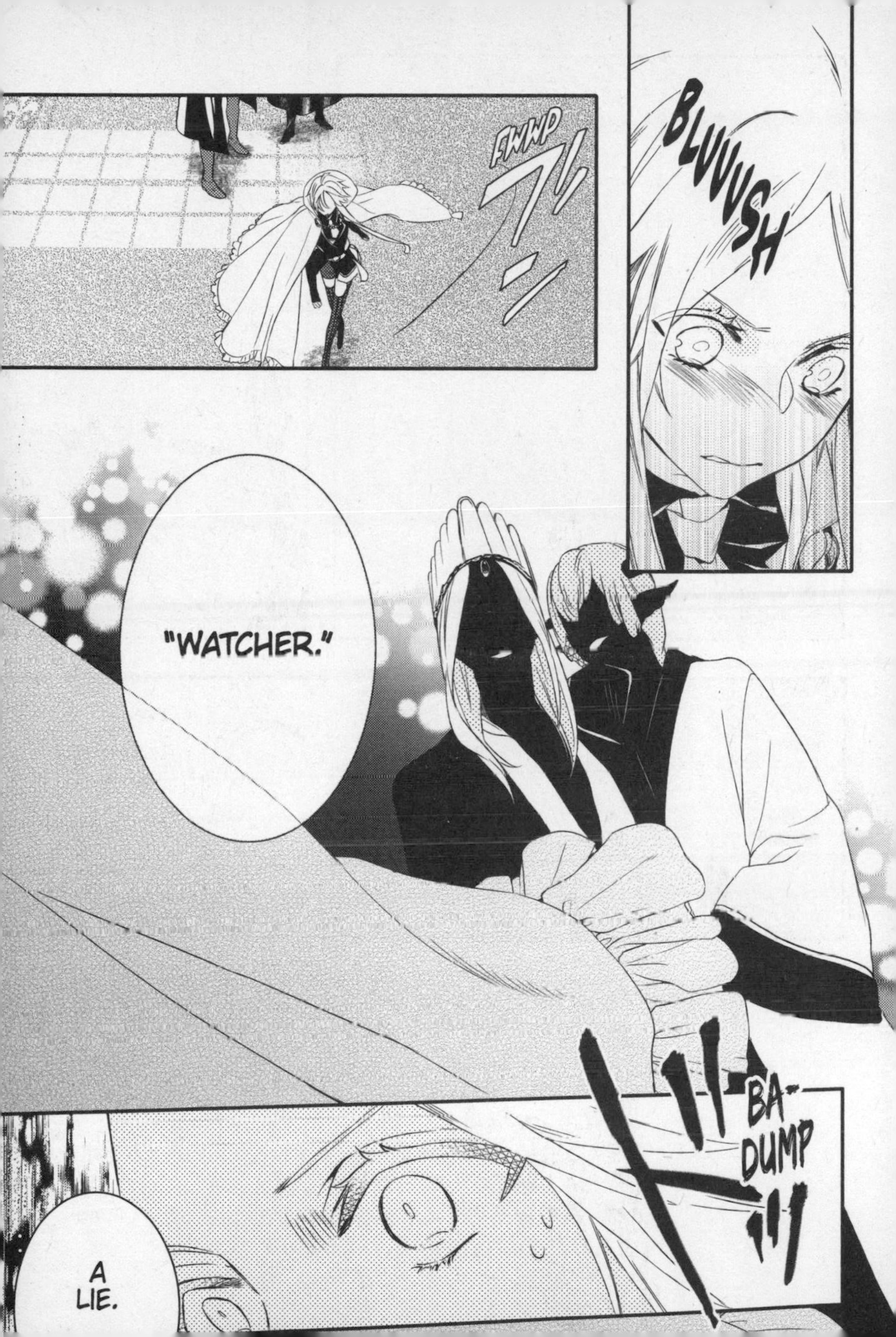
BLUUUSH
FWWP
"WATCHER."
BA-DUMP
A LIE.

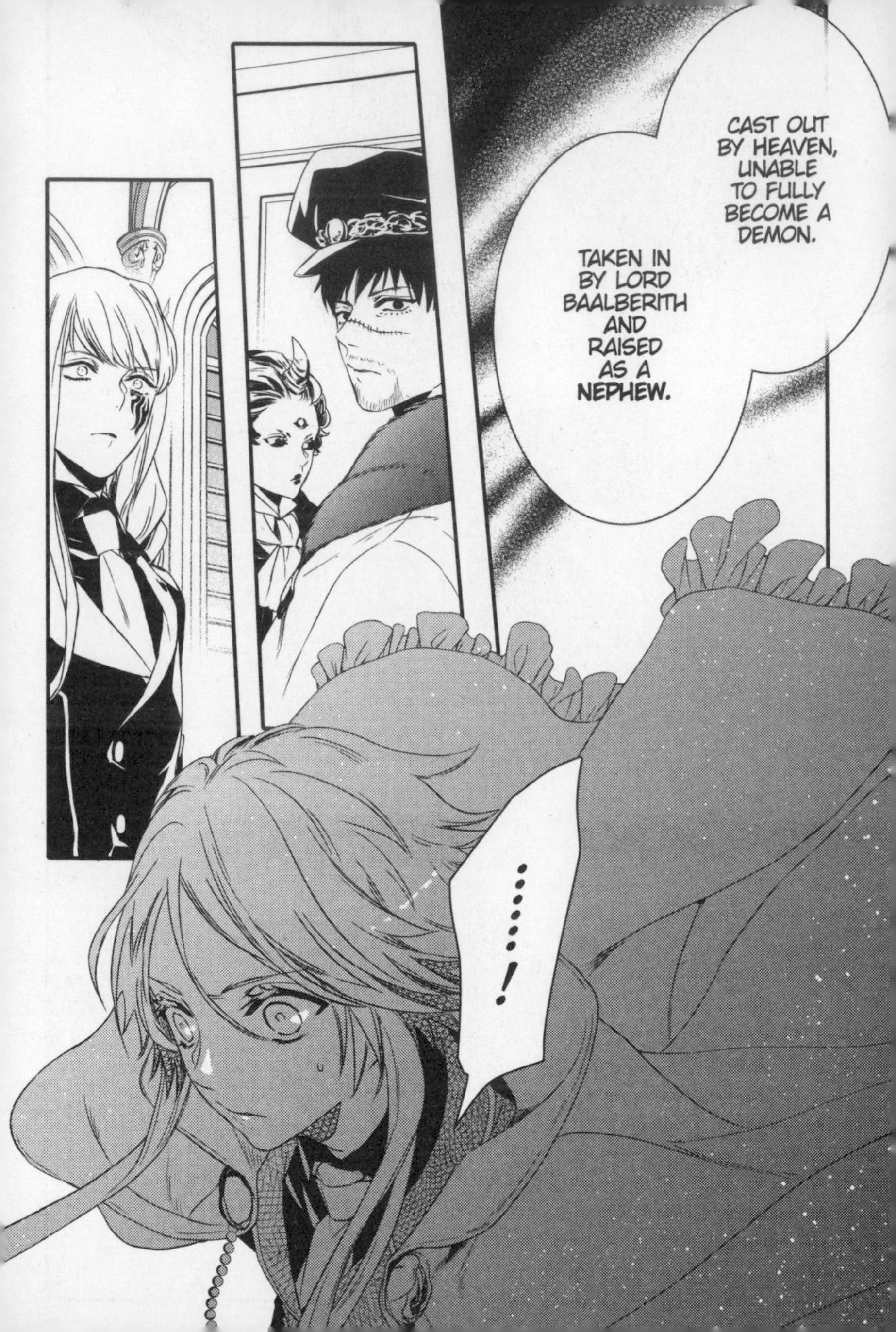
CAST OUT BY HEAVEN, UNABLE TO FULLY BECOME A DEMON.
TAKEN IN BY LORD BAALBERITH AND RAISED AS A NEPHEW.
……!

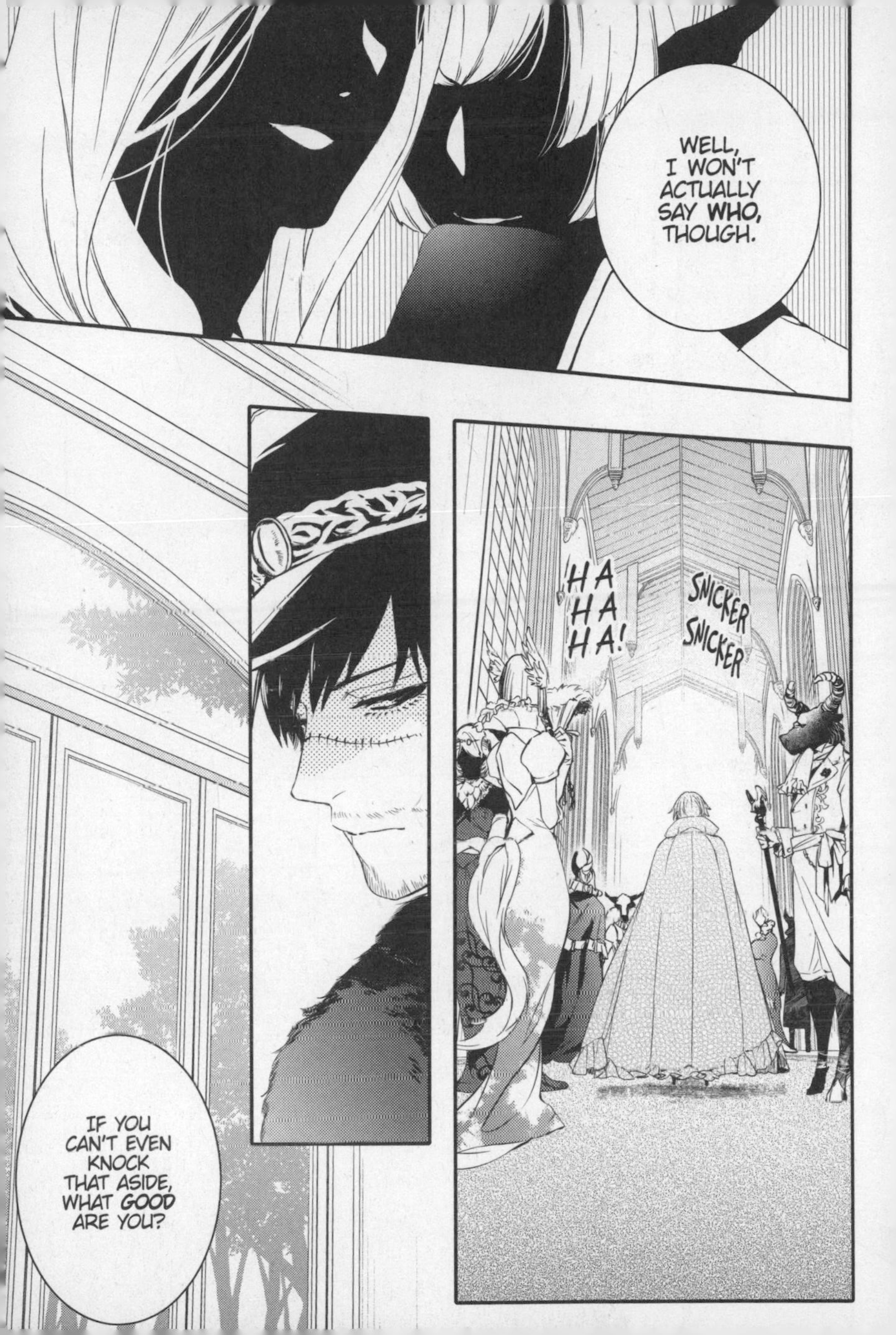
WELL, I WON'T ACTUALLY SAY WHO, THOUGH.
SNICKER SNICKER
HA HA HA HA HA HA!
IF YOU CAN'T EVEN KNOCK THAT ASIDE, WHAT GOOD ARE YOU?

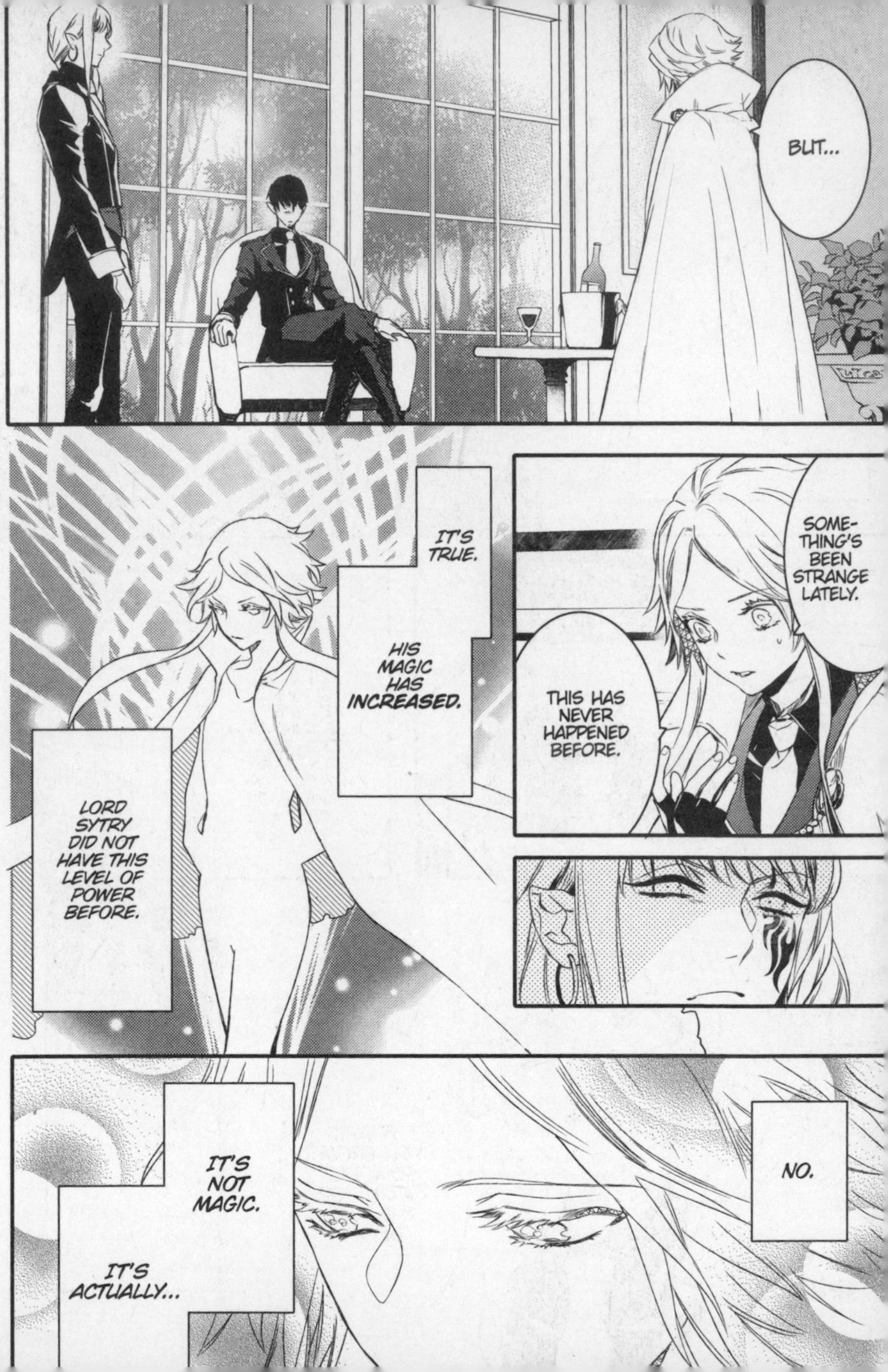
BUT...
SOME-THING'S BEEN STRANGE LATELY.
THIS HAS NEVER HAPPENED BEFORE.
IT'S TRUE.
HIS MAGIC HAS INCREASED.
LORD SYTRY DID NOT HAVE THIS LEVEL OF POWER BEFORE.
NO.
IT'S NOT MAGIC.
IT'S ACTUALLY...

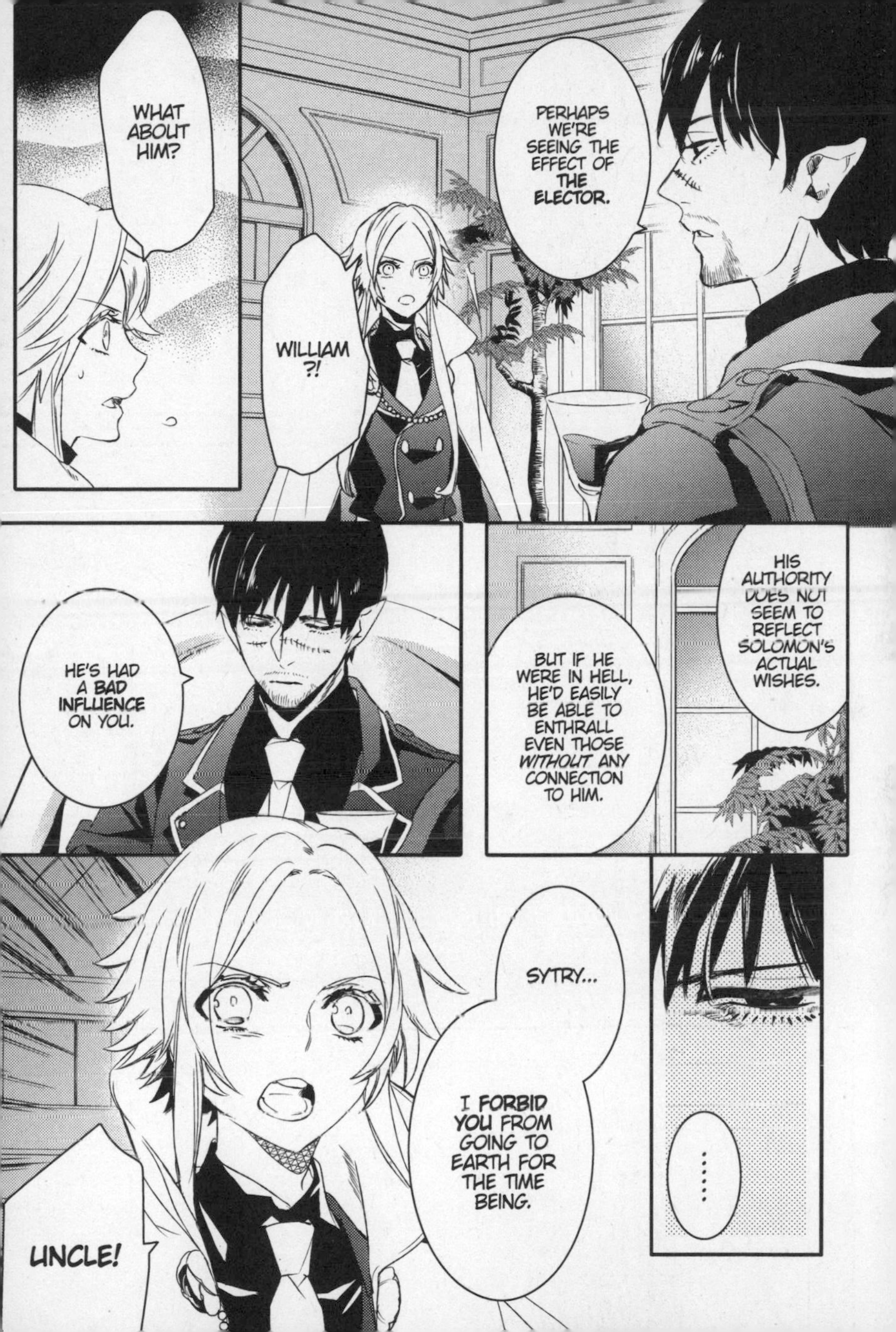
PERHAPS WE'RE SEEING THE EFFECT OF THE ELECTOR.
WILLIAM ?!
WHAT ABOUT HIM?
HIS AUTHORITY DOES NOT SEEM TO REFLECT SOLOMON'S ACTUAL WISHES.
BUT IF HE WERE IN HELL, HE'D EASILY BE ABLE TO ENTHRALL EVEN THOSE WITHOUT ANY CONNECTION TO HIM.
HE'S HAD A BAD INFLUENCE ON YOU.
......
SYTRY...
I FORBID YOU FROM GOING TO EARTH FOR THE TIME BEING.
UNCLE!

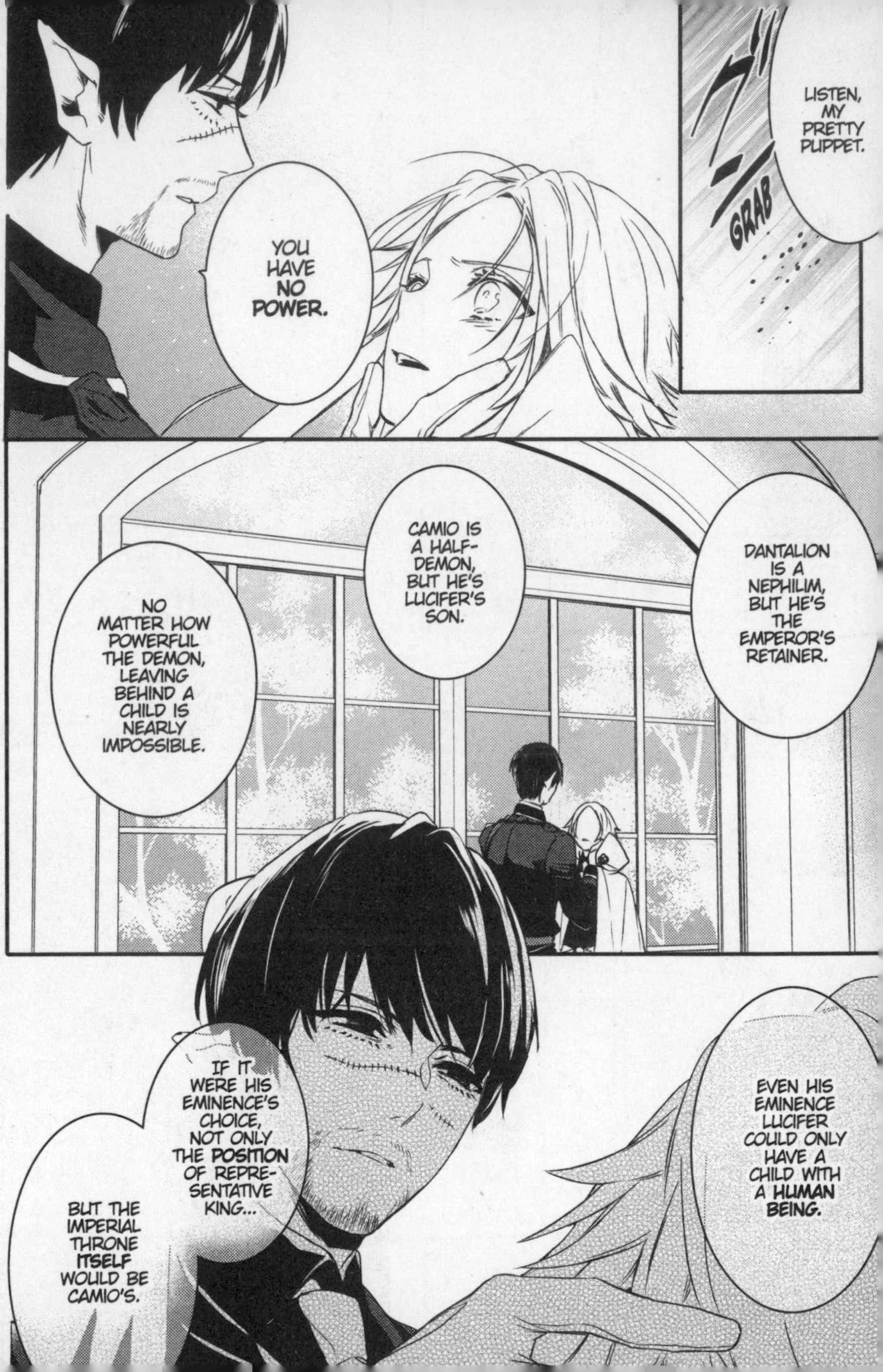
LISTEN, MY PRETTY PUPPET.
GRAB
YOU HAVE NO POWER.
DANTALION IS A NEPHILIM, BUT HE'S THE EMPEROR'S RETAINER.
CAMIO IS A HALF-DEMON, BUT HE'S LUCIFER'S SON.
NO MATTER HOW POWERFUL THE DEMON, LEAVING BEHIND A CHILD IS NEARLY IMPOSSIBLE.
EVEN HIS EMINENCE LUCIFER COULD ONLY HAVE A CHILD WITH A **HUMAN BEING.**
IF IT WERE HIS EMINENCE'S CHOICE, NOT ONLY THE **POSITION** OF REPRE-SENTATIVE KING...
BUT THE IMPERIAL THRONE **ITSELF** WOULD BE CAMIO'S.

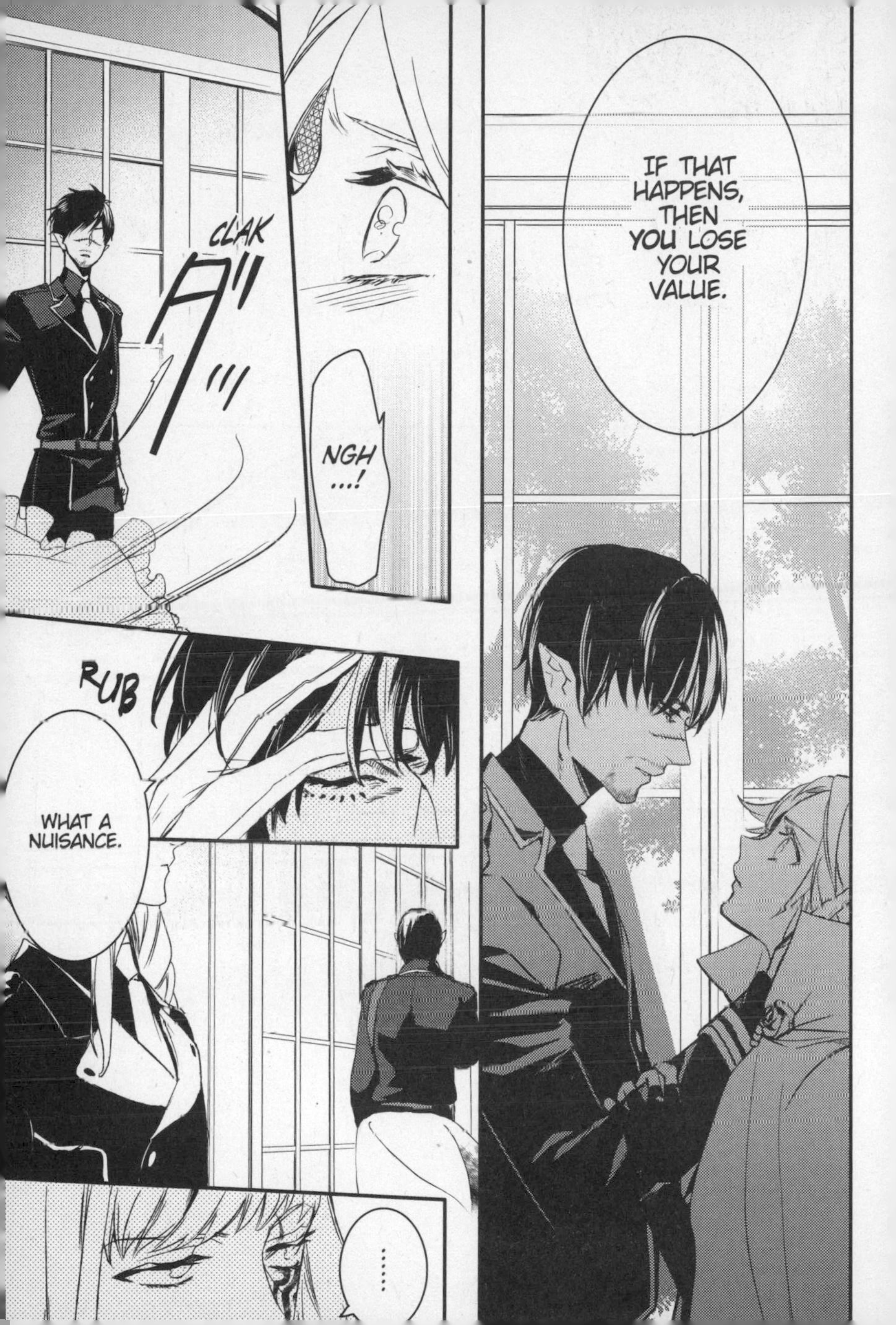
IF THAT HAPPENS, THEN YOU LOSE YOUR VALUE.
NGH ...!
CLAK
RUB
WHAT A NUISANCE.
......

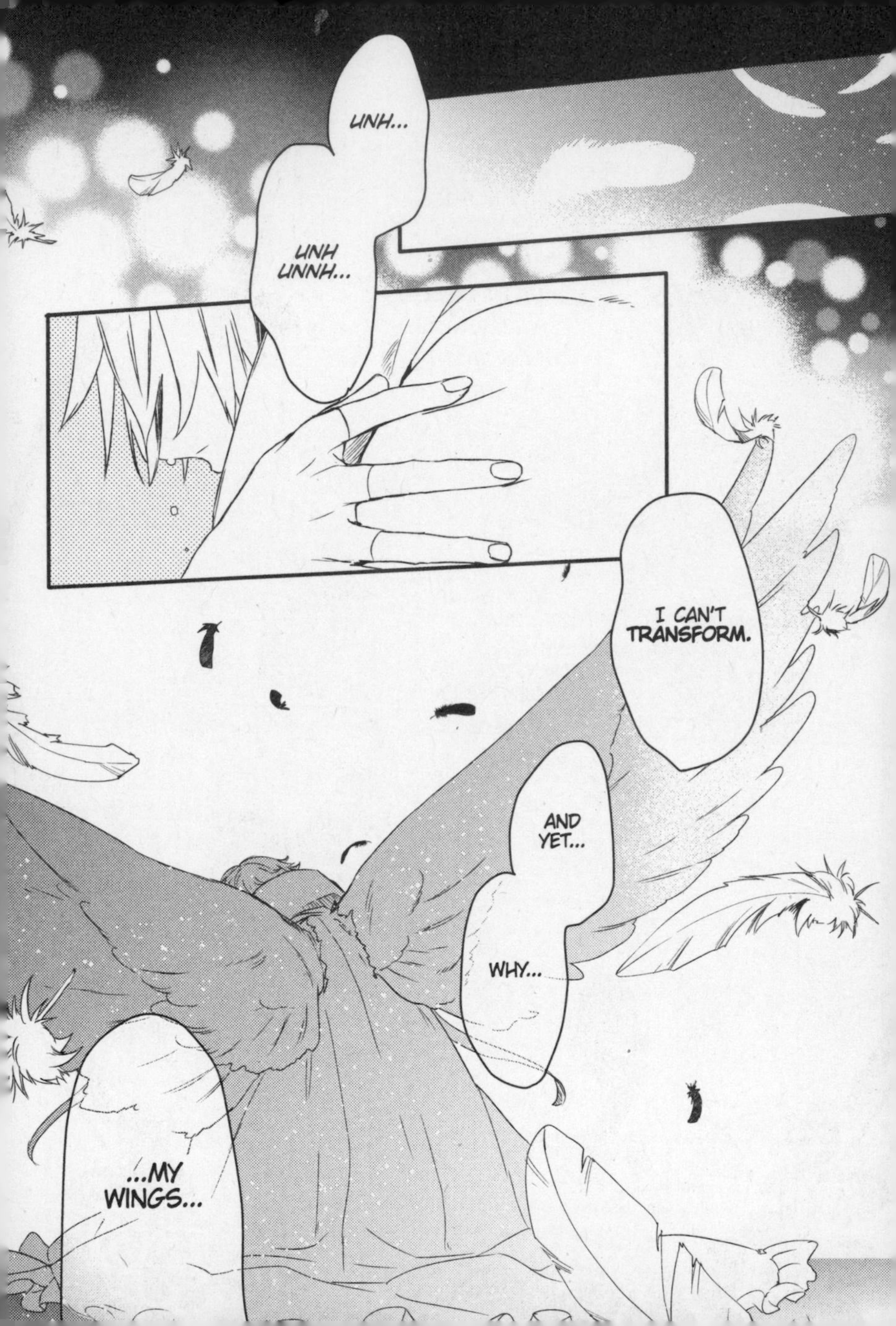
UNH...
UNH UNNH...
I CAN'T TRANSFORM.
AND YET...
WHY...
...MY WINGS...

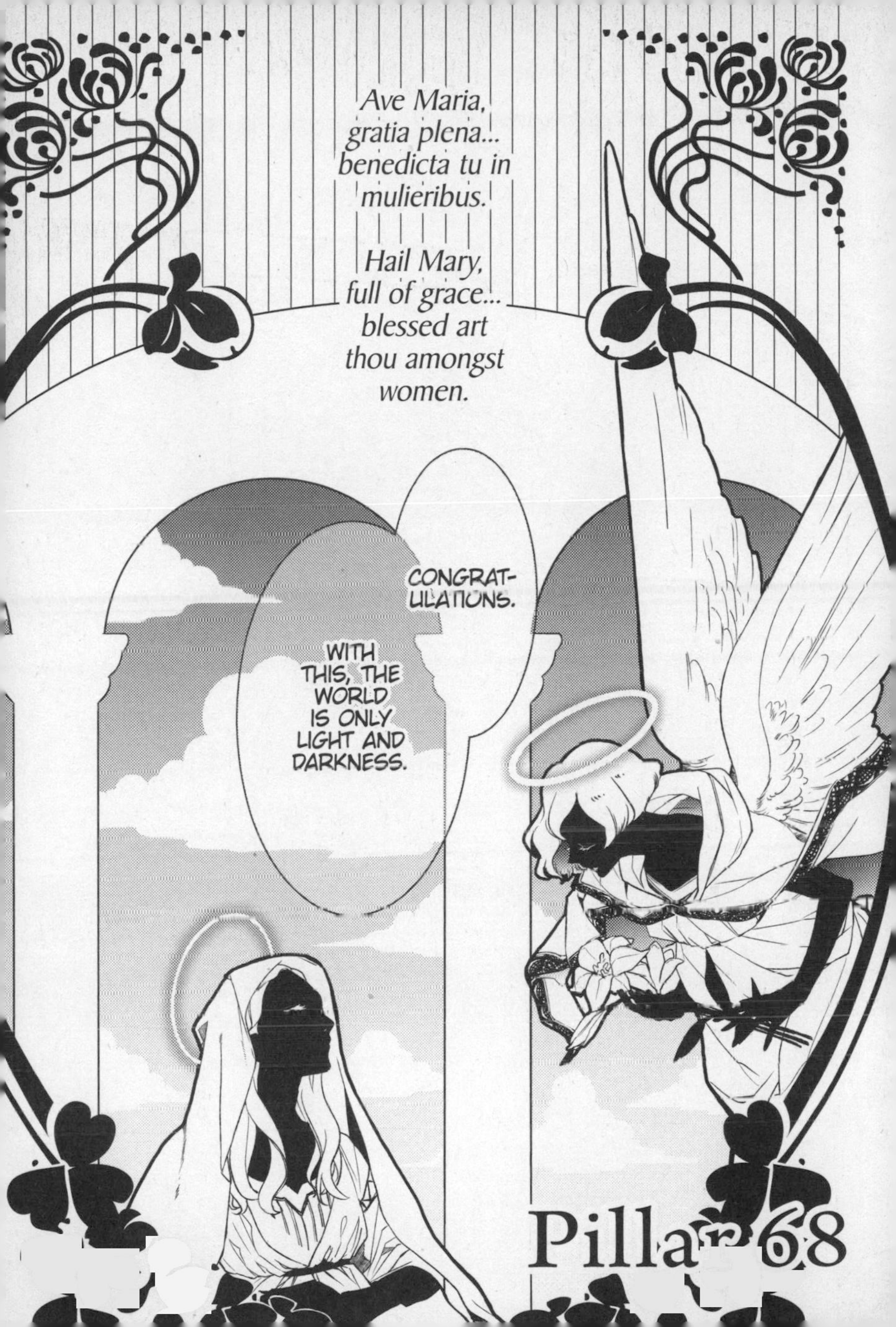
Ave Maria, gratia plena... benedicta tu in mulieribus.
Hail Mary, full of grace... blessed art thou amongst women.
CONGRAT-ULATIONS.
WITH THIS, THE WORLD IS ONLY LIGHT AND DARKNESS.
Pillar 68

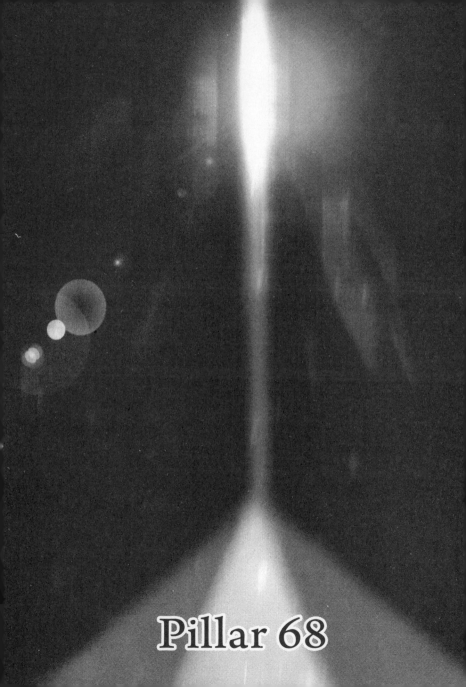

Pillar 68

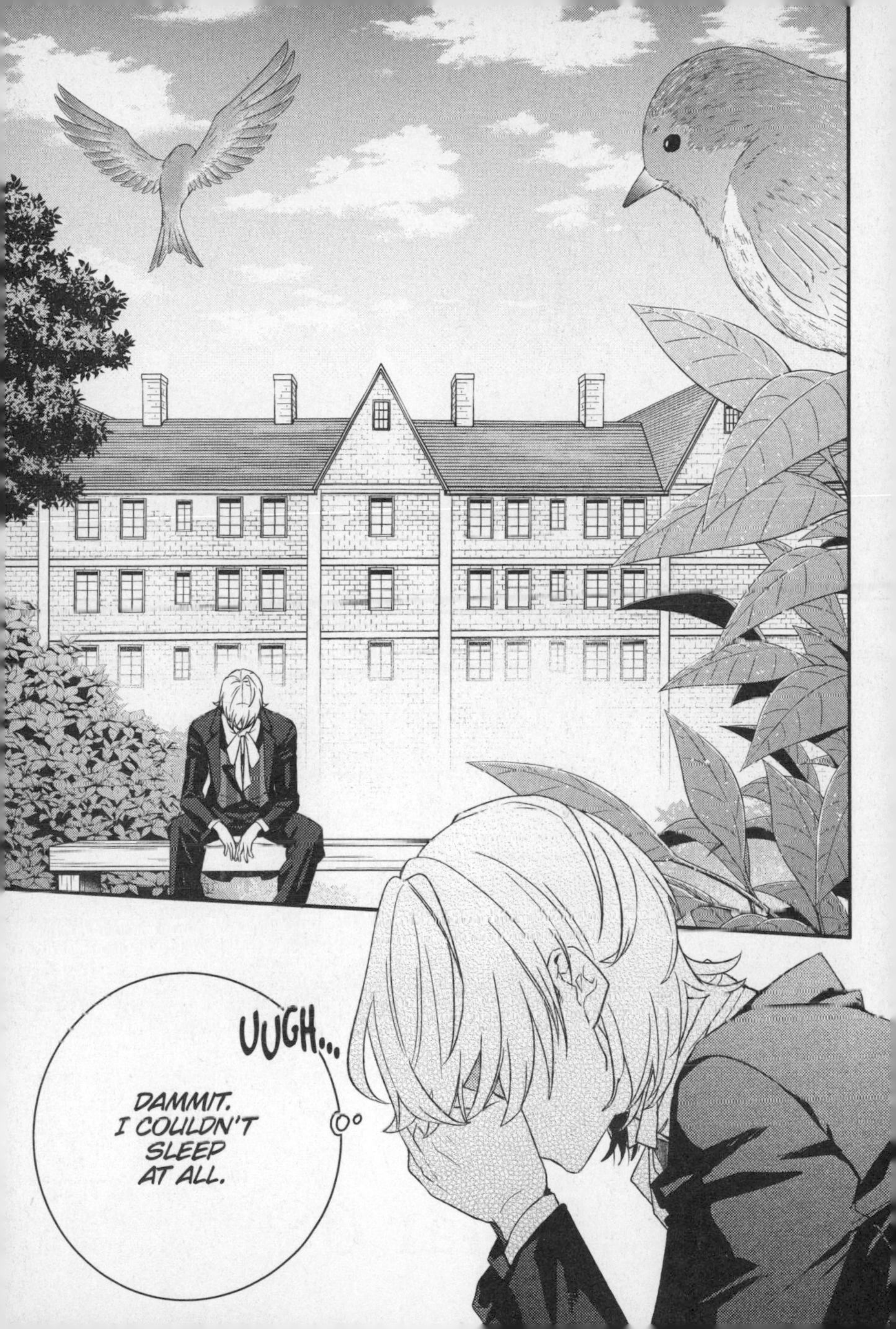
UUGH...
DAMMIT. I COULDN'T SLEEP AT ALL.

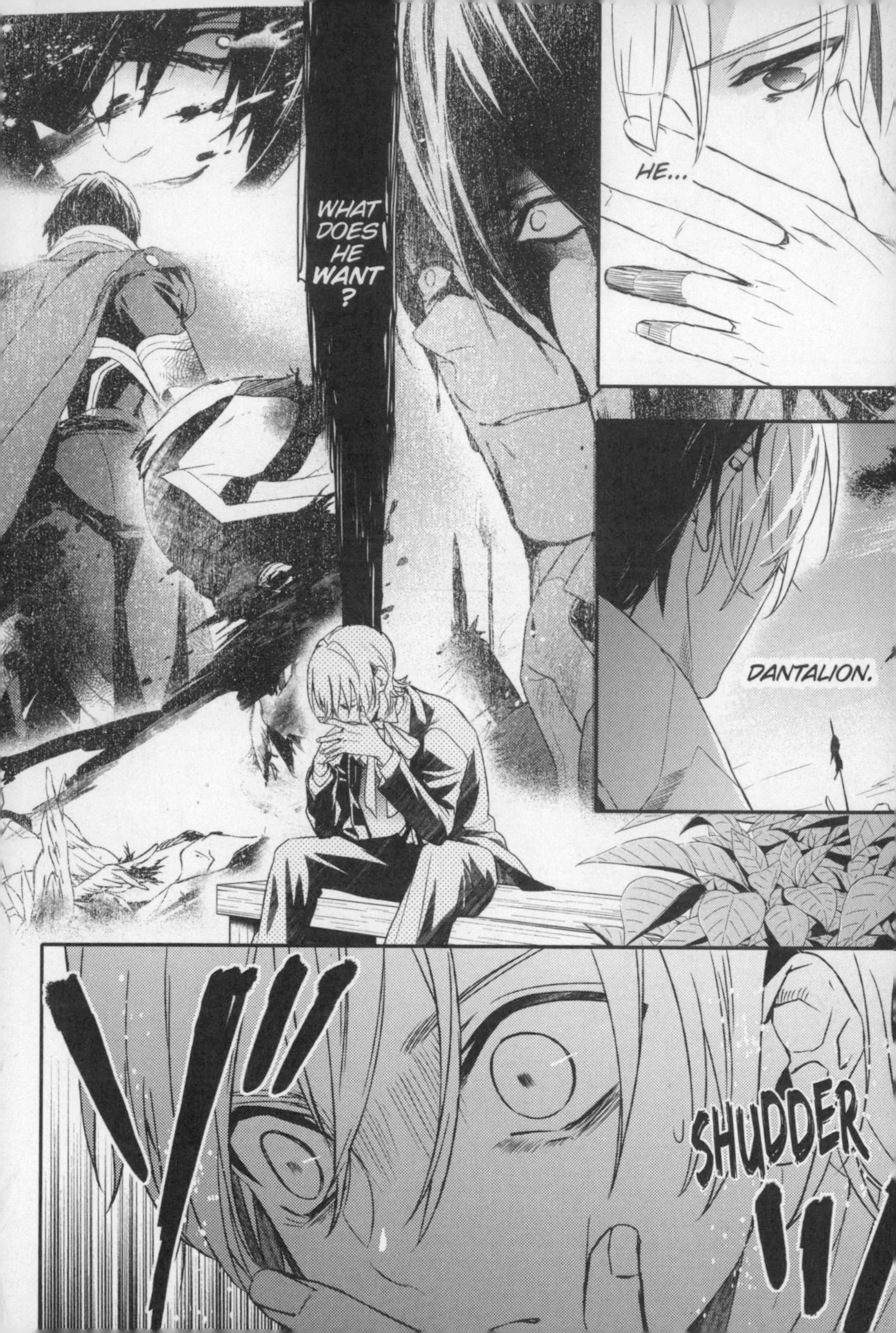
HE...
DANTALION.
WHAT DOES HE WANT ?
SHUDDER

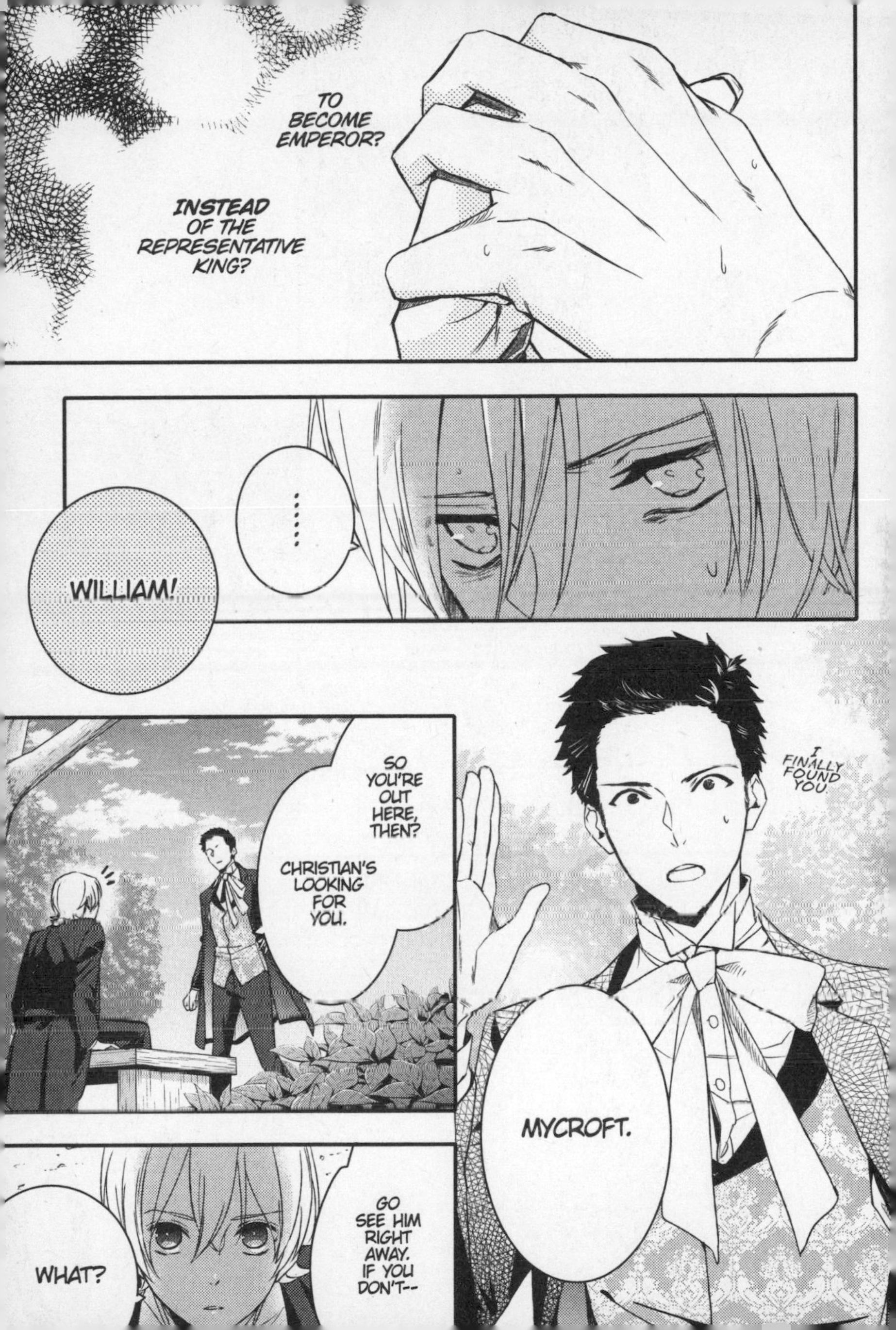
TO BECOME EMPEROR?
INSTEAD OF THE REPRESENTATIVE KING?
......
WILLIAM!
I FINALLY FOUND YOU.
MYCROFT.
SO YOU'RE OUT HERE, THEN?
CHRISTIAN'S LOOKING FOR YOU.
GO SEE HIM RIGHT AWAY. IF YOU DON'T--
WHAT?

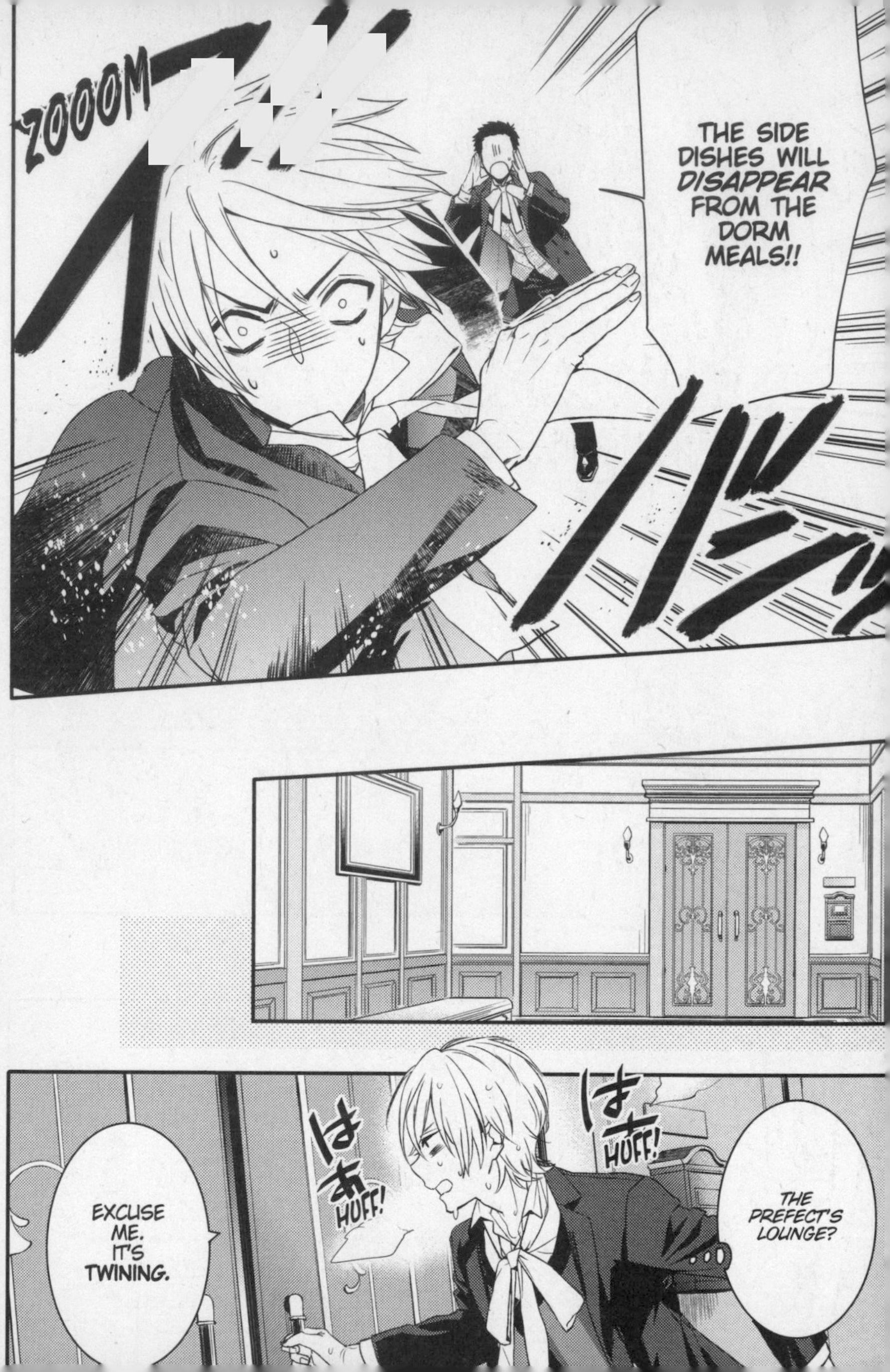
THE SIDE DISHES WILL DISAPPEAR FROM THE DORM MEALS!!
ZOOOM
THE PREFECT'S LOUNGE?
HUFF!
HUFF!
EXCUSE ME. IT'S TWINING.

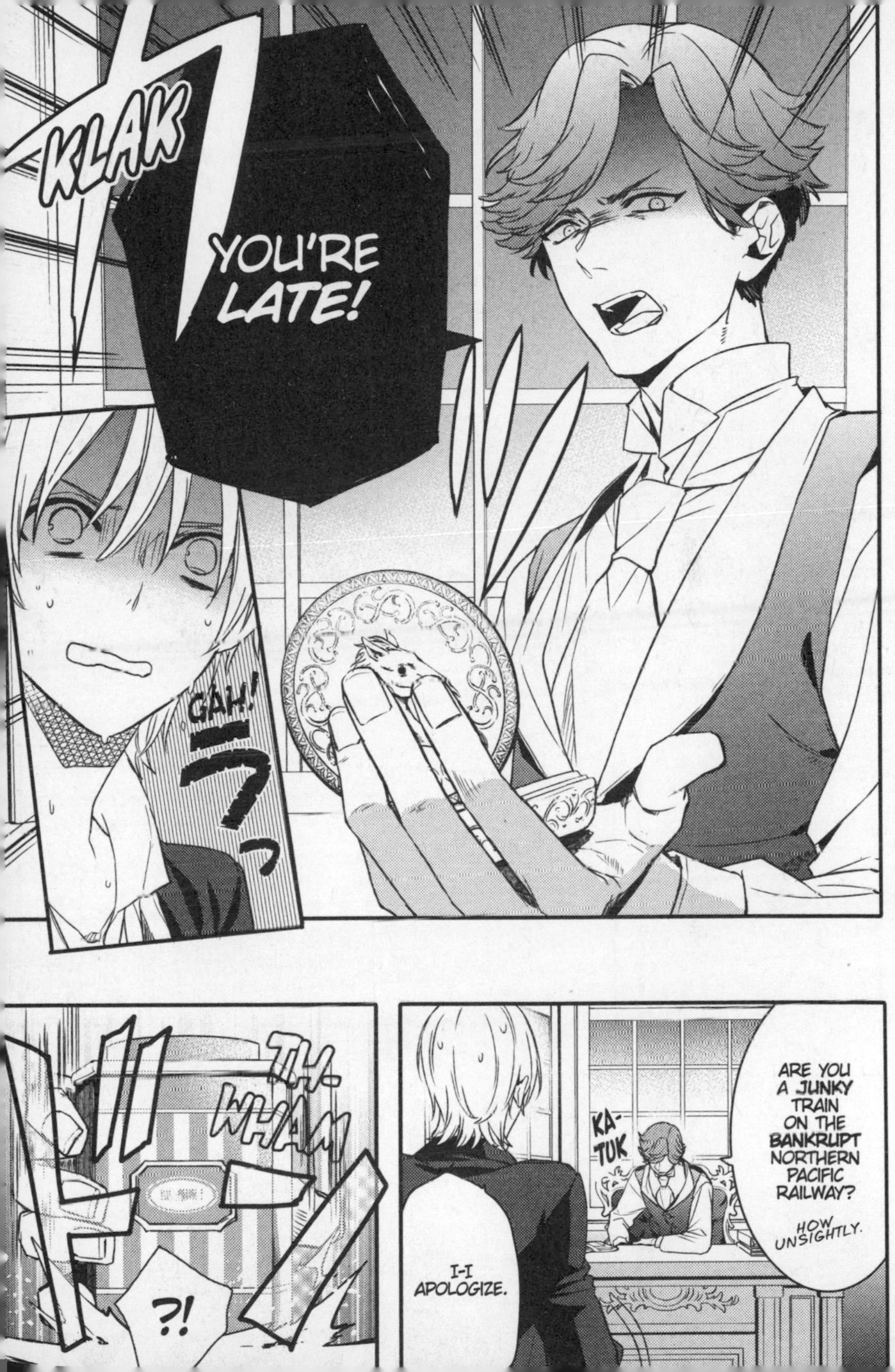
KLAK
YOU'RE LATE!
GAH!
ARE YOU A JUNKY TRAIN ON THE BANKRUPT NORTHERN PACIFIC RAILWAY?
HOW UNSIGHTLY.
KA-TUK
I-I APOLOGIZE.
THA-WHAM
?!

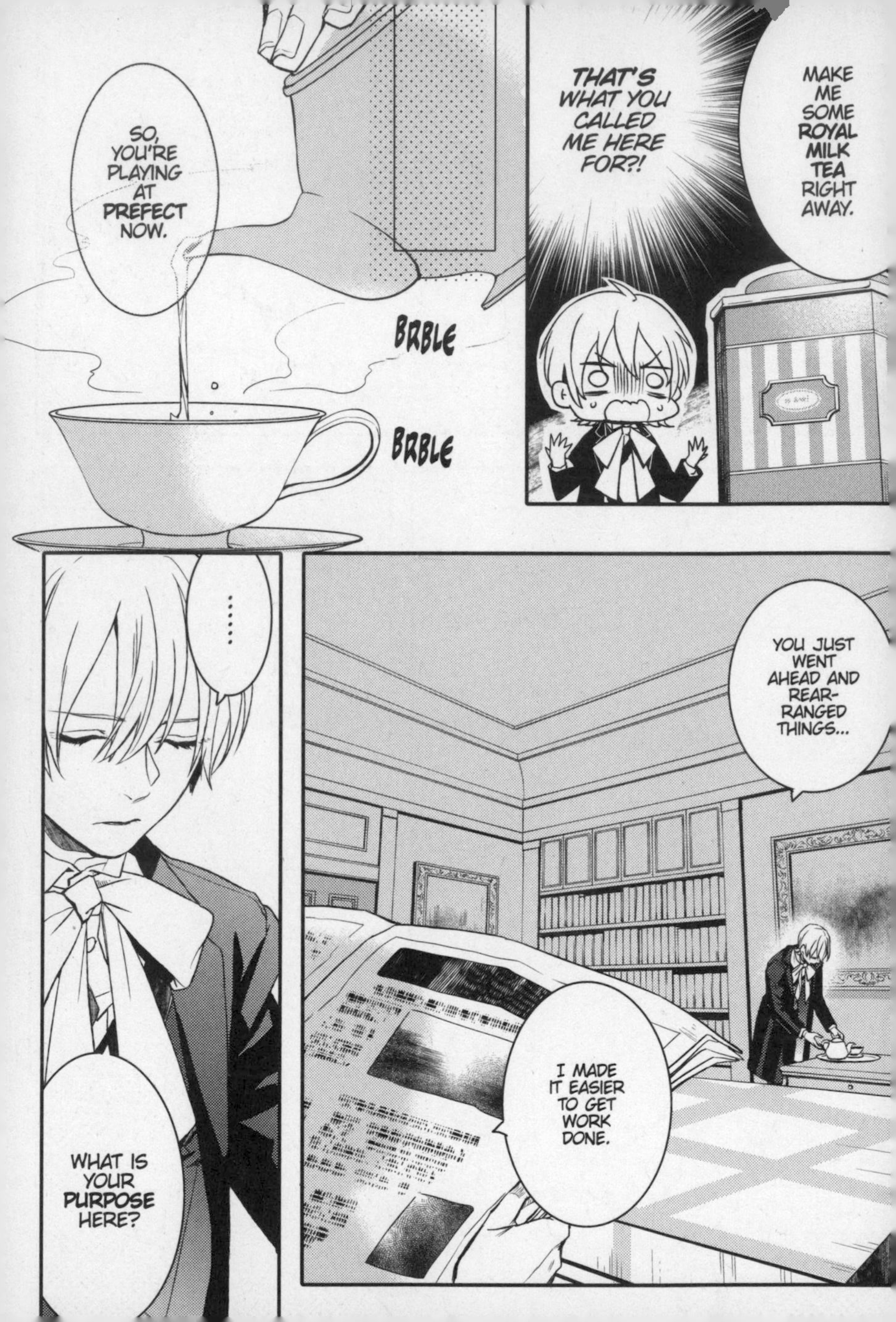
MAKE ME SOME ROYAL MILK TEA RIGHT AWAY.
THAT'S WHAT YOU CALLED ME HERE FOR?!
SO, YOU'RE PLAYING AT PREFECT NOW.
BRBLE
BRBLE
YOU JUST WENT AHEAD AND REAR-RANGED THINGS...
I MADE IT EASIER TO GET WORK DONE.
......
WHAT IS YOUR PURPOSE HERE?

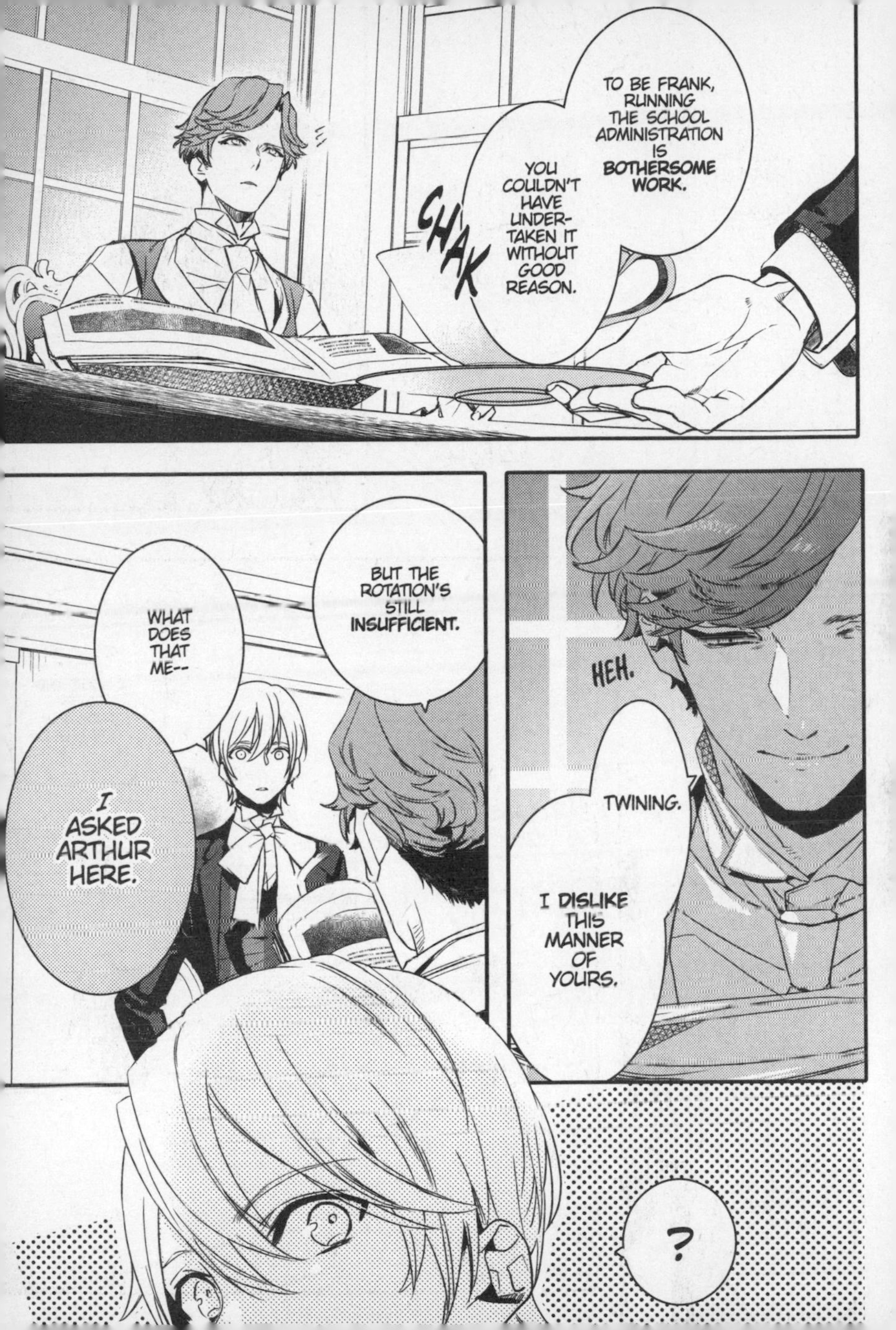
TO BE FRANK, RUNNING THE SCHOOL ADMINISTRATION IS BOTHERSOME WORK.
YOU COULDN'T HAVE UNDER-TAKEN IT WITHOUT GOOD REASON.
CHAK
HEH.
TWINING.
I DISLIKE THIS MANNER OF YOURS.
BUT THE ROTATION'S STILL INSUFFICIENT.
WHAT DOES THAT ME--
I ASKED ARTHUR HERE.
?

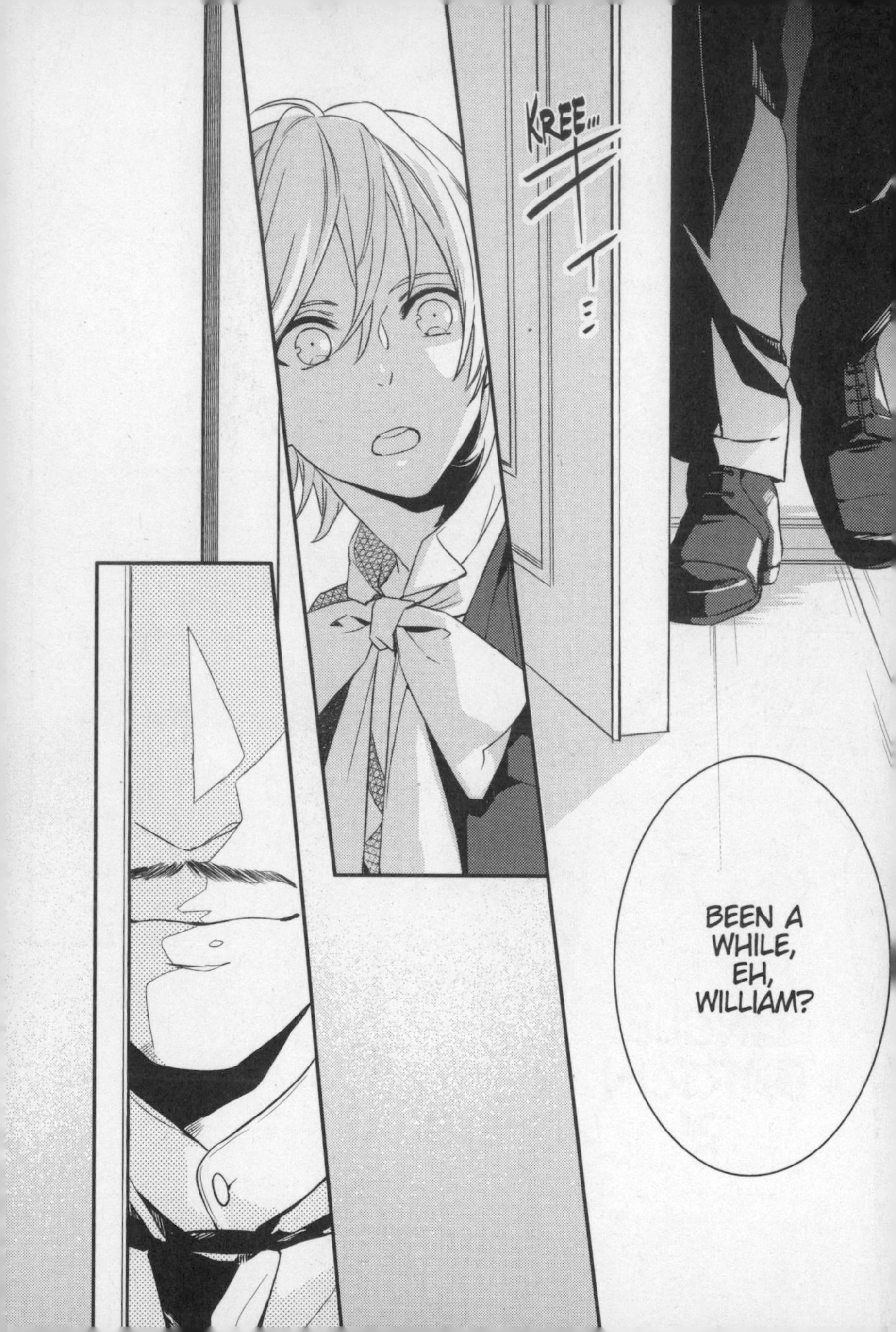
KREE...
BEEN A WHILE, EH, WILLIAM?

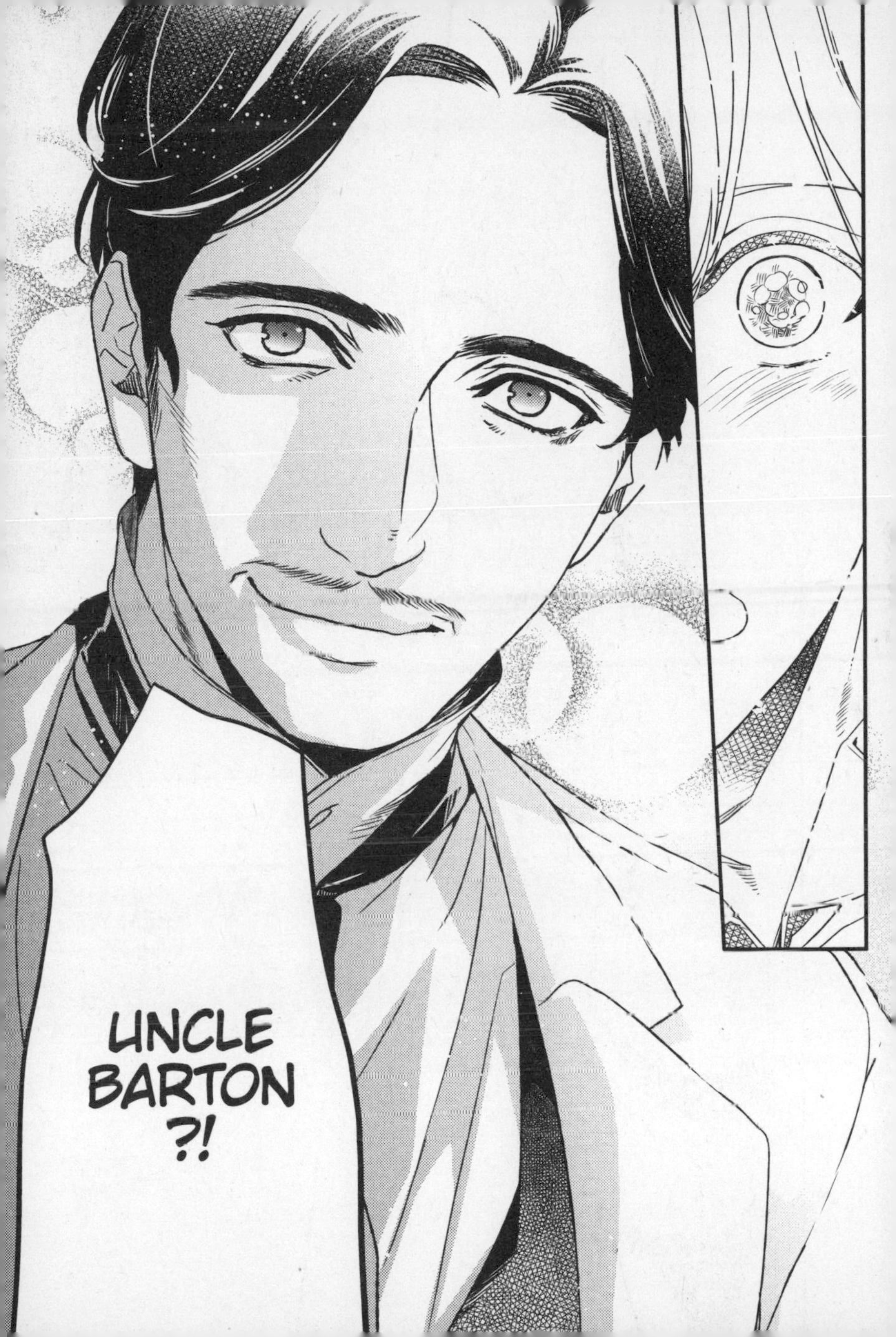
UNCLE BARTON ?!

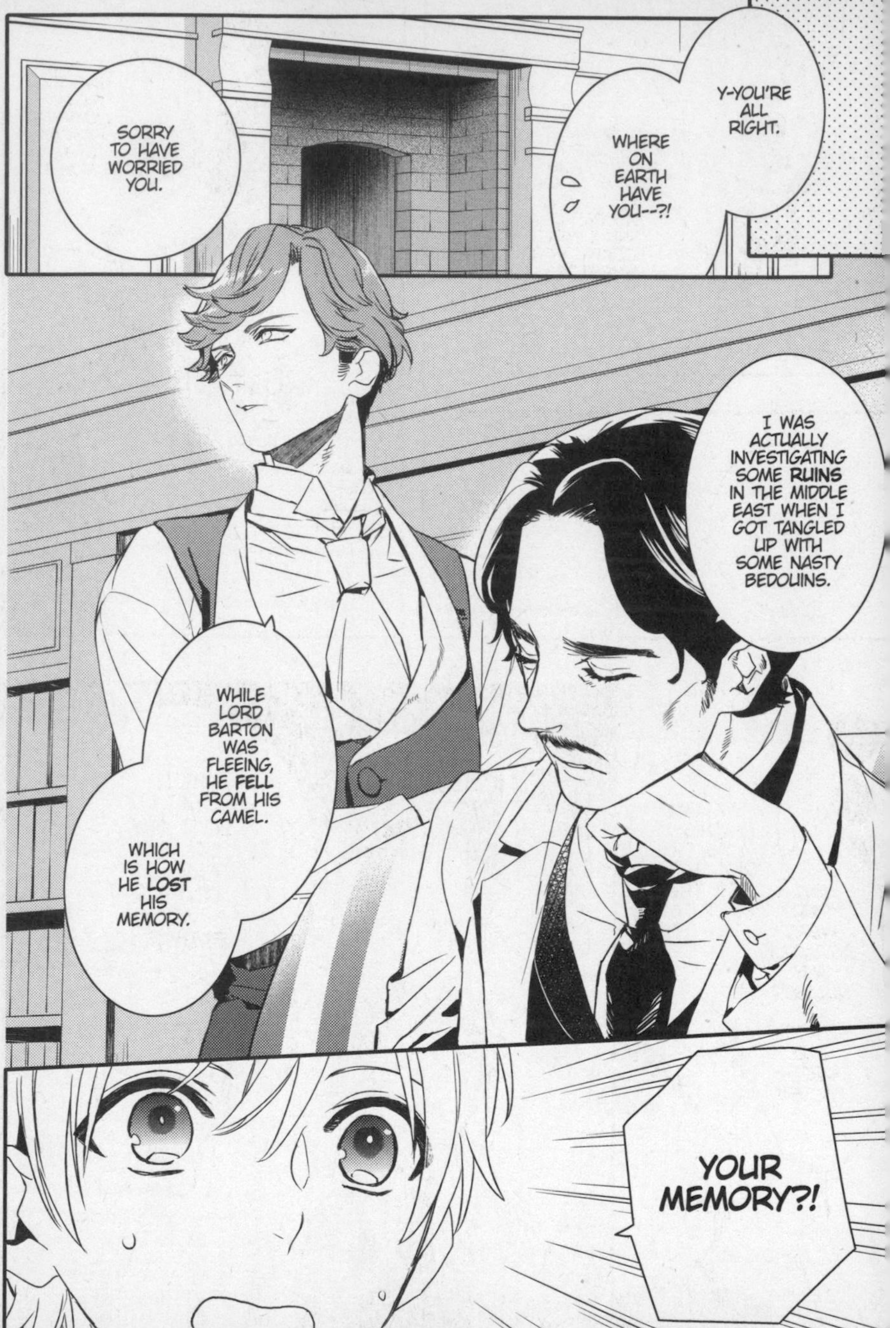
Y-YOU'RE ALL RIGHT.
WHERE ON EARTH HAVE YOU--?!
SORRY TO HAVE WORRIED YOU.
I WAS ACTUALLY INVESTIGATING SOME RUINS IN THE MIDDLE EAST WHEN I GOT TANGLED UP WITH SOME NASTY BEDOUINS.
WHILE LORD BARTON WAS FLEEING, HE FELL FROM HIS CAMEL.
WHICH IS HOW HE LOST HIS MEMORY.
YOUR MEMORY?!

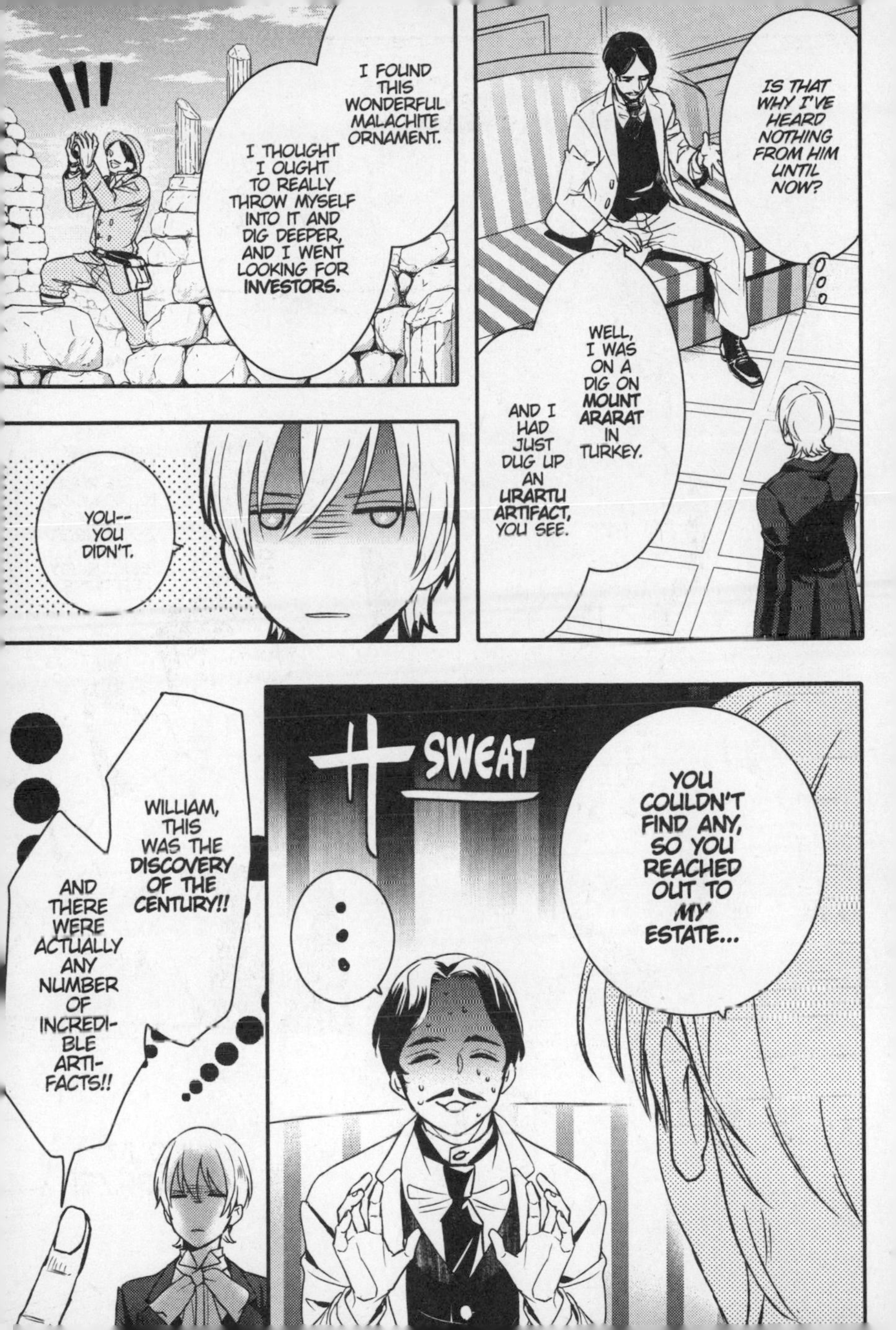
IS THAT WHY I'VE HEARD NOTHING FROM HIM UNTIL NOW?
WELL, I WAS ON A DIG ON MOUNT ARARAT IN TURKEY.
AND I HAD JUST DUG UP AN URARTU ARTIFACT, YOU SEE.
I FOUND THIS WONDERFUL MALACHITE ORNAMENT.
I THOUGHT I OUGHT TO REALLY THROW MYSELF INTO IT AND DIG DEEPER, AND I WENT LOOKING FOR INVESTORS.
YOU--YOU DIDN'T.
YOU COULDN'T FIND ANY, SO YOU REACHED OUT TO MY ESTATE...
SWEAT
...
WILLIAM, THIS WAS THE DISCOVERY OF THE CENTURY!!
AND THERE WERE ACTUALLY ANY NUMBER OF INCREDIBLE ARTIFACTS!!

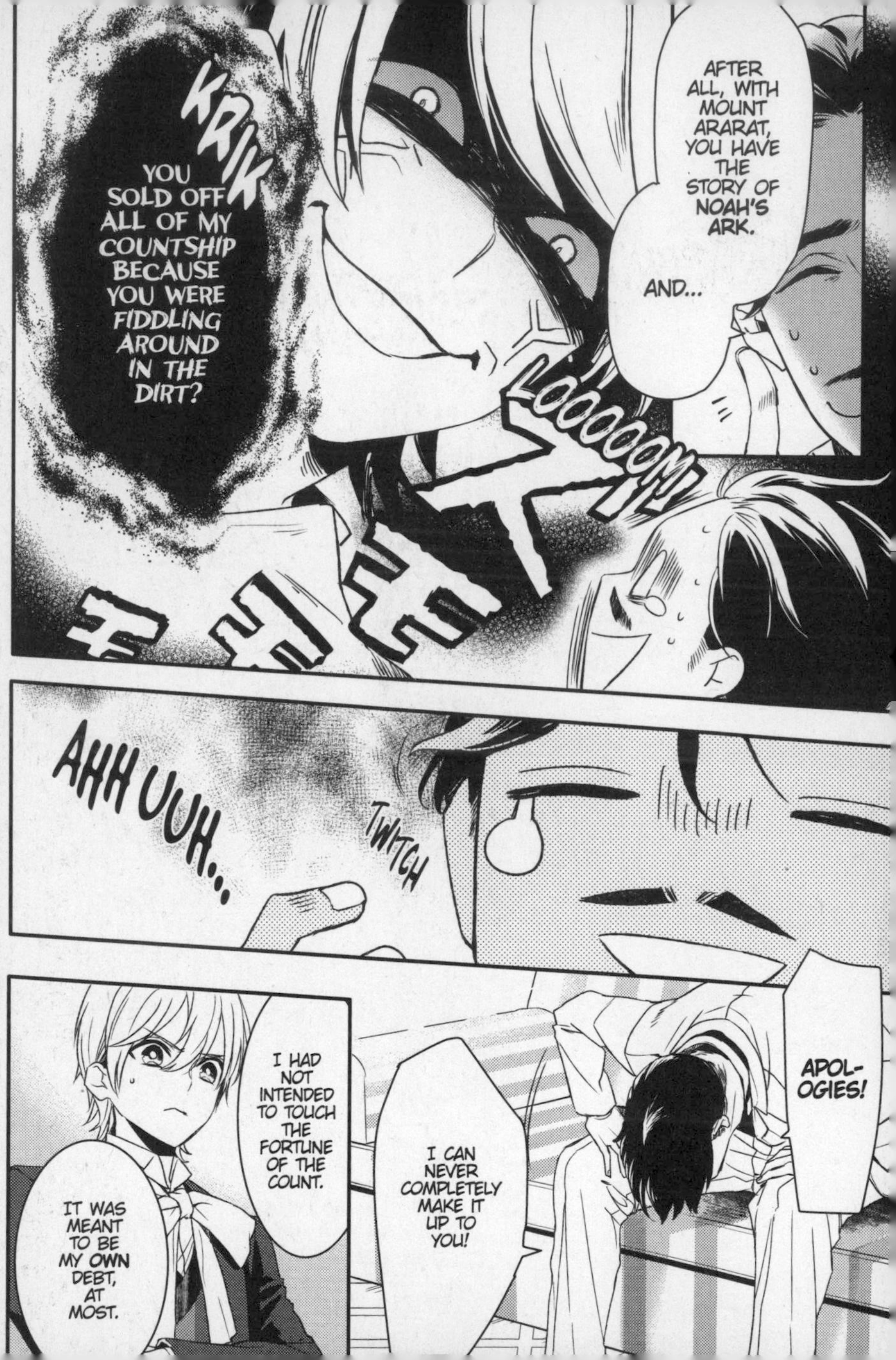
AFTER ALL, WITH MOUNT ARARAT, YOU HAVE THE STORY OF NOAH'S ARK.
AND...
KRIK
YOU SOLD OFF ALL OF MY COUNTSHIP BECAUSE YOU WERE FIDDLING AROUND IN THE DIRT?
LOOOOOM!!
AHH UUH...
TWITCH
APOL-OGIES!
I CAN NEVER COMPLETELY MAKE IT UP TO YOU!
I HAD NOT INTENDED TO TOUCH THE FORTUNE OF THE COUNT.
IT WAS MEANT TO BE MY OWN DEBT, AT MOST.

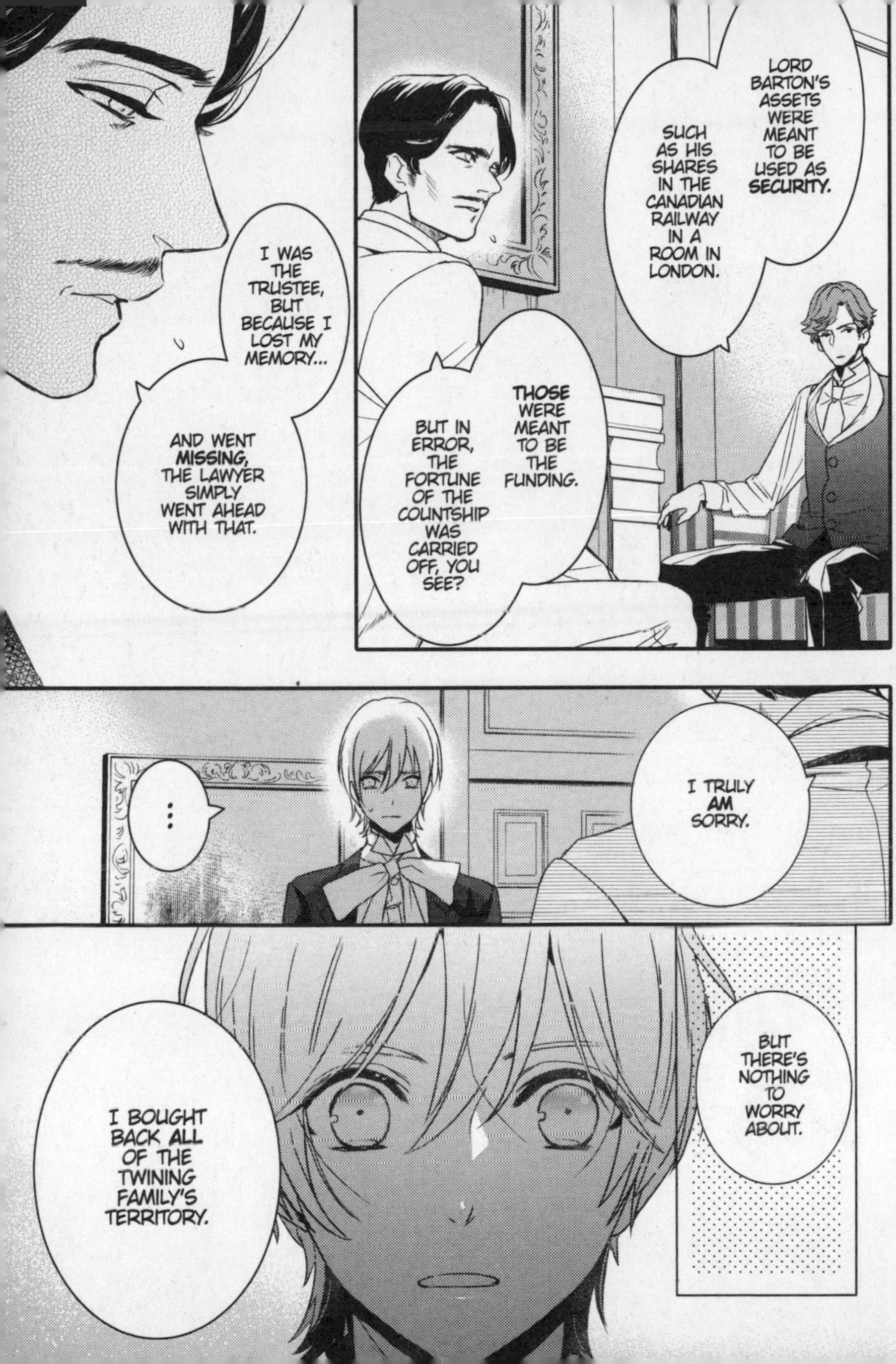
LORD BARTON'S ASSETS WERE MEANT TO BE USED AS SECURITY.
SUCH AS HIS SHARES IN THE CANADIAN RAILWAY IN A ROOM IN LONDON.
THOSE WERE MEANT TO BE THE FUNDING.
BUT IN ERROR, THE FORTUNE OF THE COUNTSHIP WAS CARRIED OFF, YOU SEE?
I WAS THE TRUSTEE, BUT BECAUSE I LOST MY MEMORY...
AND WENT MISSING, THE LAWYER SIMPLY WENT AHEAD WITH THAT.
I TRULY AM SORRY.
...
BUT THERE'S NOTHING TO WORRY ABOUT.
I BOUGHT BACK ALL OF THE TWINING FAMILY'S TERRITORY.

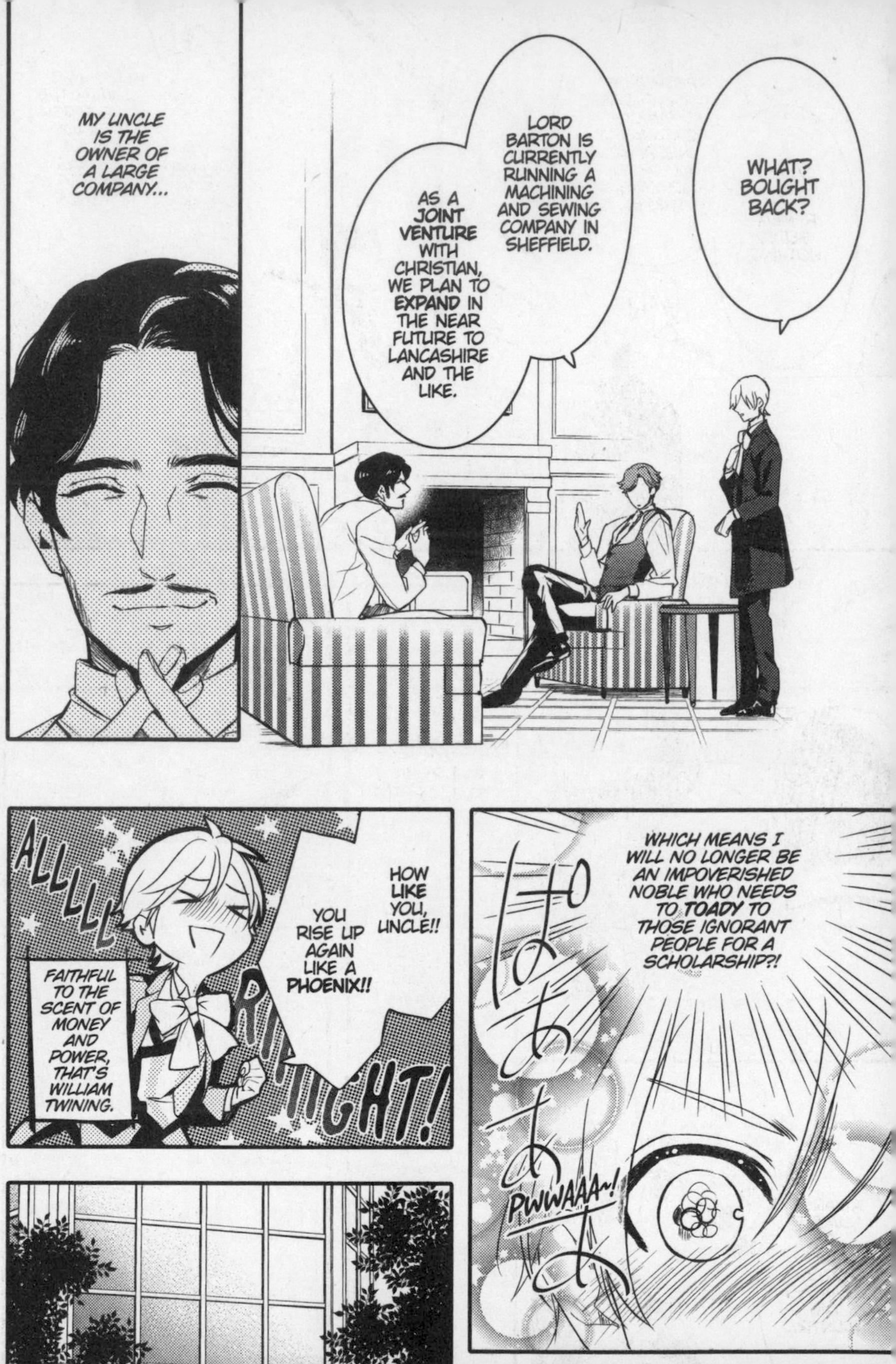
WHAT? BOUGHT BACK?
LORD BARTON IS CURRENTLY RUNNING A MACHINING AND SEWING COMPANY IN SHEFFIELD.
AS A JOINT VENTURE WITH CHRISTIAN, WE PLAN TO EXPAND IN THE NEAR FUTURE TO LANCASHIRE AND THE LIKE.
MY UNCLE IS THE OWNER OF A LARGE COMPANY...
WHICH MEANS I WILL NO LONGER BE AN IMPOVERISHED NOBLE WHO NEEDS TO TOADY TO THOSE IGNORANT PEOPLE FOR A SCHOLARSHIP?!
PWWAAA~!
HOW LIKE YOU, UNCLE!!
YOU RISE UP AGAIN LIKE A PHOENIX!!
ALLLLL RIIIGHT!
FAITHFUL TO THE SCENT OF MONEY AND POWER, THAT'S WILLIAM TWINING.

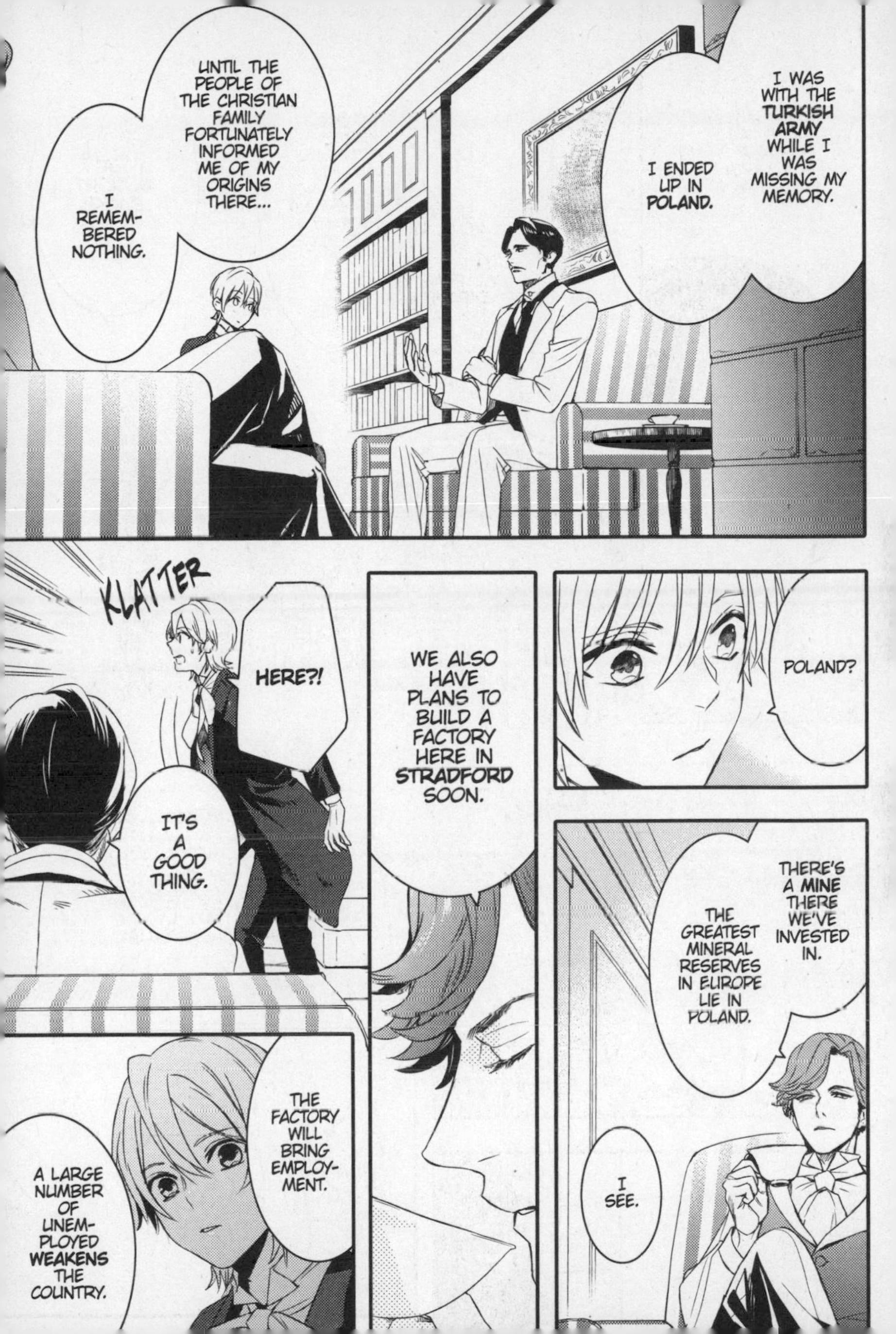

I WAS WITH THE TURKISH ARMY WHILE I WAS MISSING MY MEMORY.
I ENDED UP IN POLAND.
UNTIL THE PEOPLE OF THE CHRISTIAN FAMILY FORTUNATELY INFORMED ME OF MY ORIGINS THERE...
I REMEMBERED NOTHING.
POLAND?
THERE'S A MINE THERE WE'VE INVESTED IN.
THE GREATEST MINERAL RESERVES IN EUROPE LIE IN POLAND.
I SEE.
WE ALSO HAVE PLANS TO BUILD A FACTORY HERE IN STRADFORD SOON.
KLATTER
HERE?!
IT'S A GOOD THING.
THE FACTORY WILL BRING EMPLOYMENT.
A LARGE NUMBER OF UNEMPLOYED WEAKENS THE COUNTRY.

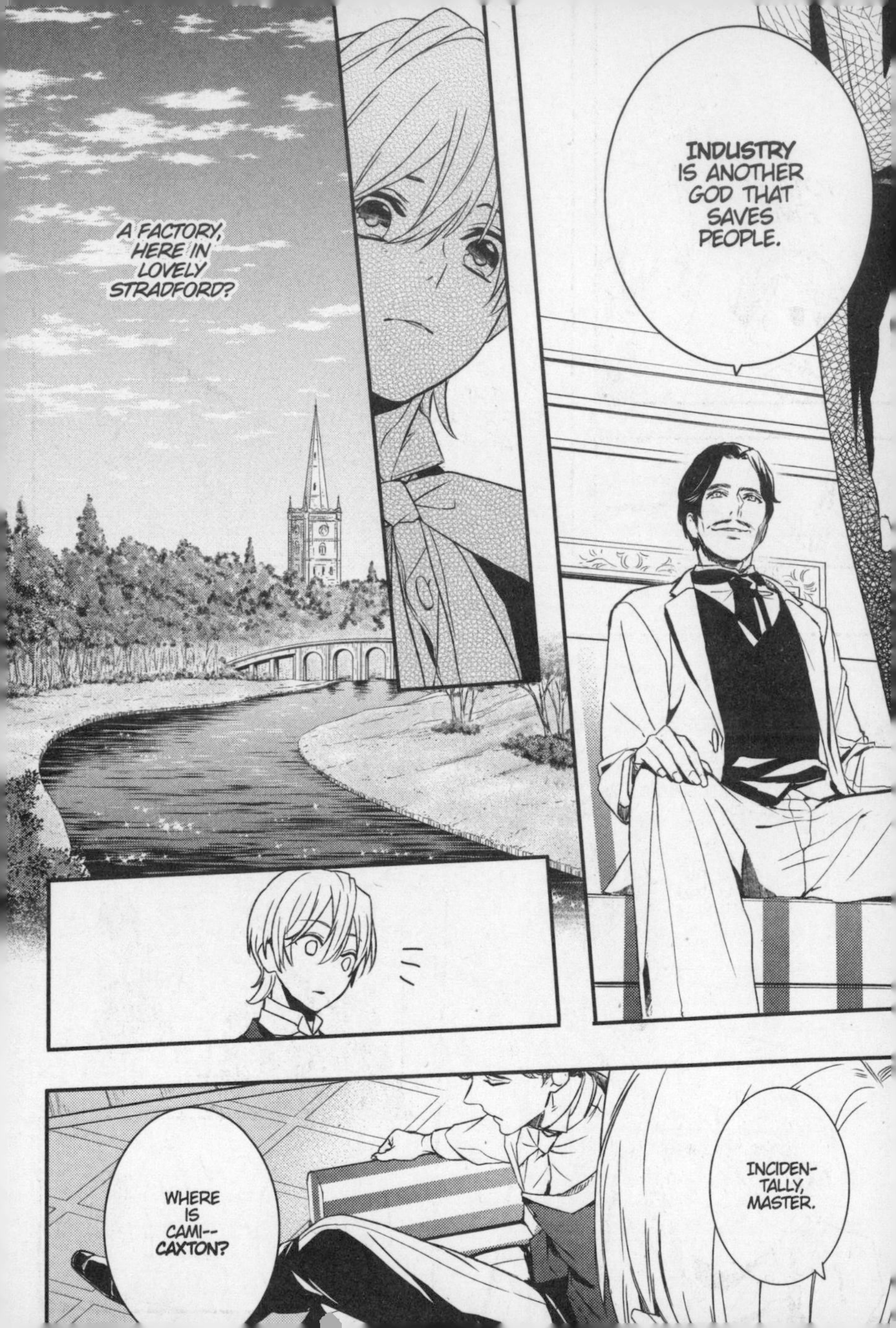
INDUSTRY IS ANOTHER GOD THAT SAVES PEOPLE.
A FACTORY, HERE IN LOVELY STRADFORD?
INCIDENTALLY, MASTER.
WHERE IS CAMI--CAXTON?

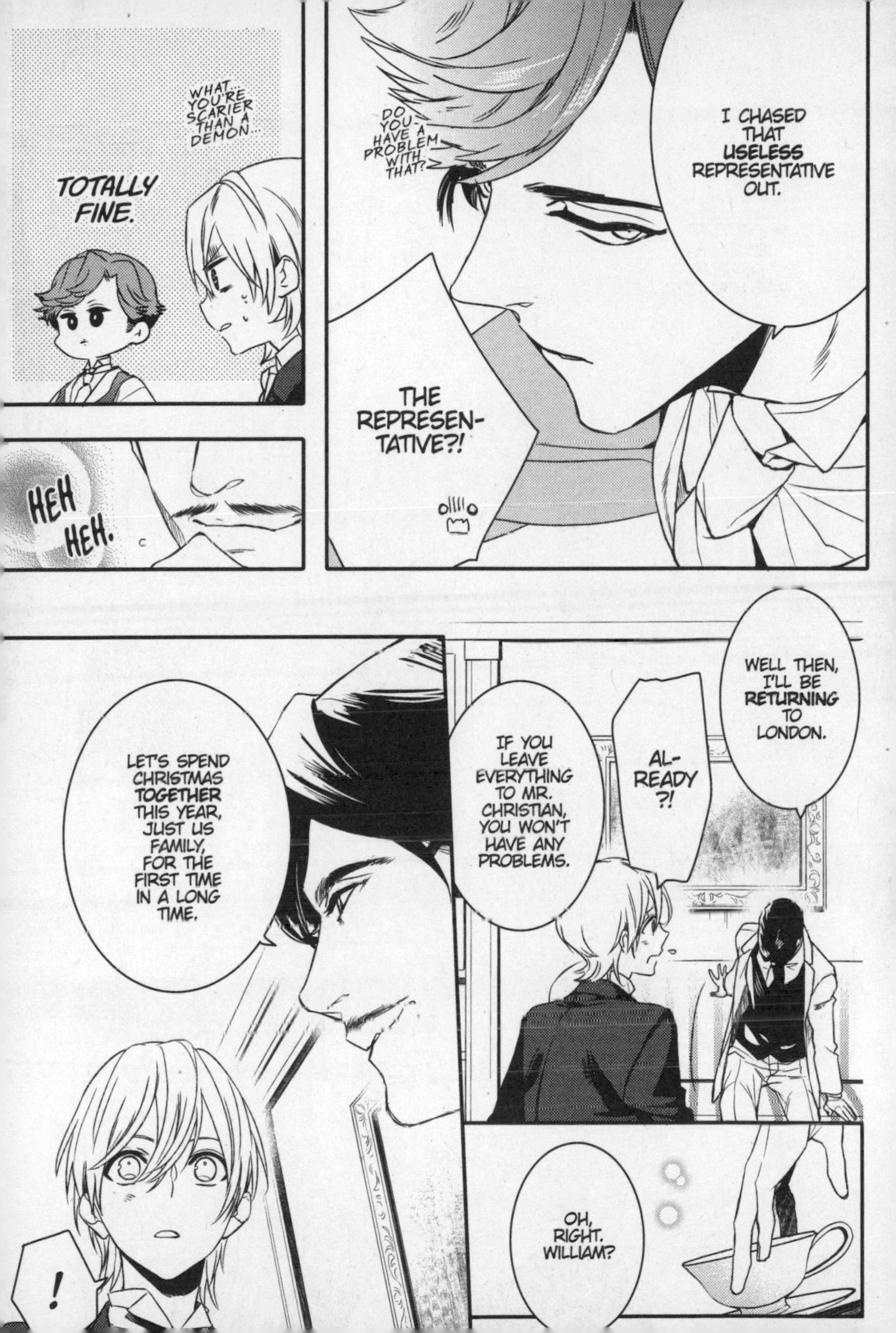
I CHASED THAT USELESS REPRESENTATIVE OUT.
DO YOU HAVE A PROBLEM WITH THAT?
THE REPRESENTATIVE?!
WHAT... YOU'RE SCARIER THAN A DEMON...
TOTALLY FINE.
HEH HEH.
WELL THEN, I'LL BE RETURNING TO LONDON.
ALREADY?!
IF YOU LEAVE EVERYTHING TO MR. CHRISTIAN, YOU WON'T HAVE ANY PROBLEMS.
OH, RIGHT. WILLIAM?
LET'S SPEND CHRISTMAS TOGETHER THIS YEAR, JUST US FAMILY, FOR THE FIRST TIME IN A LONG TIME.
!

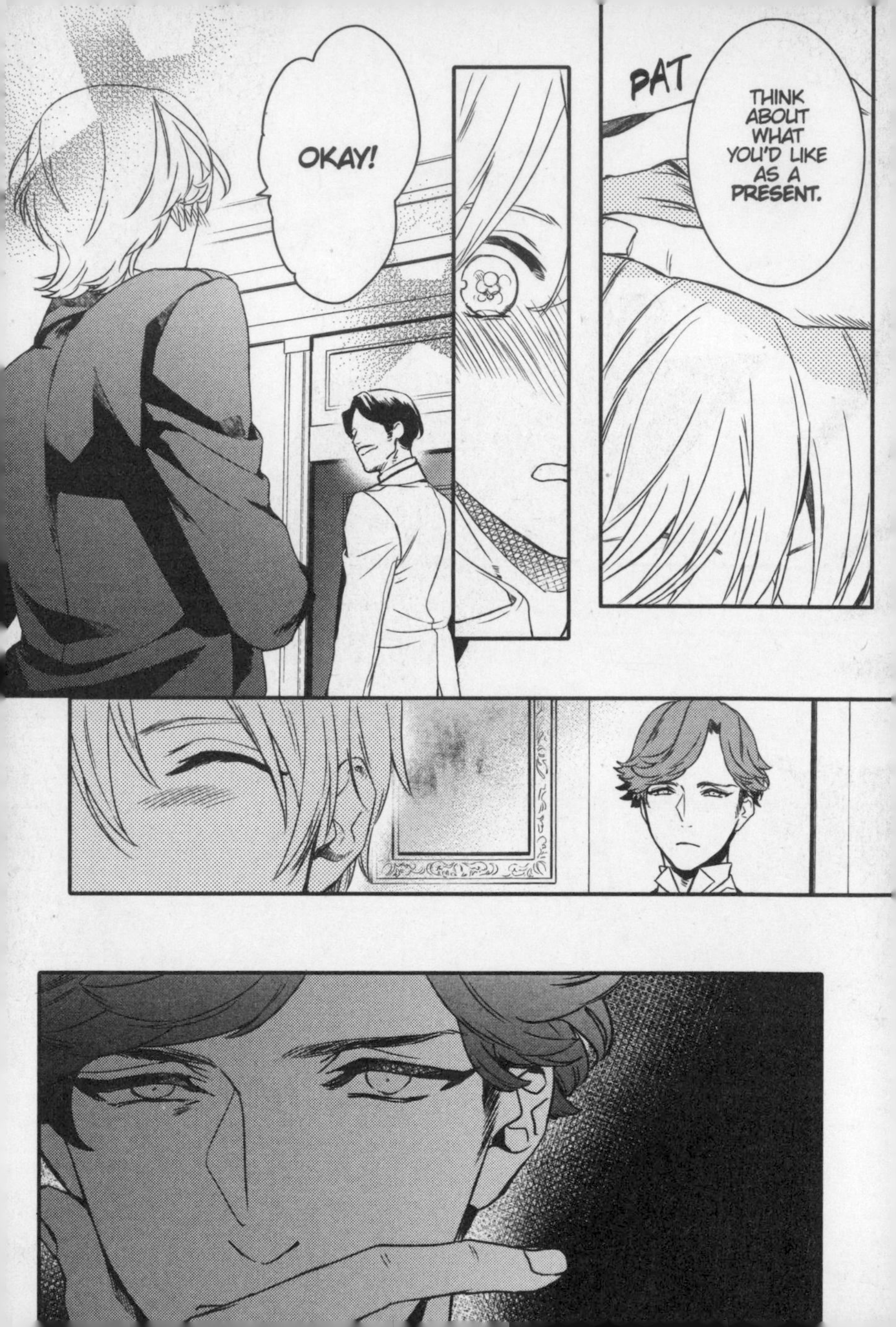
PAT
THINK ABOUT WHAT YOU'D LIKE AS A PRESENT.
OKAY!

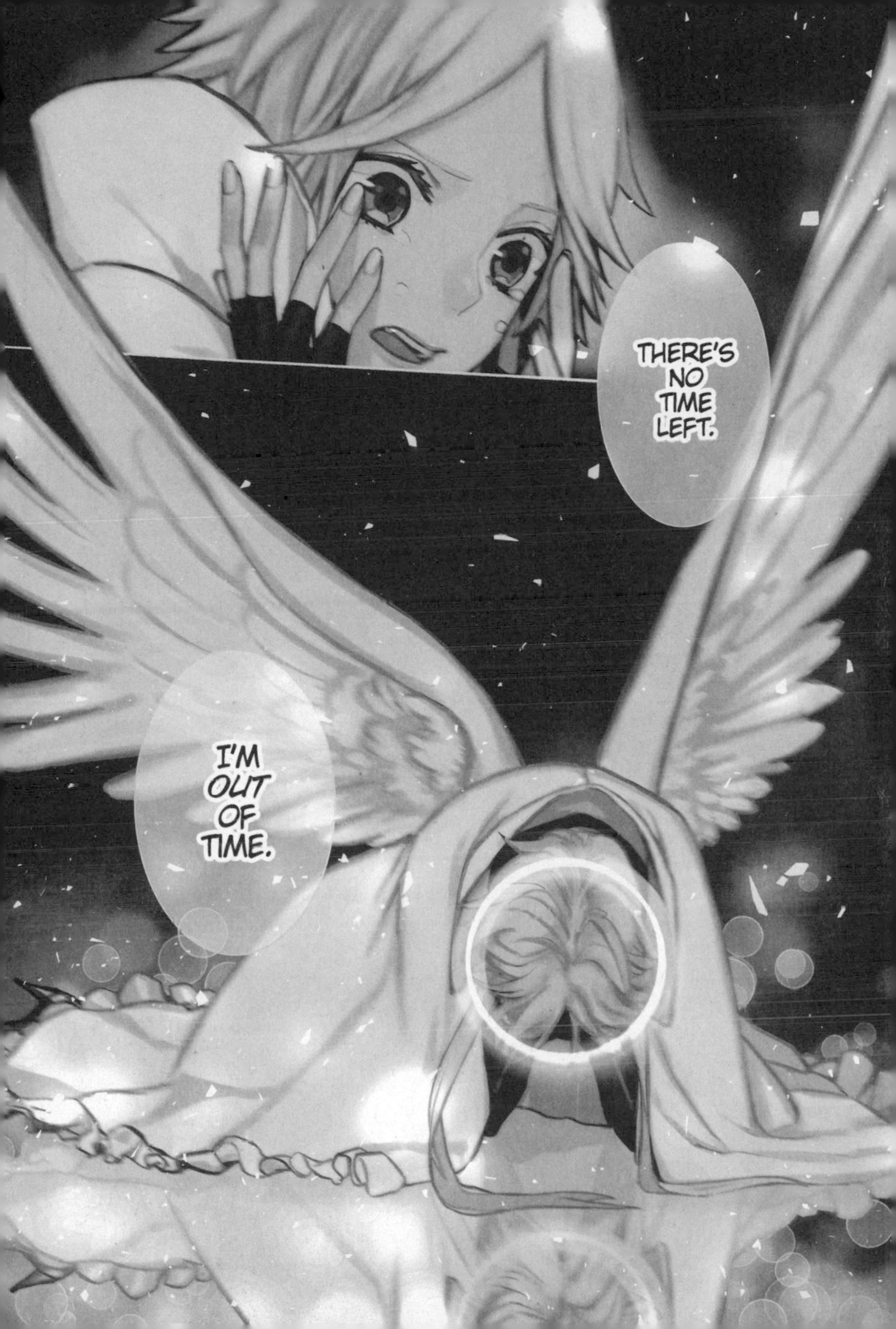
THERE'S NO TIME LEFT.
I'M OUT OF TIME.

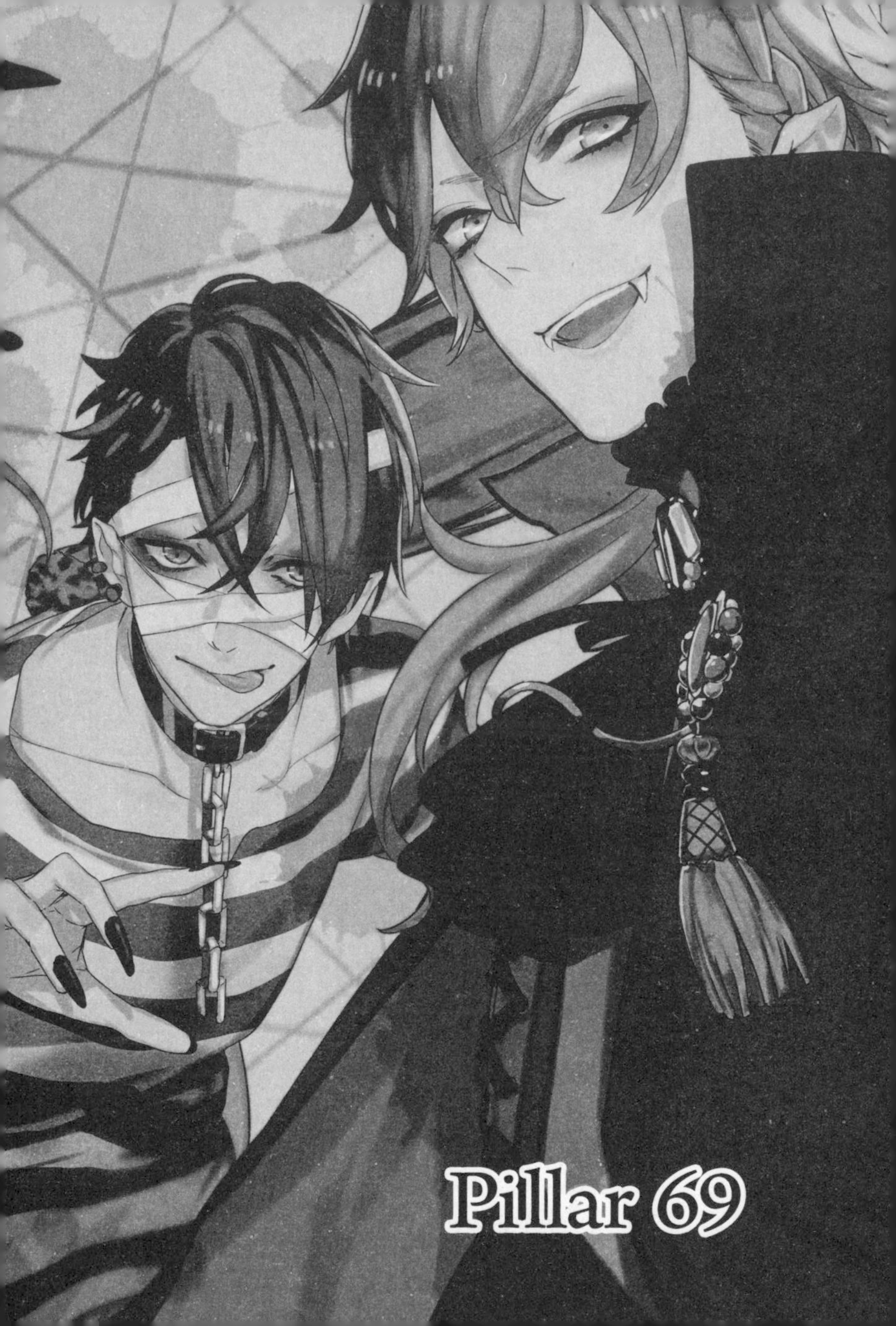
Pillar 69

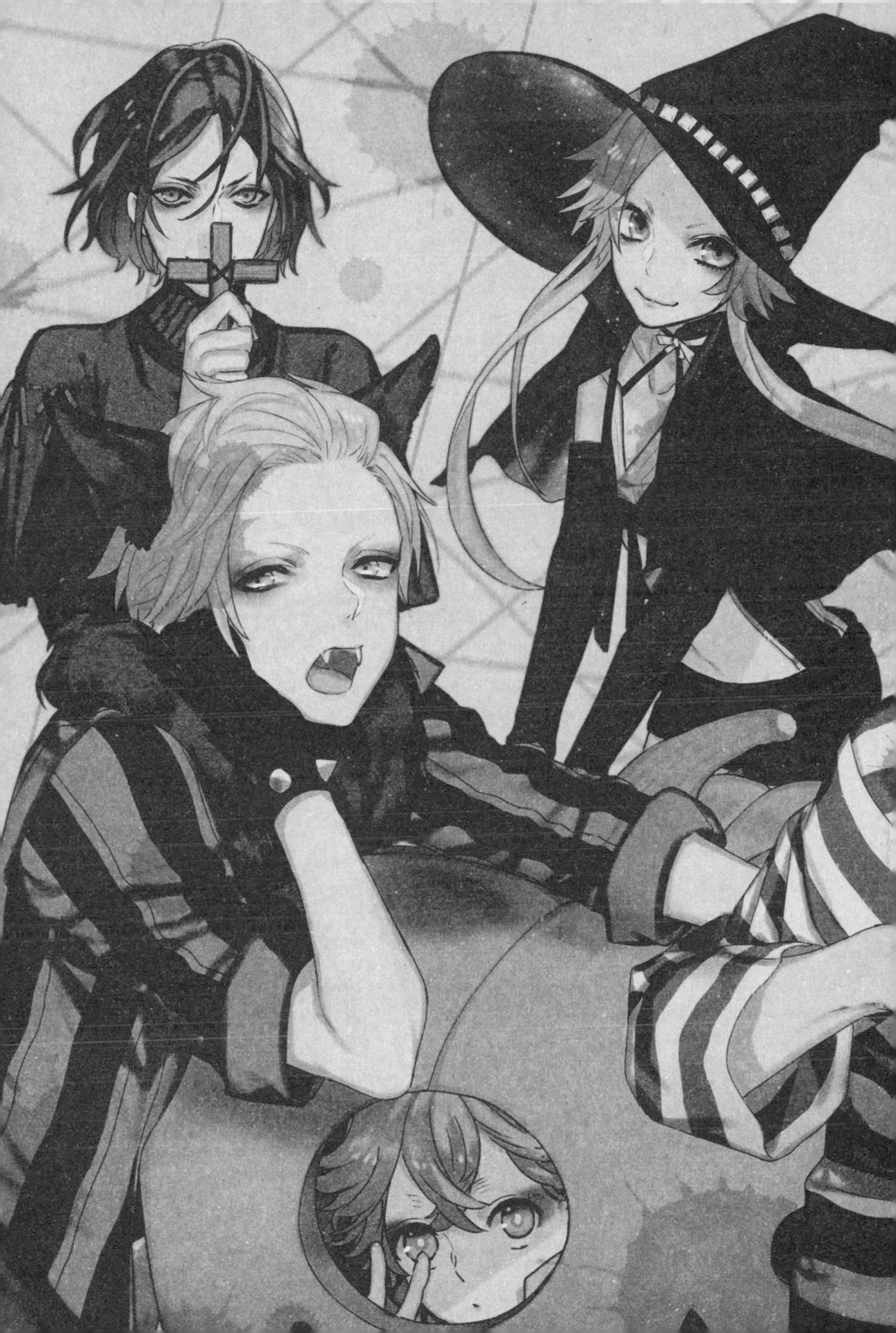

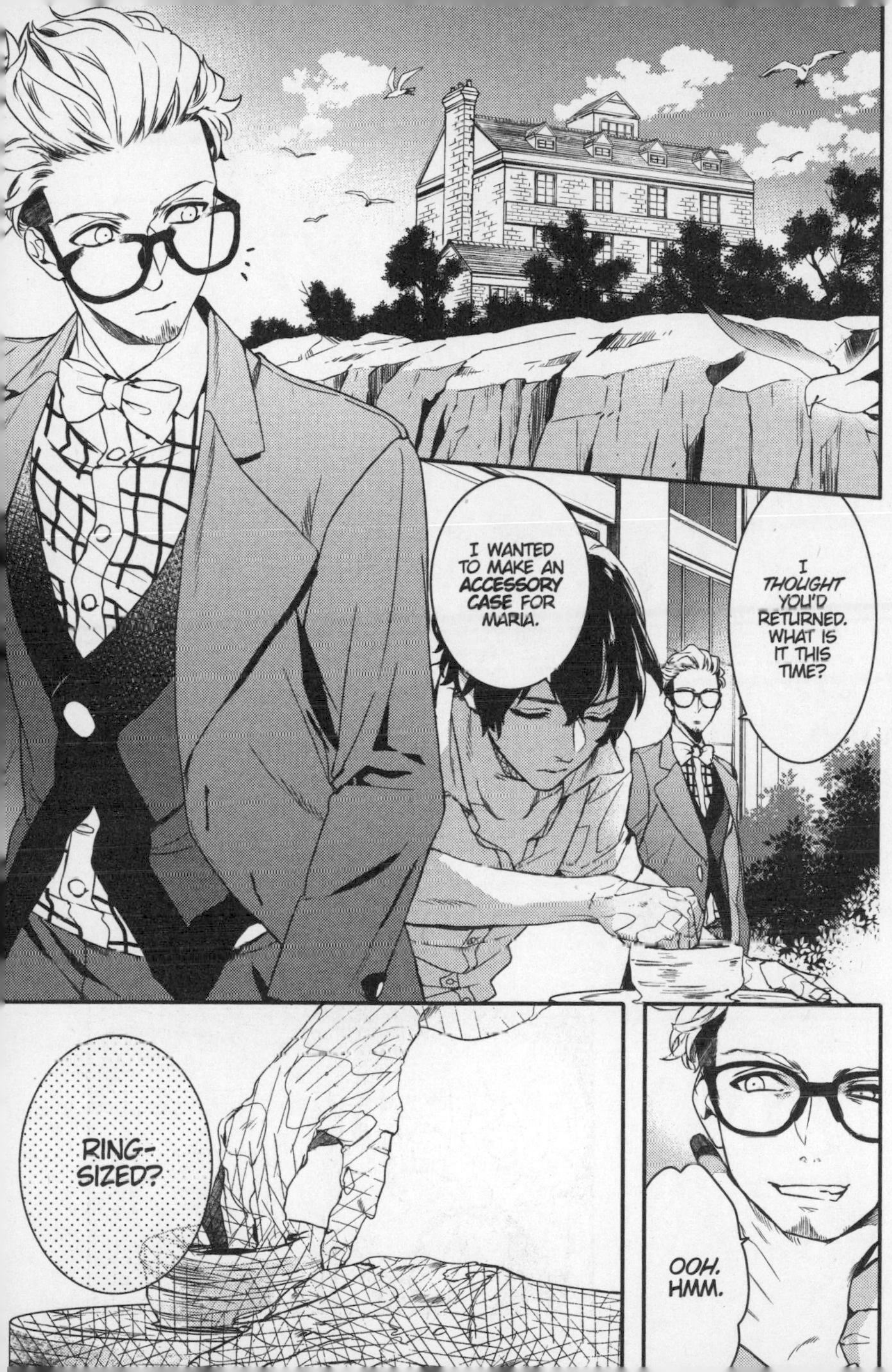
I THOUGHT YOU'D RETURNED. WHAT IS IT THIS TIME?
I WANTED TO MAKE AN ACCESSORY CASE FOR MARIA.
OOH. HMM.
RING-SIZED?

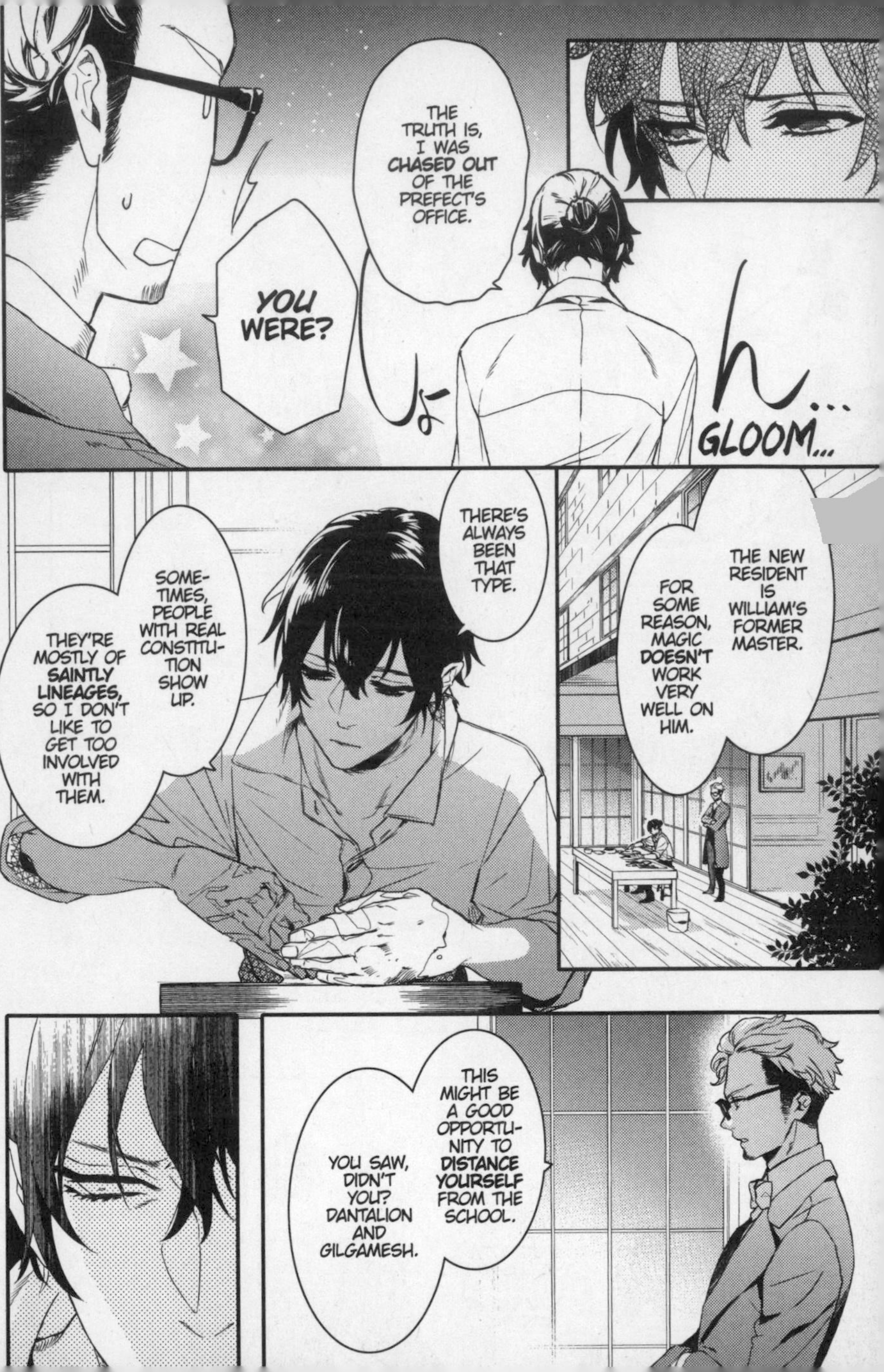
h...
GLOOM...
THE TRUTH IS, I WAS CHASED OUT OF THE PREFECT'S OFFICE.
YOU WERE?
THE NEW RESIDENT IS WILLIAM'S FORMER MASTER.
FOR SOME REASON, MAGIC DOESN'T WORK VERY WELL ON HIM.
THERE'S ALWAYS BEEN THAT TYPE.
SOME-TIMES, PEOPLE WITH REAL CONSTITU-TION SHOW UP.
THEY'RE MOSTLY OF SAINTLY LINEAGES, SO I DON'T LIKE TO GET TOO INVOLVED WITH THEM.
THIS MIGHT BE A GOOD OPPORTU-NITY TO DISTANCE YOURSELF FROM THE SCHOOL.
YOU SAW, DIDN'T YOU? DANTALION AND GILGAMESH.

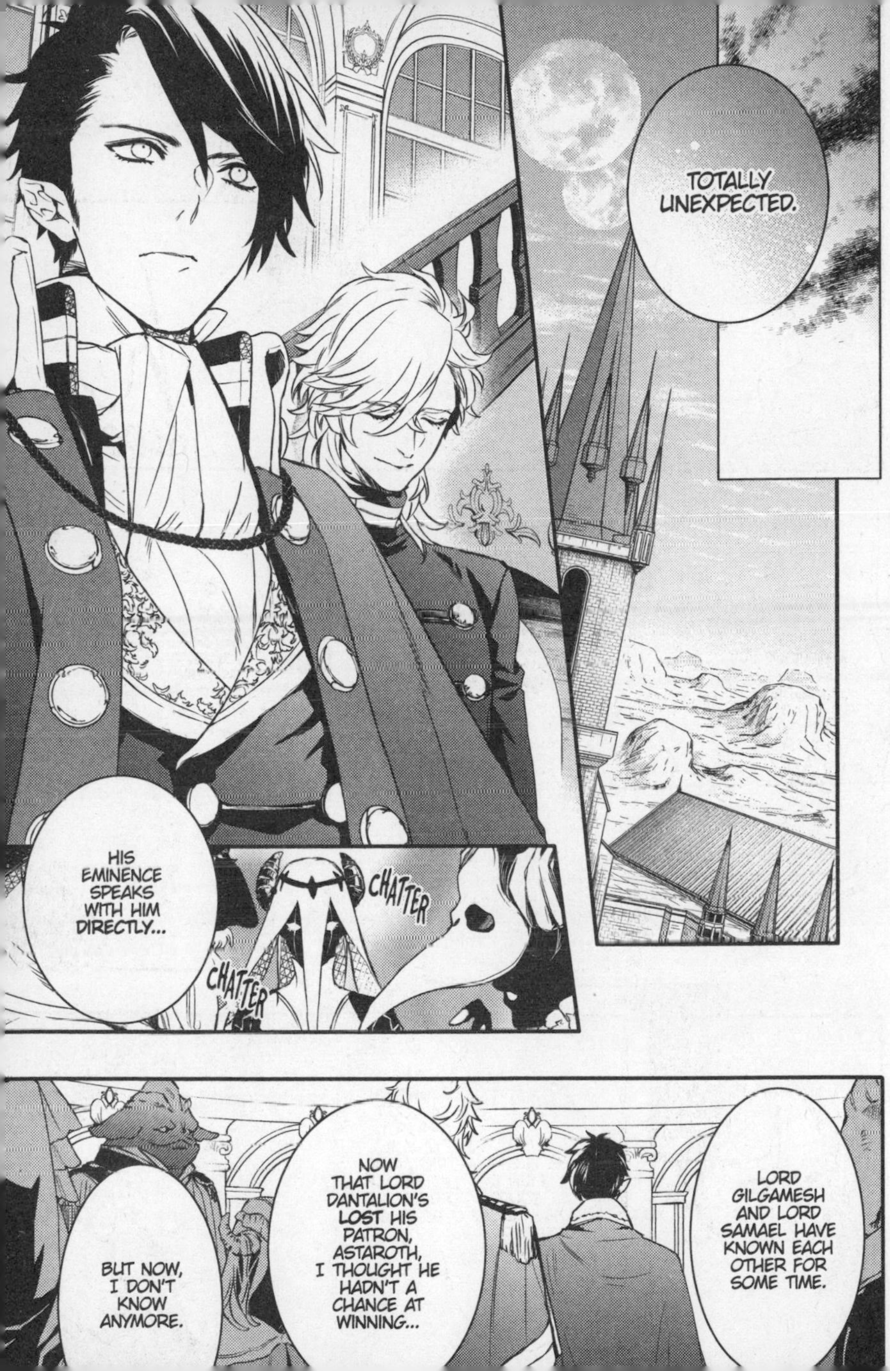
TOTALLY UNEXPECTED.
HIS EMINENCE SPEAKS WITH HIM DIRECTLY...
CHATTER
CHATTER
LORD GILGAMESH AND LORD SAMAEL HAVE KNOWN EACH OTHER FOR SOME TIME.
NOW THAT LORD DANTALION'S LOST HIS PATRON, ASTAROTH, I THOUGHT HE HADN'T A CHANCE AT WINNING...
BUT NOW, I DON'T KNOW ANYMORE.

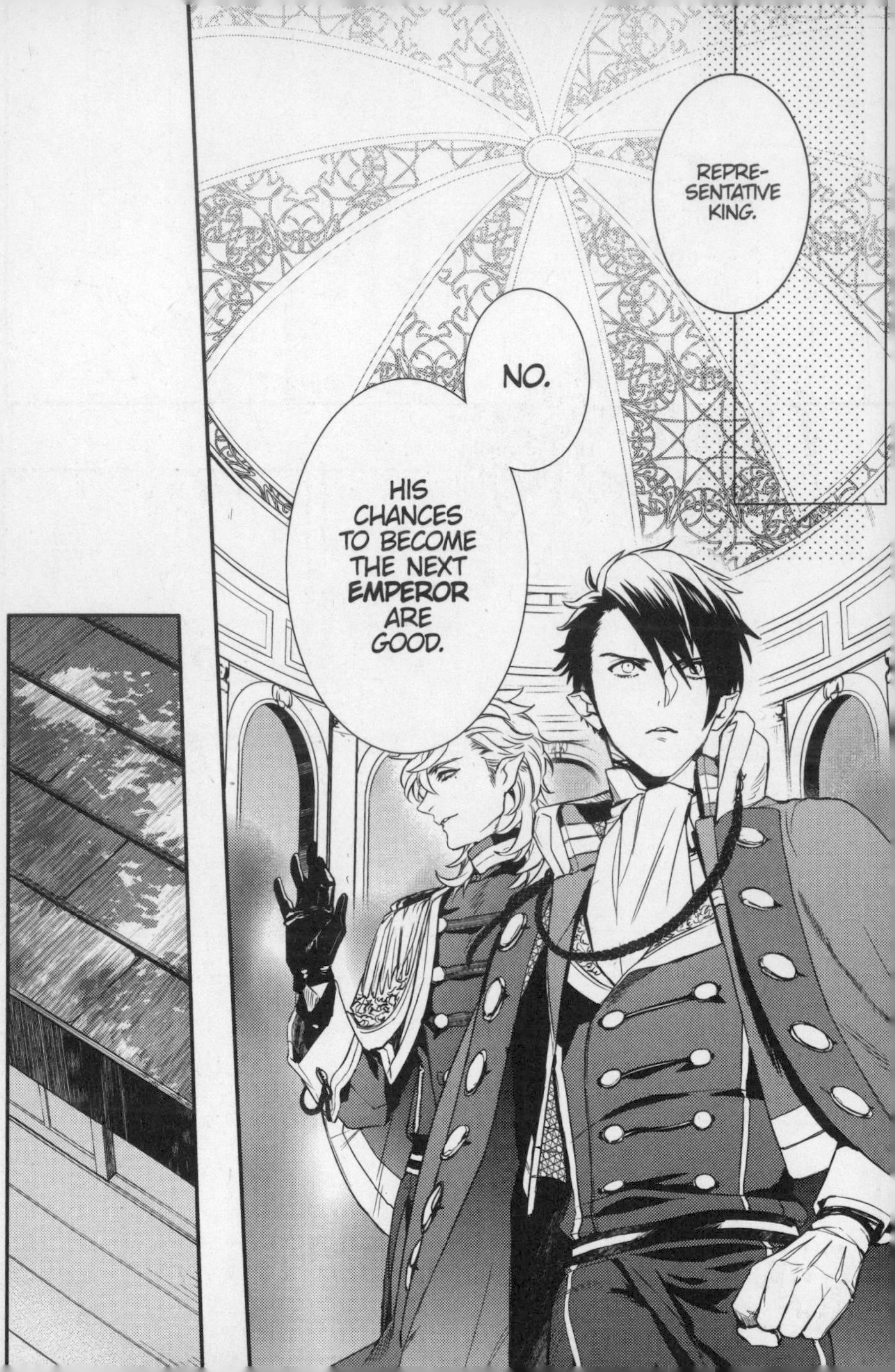
REPRE-SENTATIVE KING.
NO.
HIS CHANCES TO BECOME THE NEXT EMPEROR ARE GOOD.

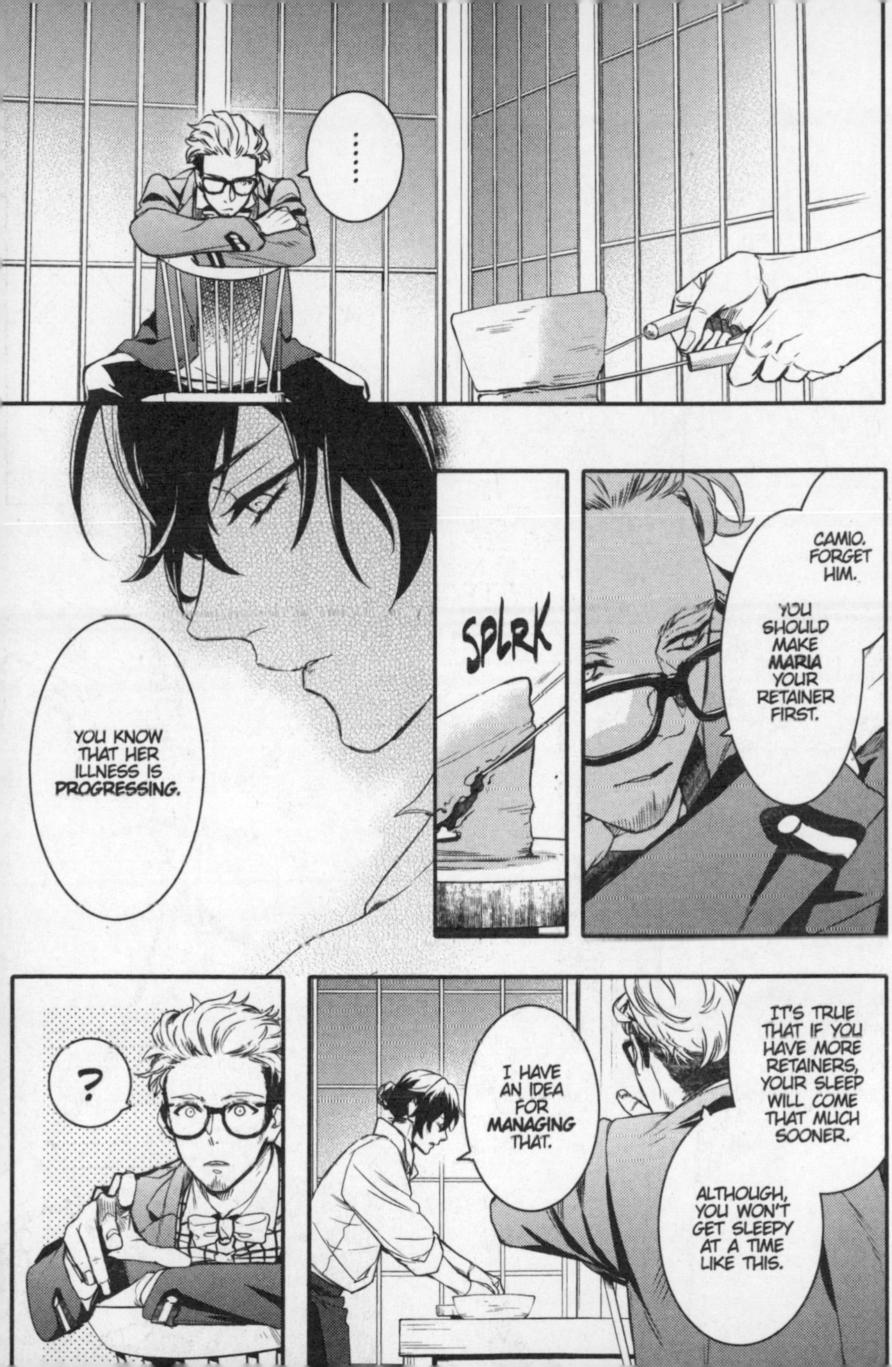
......
CAMIO. FORGET HIM.
YOU SHOULD MAKE MARIA YOUR RETAINER FIRST.
SPLRK
YOU KNOW THAT HER ILLNESS IS PROGRESSING.
IT'S TRUE THAT IF YOU HAVE MORE RETAINERS, YOUR SLEEP WILL COME THAT MUCH SOONER.
ALTHOUGH, YOU WON'T GET SLEEPY AT A TIME LIKE THIS.
I HAVE AN IDEA FOR MANAGING THAT.
?

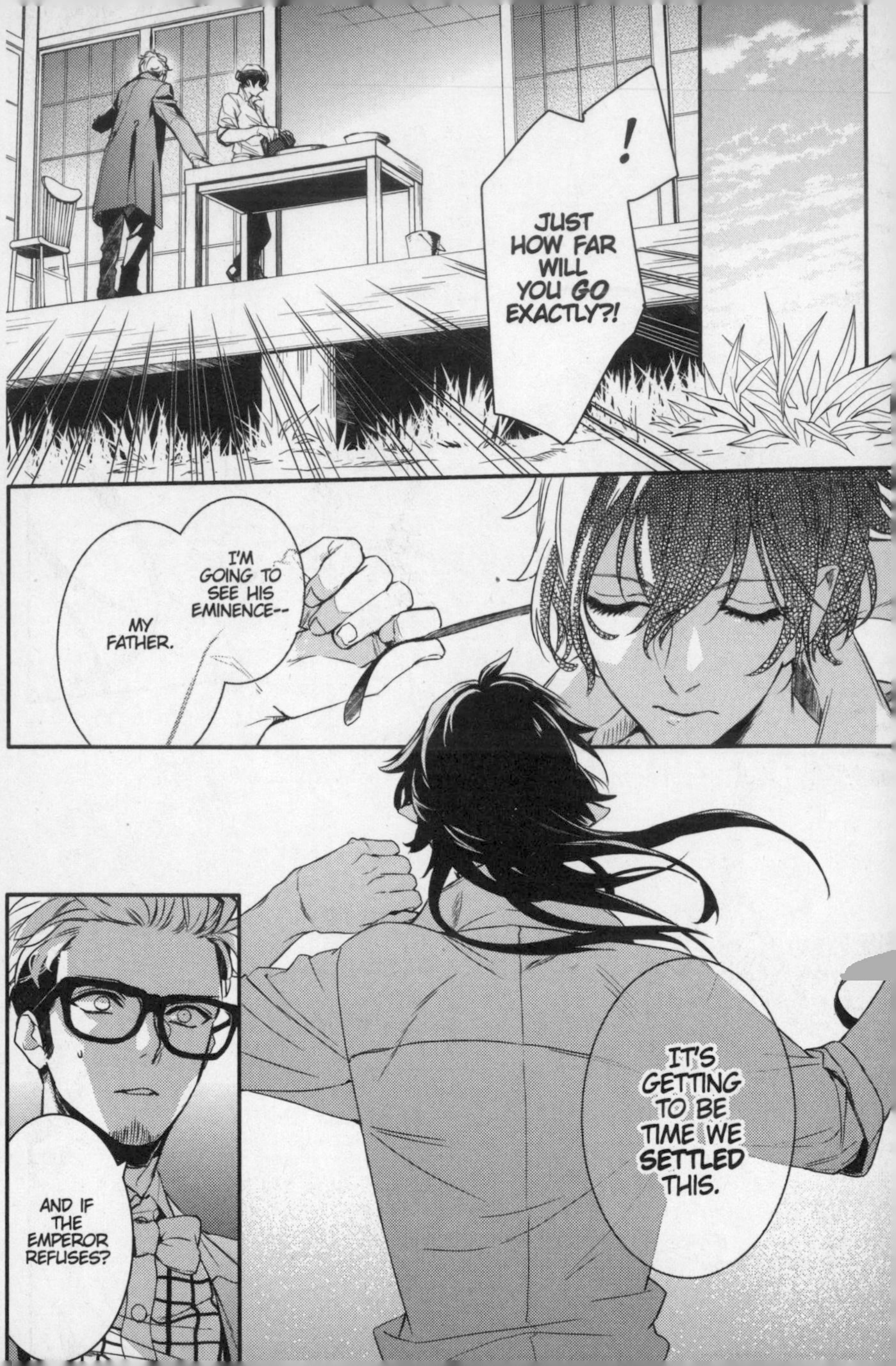
!
JUST HOW FAR WILL YOU GO EXACTLY?!
I'M GOING TO SEE HIS EMINENCE--
MY FATHER.
IT'S GETTING TO BE TIME WE SETTLED THIS.
AND IF THE EMPEROR REFUSES?

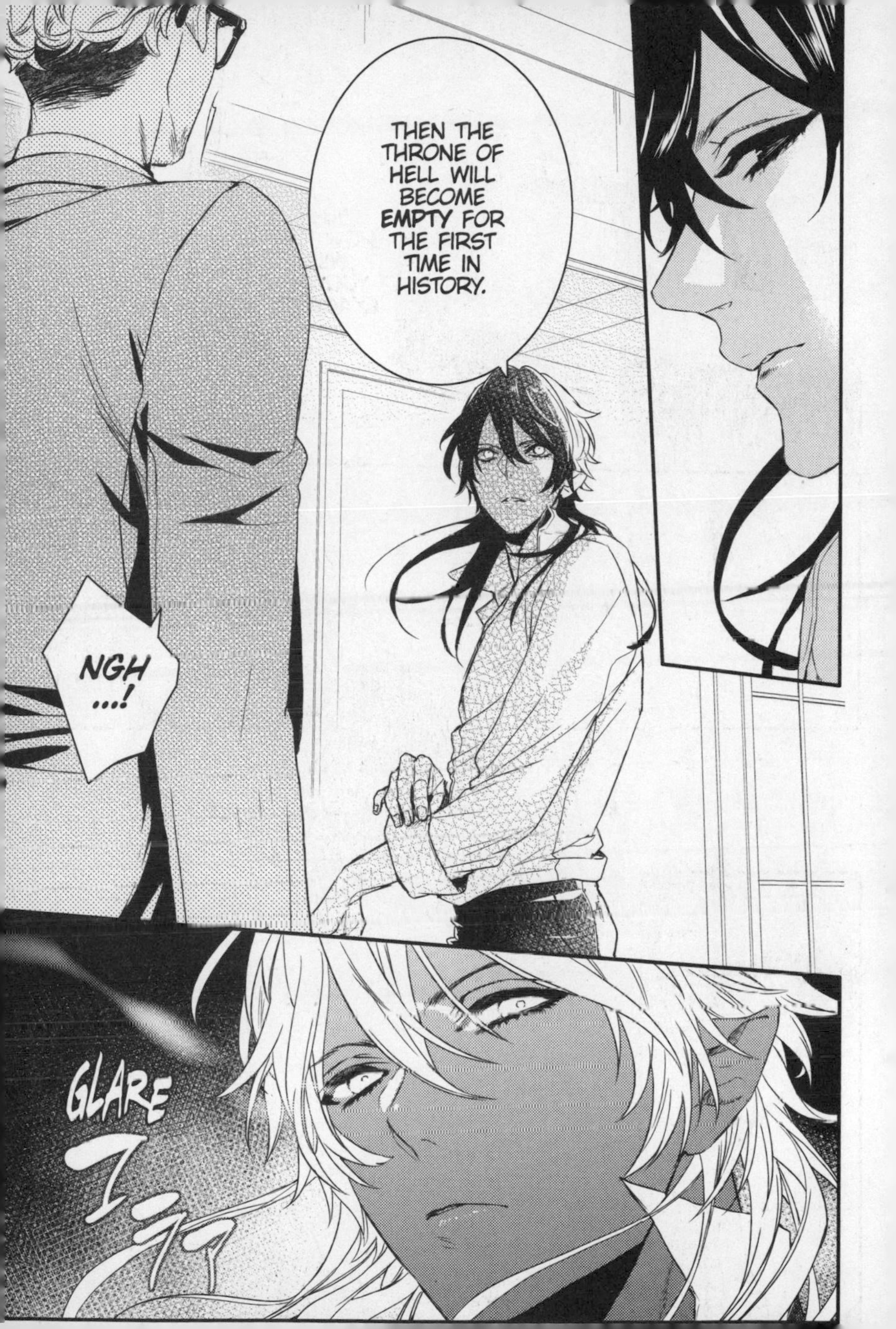
THEN THE THRONE OF HELL WILL BECOME EMPTY FOR THE FIRST TIME IN HISTORY.
NGH ...!
GLARE

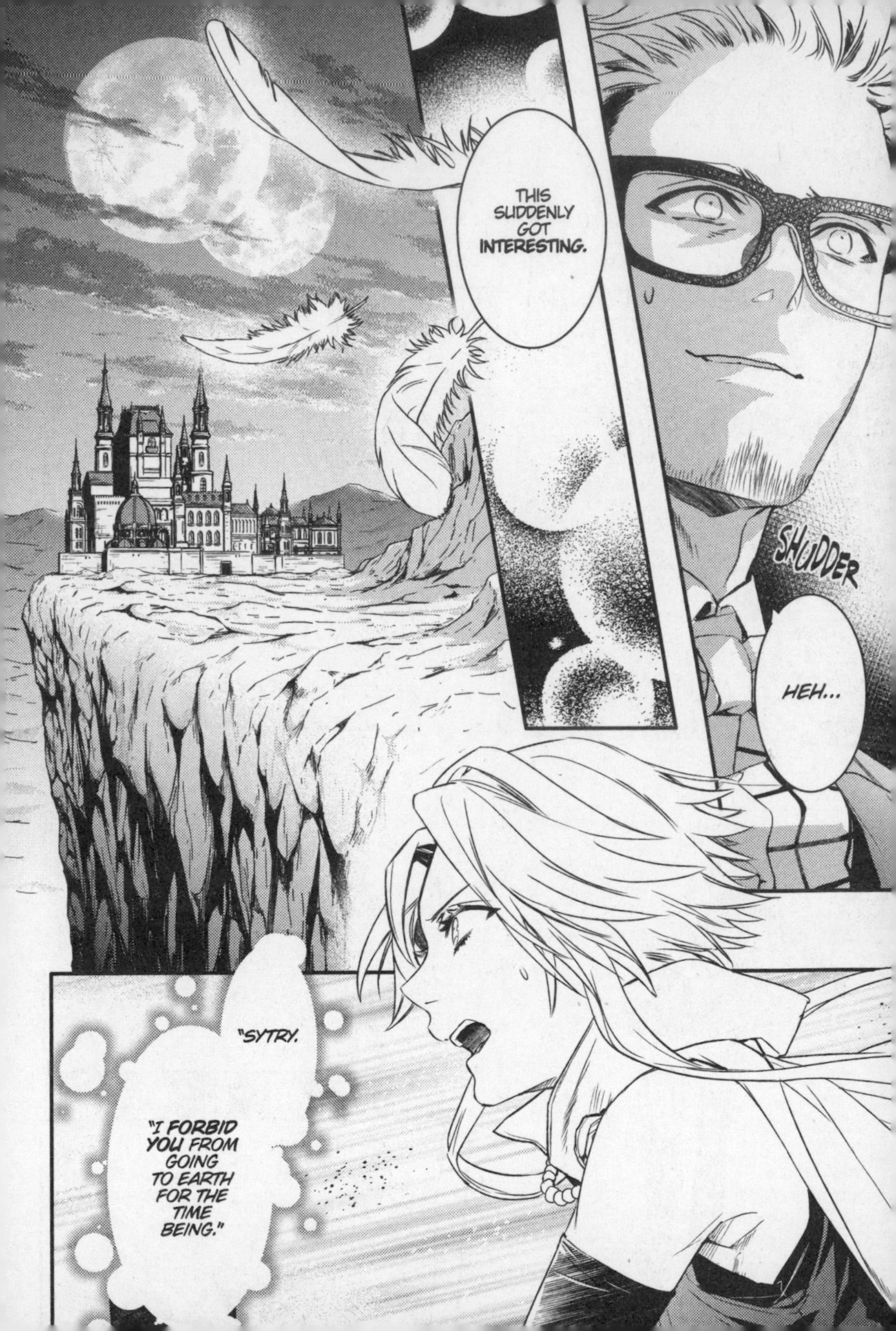
SHUDDER
HEH...
THIS SUDDENLY GOT INTERESTING.
"SYTRY.
"I FORBID YOU FROM GOING TO EARTH FOR THE TIME BEING."

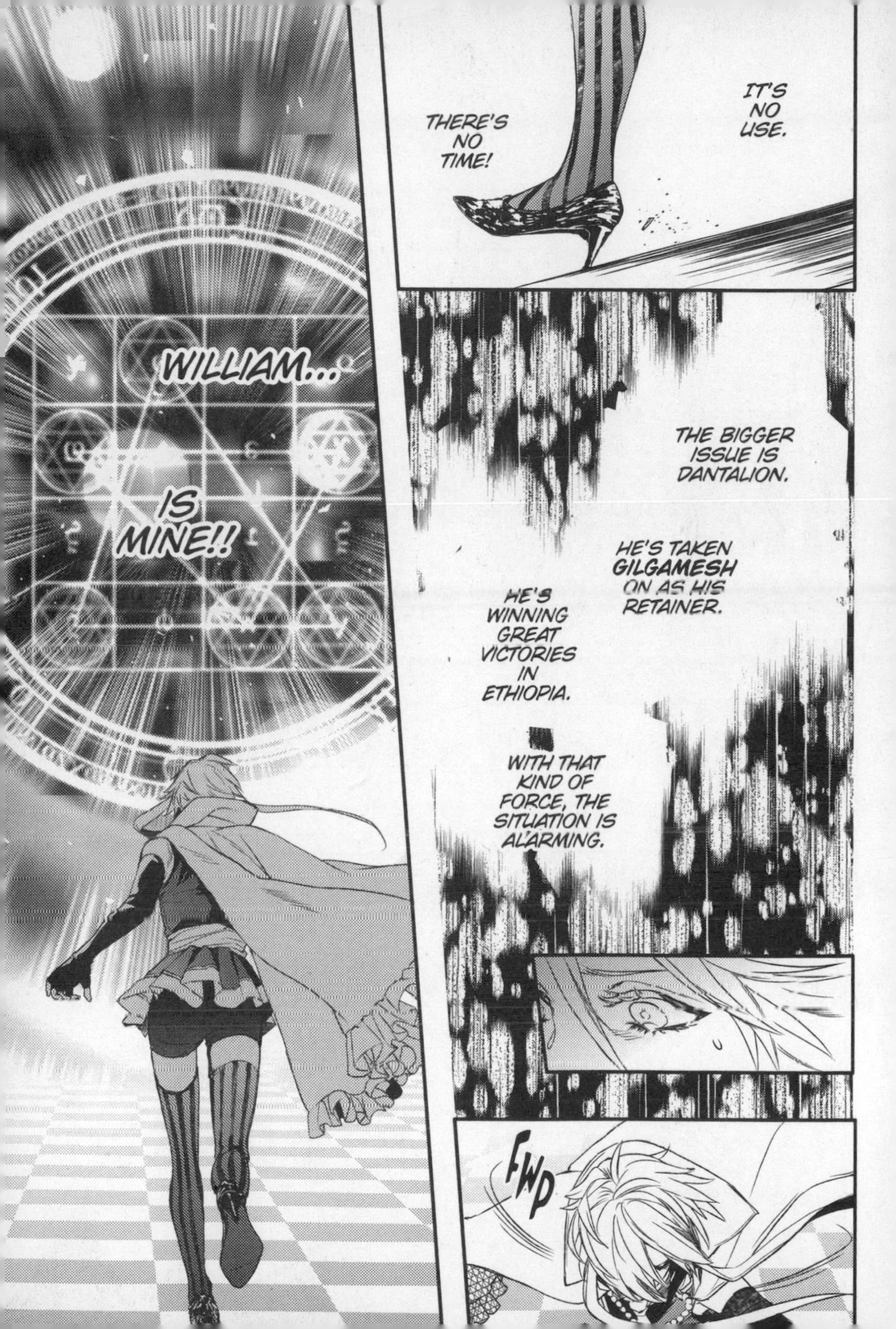
IT'S NO USE.
THERE'S NO TIME!
THE BIGGER ISSUE IS DANTALION.
HE'S TAKEN GILGAMESH ON AS HIS RETAINER.
HE'S WINNING GREAT VICTORIES IN ETHIOPIA.
WITH THAT KIND OF FORCE, THE SITUATION IS ALARMING.
FWP
WILLIAM...
IS MINE!!

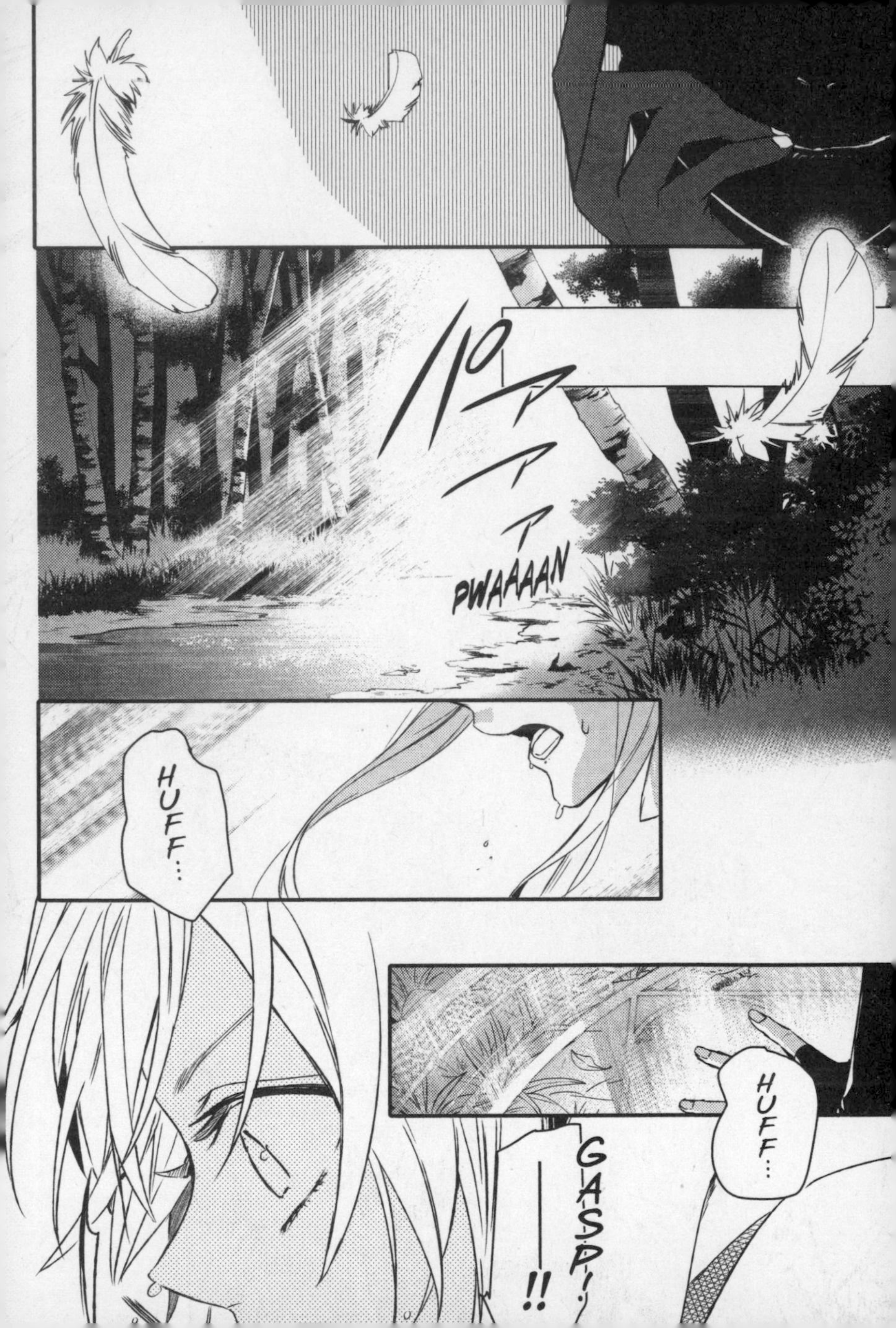
パァァァ
PWAAAAN
HUFF...
HUFF...
GASP!
——!!

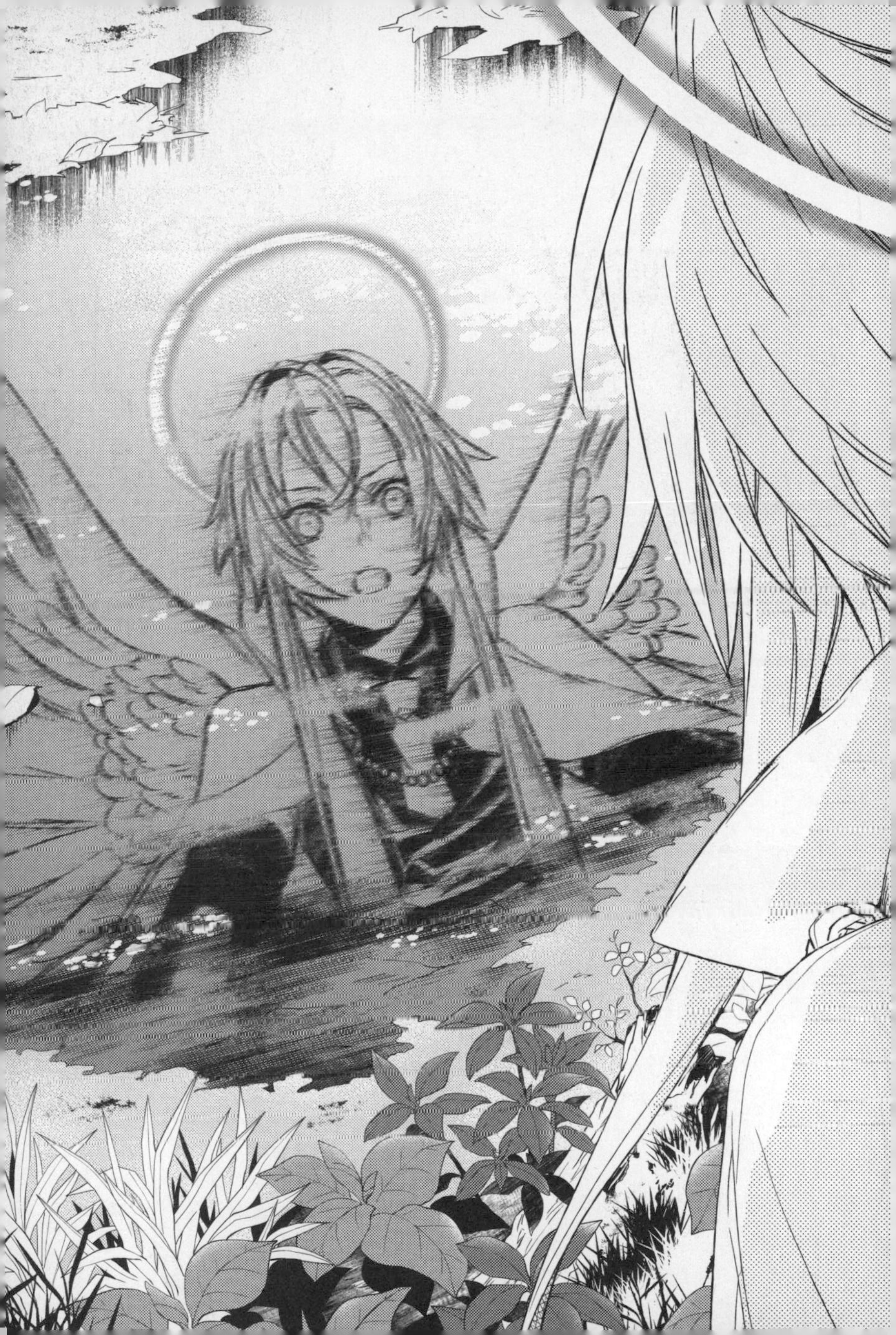

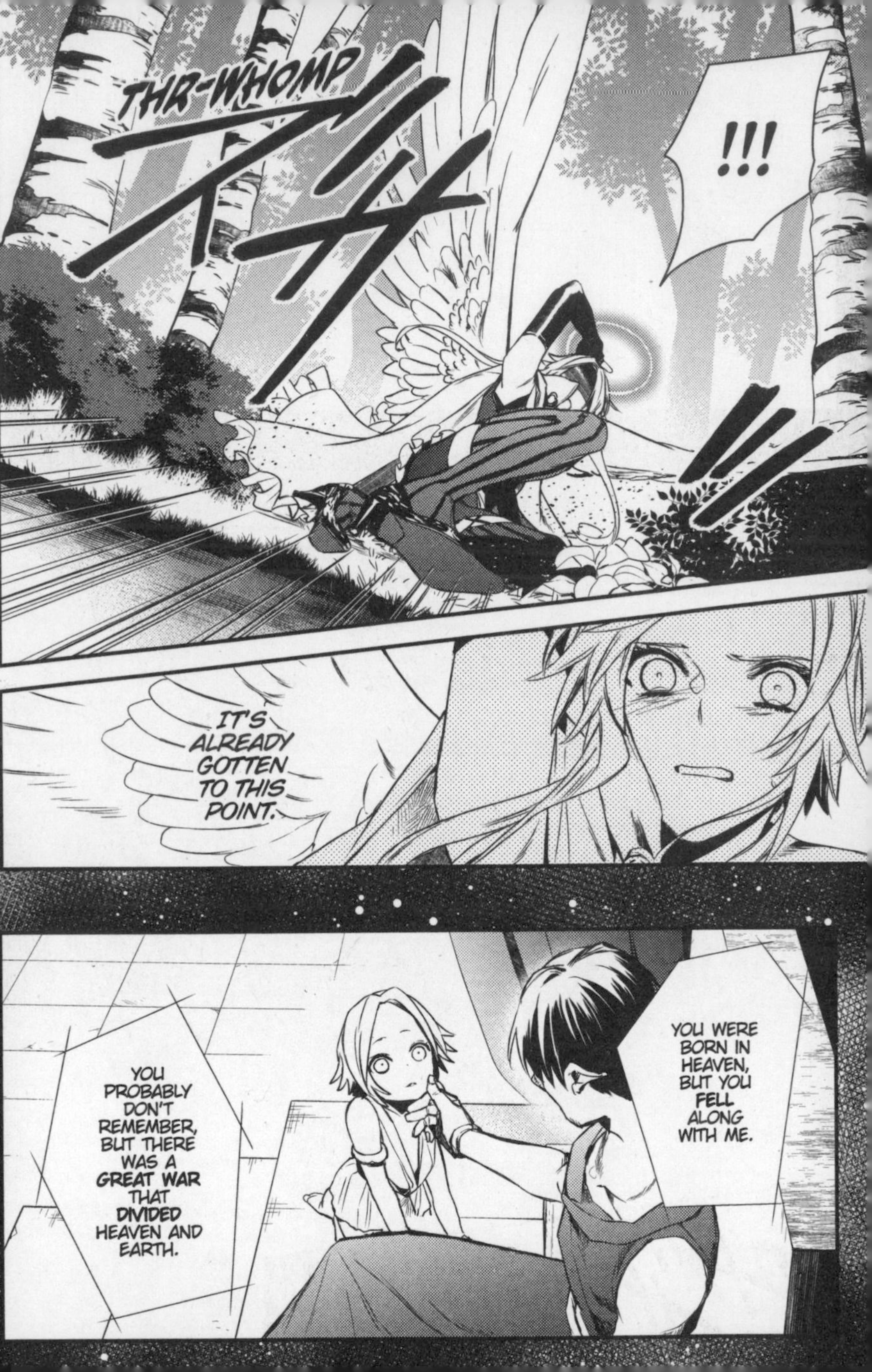
!!!
THR-WHOMP
IT'S ALREADY GOTTEN TO THIS POINT.
YOU WERE BORN IN HEAVEN, BUT YOU FELL ALONG WITH ME.
YOU PROBABLY DON'T REMEMBER, BUT THERE WAS A GREAT WAR THAT DIVIDED HEAVEN AND EARTH.

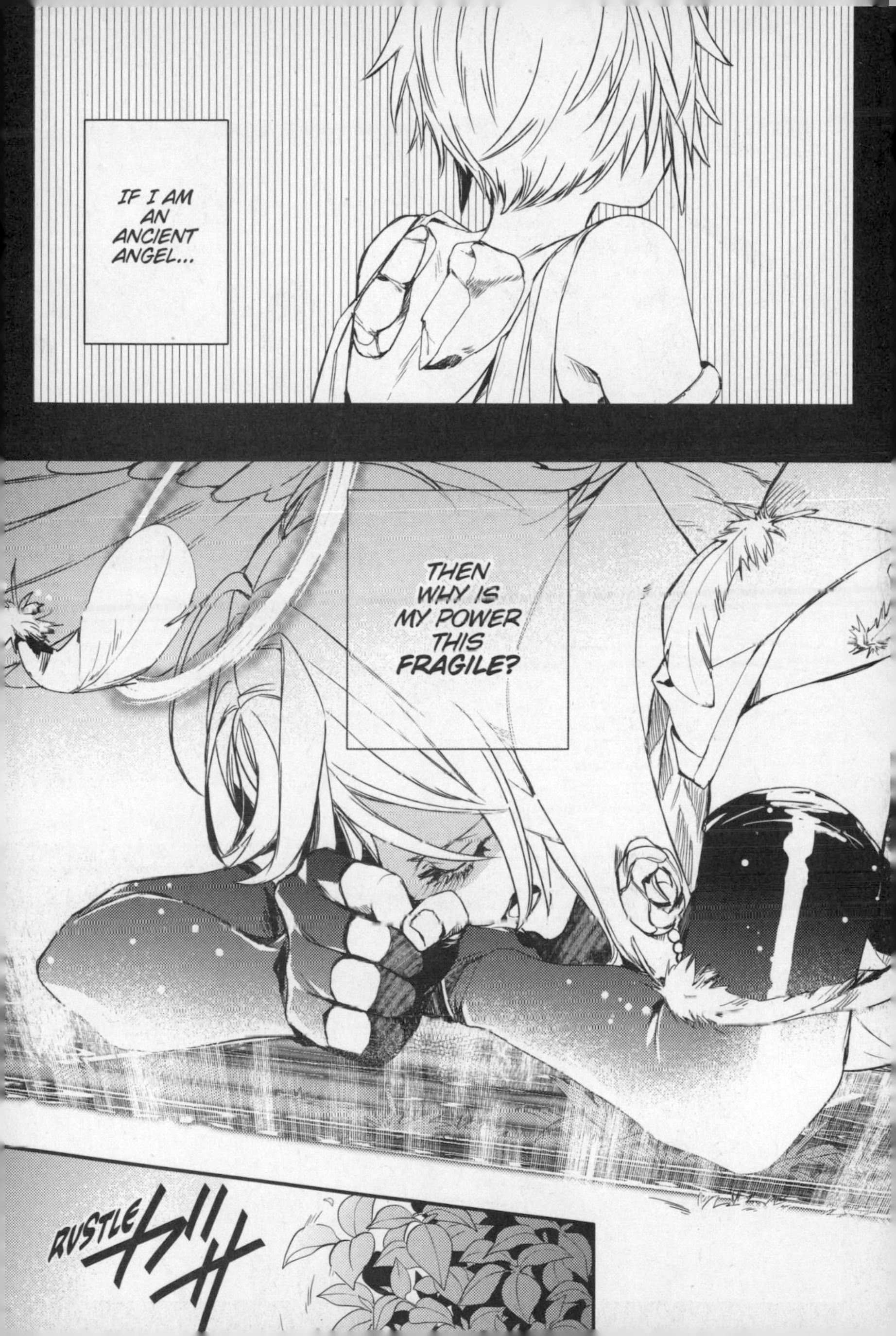
IF I AM AN ANCIENT ANGEL...
THEN WHY IS MY POWER THIS FRAGILE?
RUSTLE

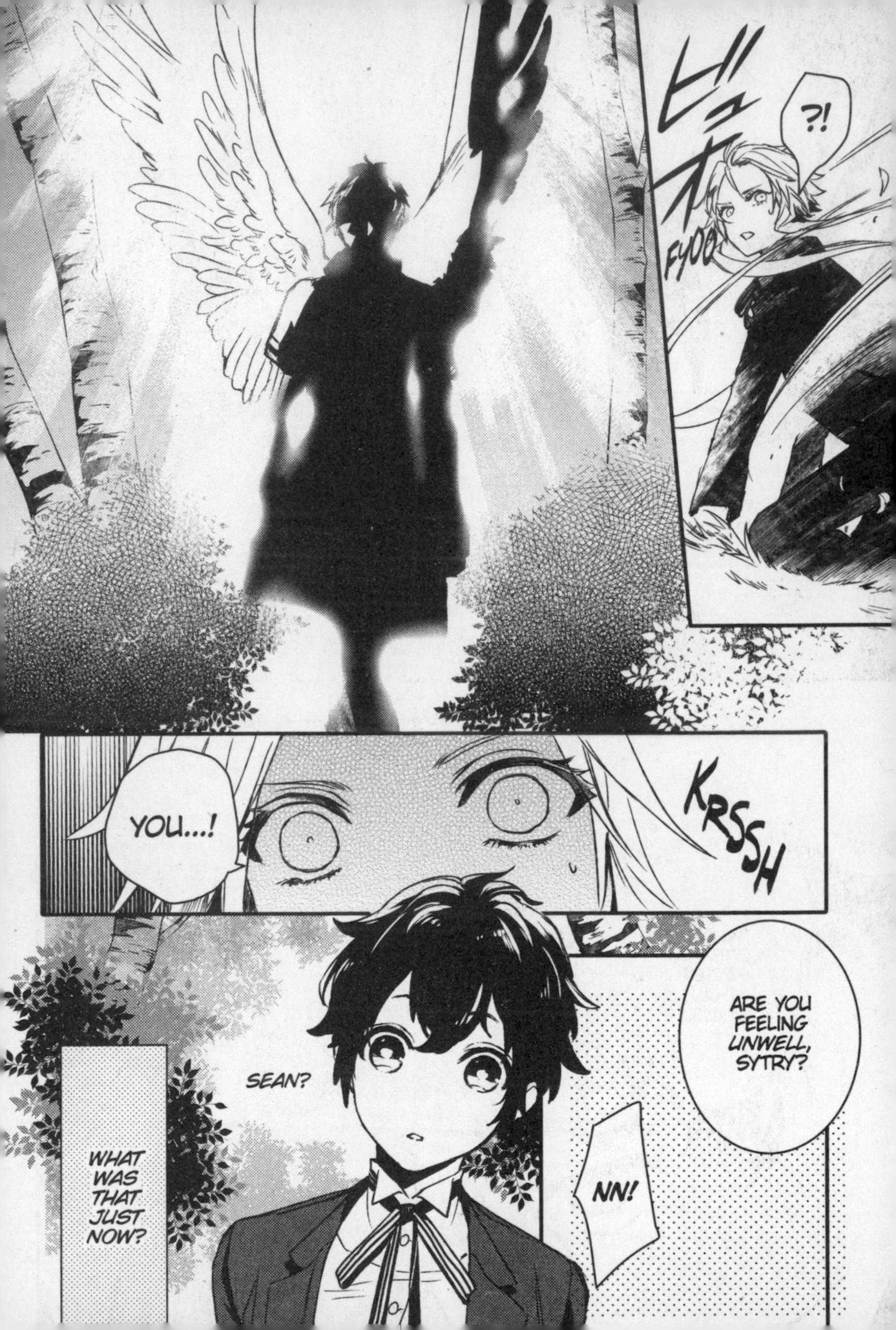
?!
ビュオ
FYOO
KRSSH
YOU...!
ARE YOU FEELING UNWELL, SYTRY?
NN!
SEAN?
WHAT WAS THAT JUST NOW?

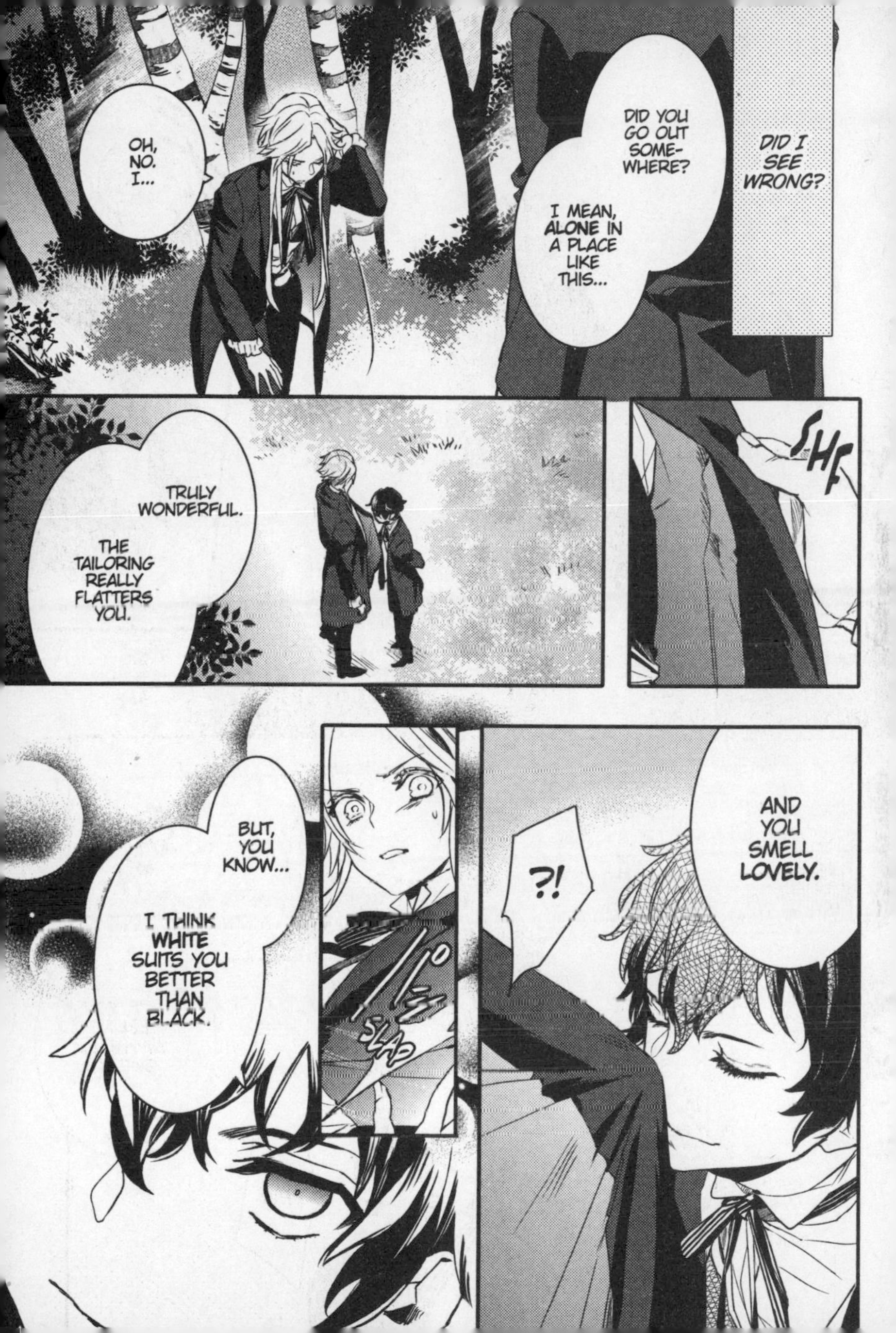
DID I SEE WRONG?
DID YOU GO OUT SOME-WHERE?
I MEAN, ALONE IN A PLACE LIKE THIS...
OH, NO. I...
SHF
TRULY WONDERFUL.
THE TAILORING REALLY FLATTERS YOU.
AND YOU SMELL LOVELY.
?!
BUT, YOU KNOW...
I THINK WHITE SUITS YOU BETTER THAN BLACK.

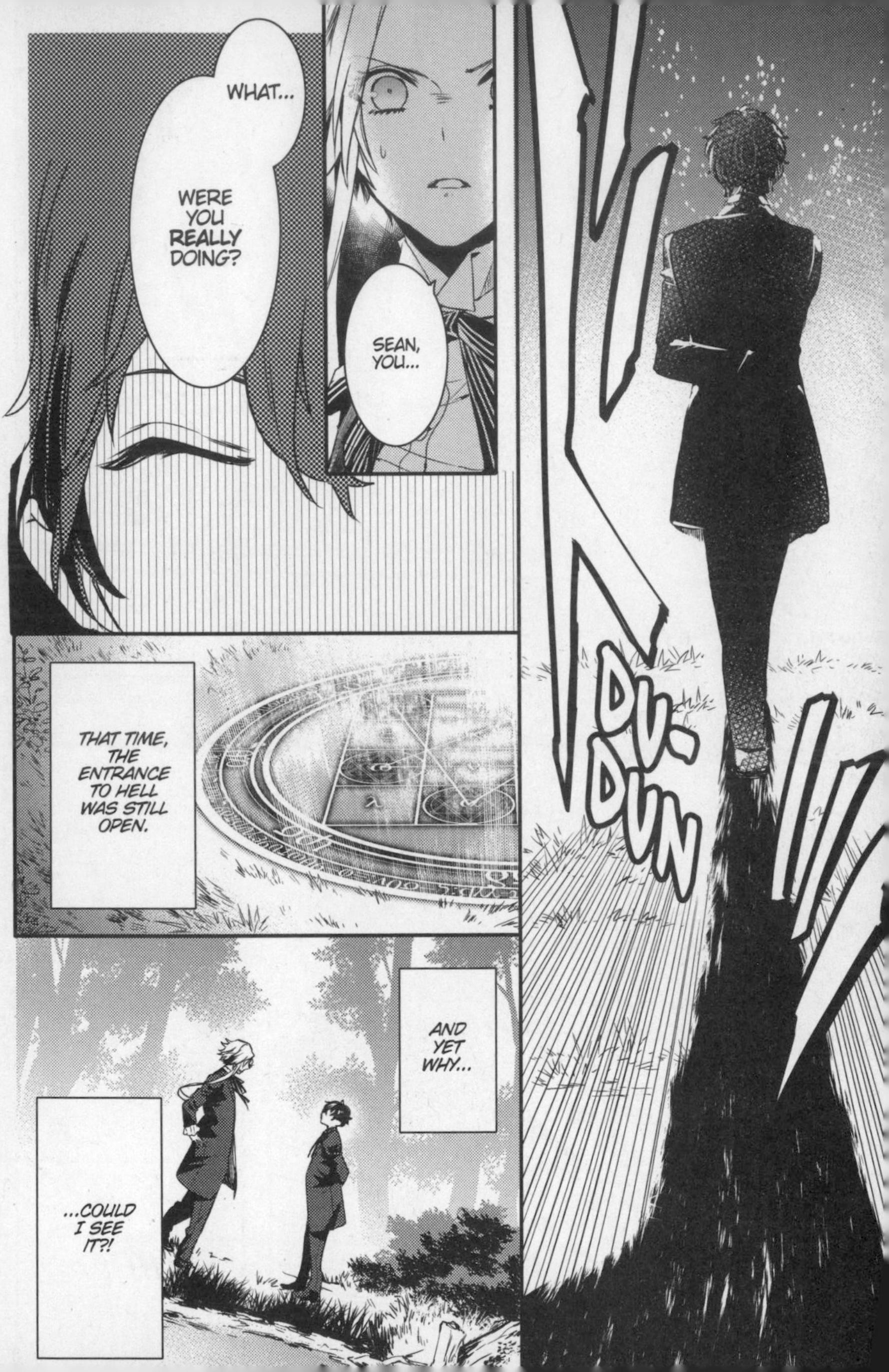
DU-DUN
SEAN, YOU...
WHAT...
WERE YOU REALLY DOING?
THAT TIME, THE ENTRANCE TO HELL WAS STILL OPEN.
AND YET WHY...
...COULD I SEE IT?!

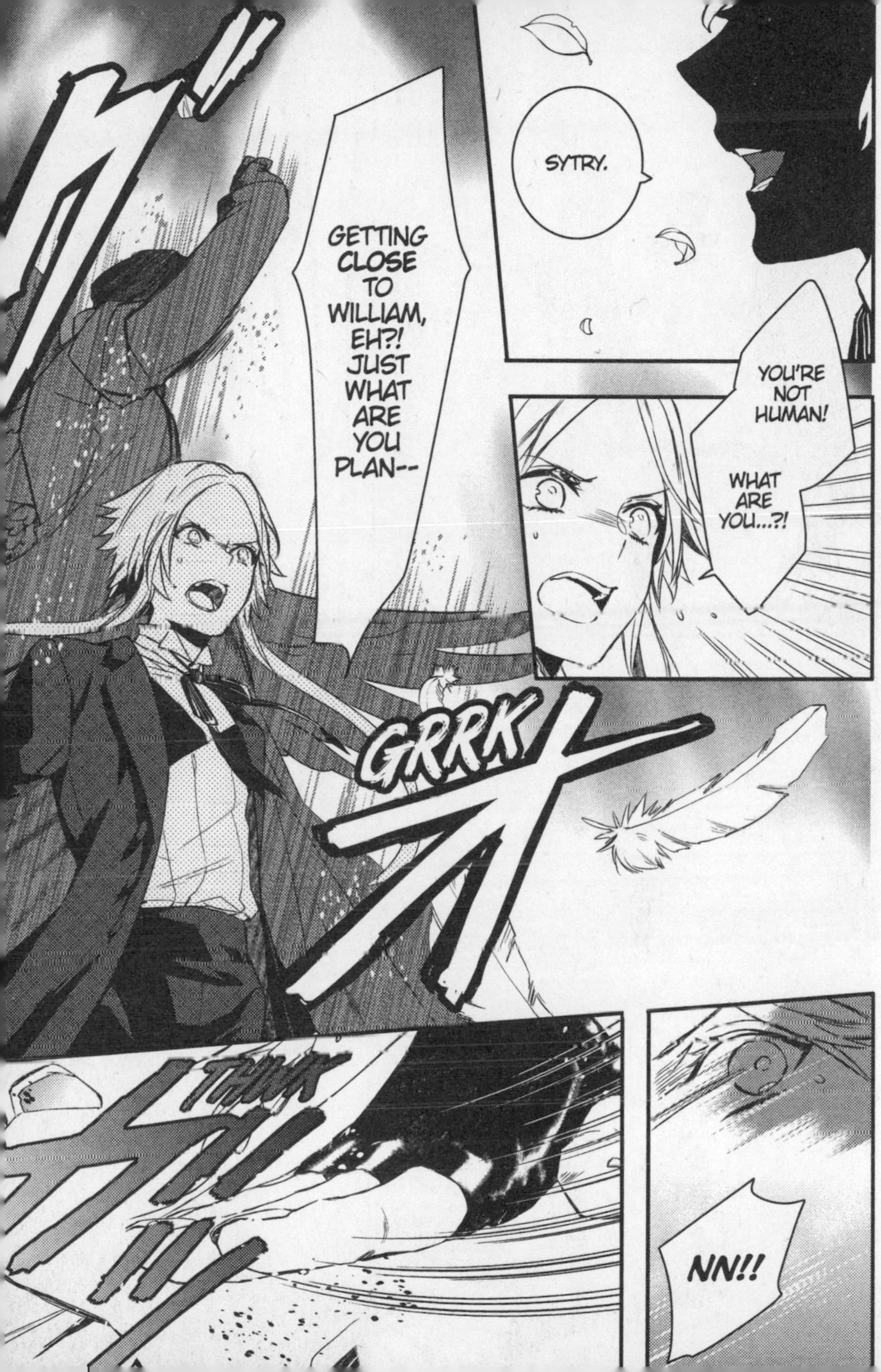
SYTRY.
YOU'RE NOT HUMAN!
WHAT ARE YOU...?!
GETTING CLOSE TO WILLIAM, EH?! JUST WHAT ARE YOU PLAN--
GRRK
NN!!
THUK

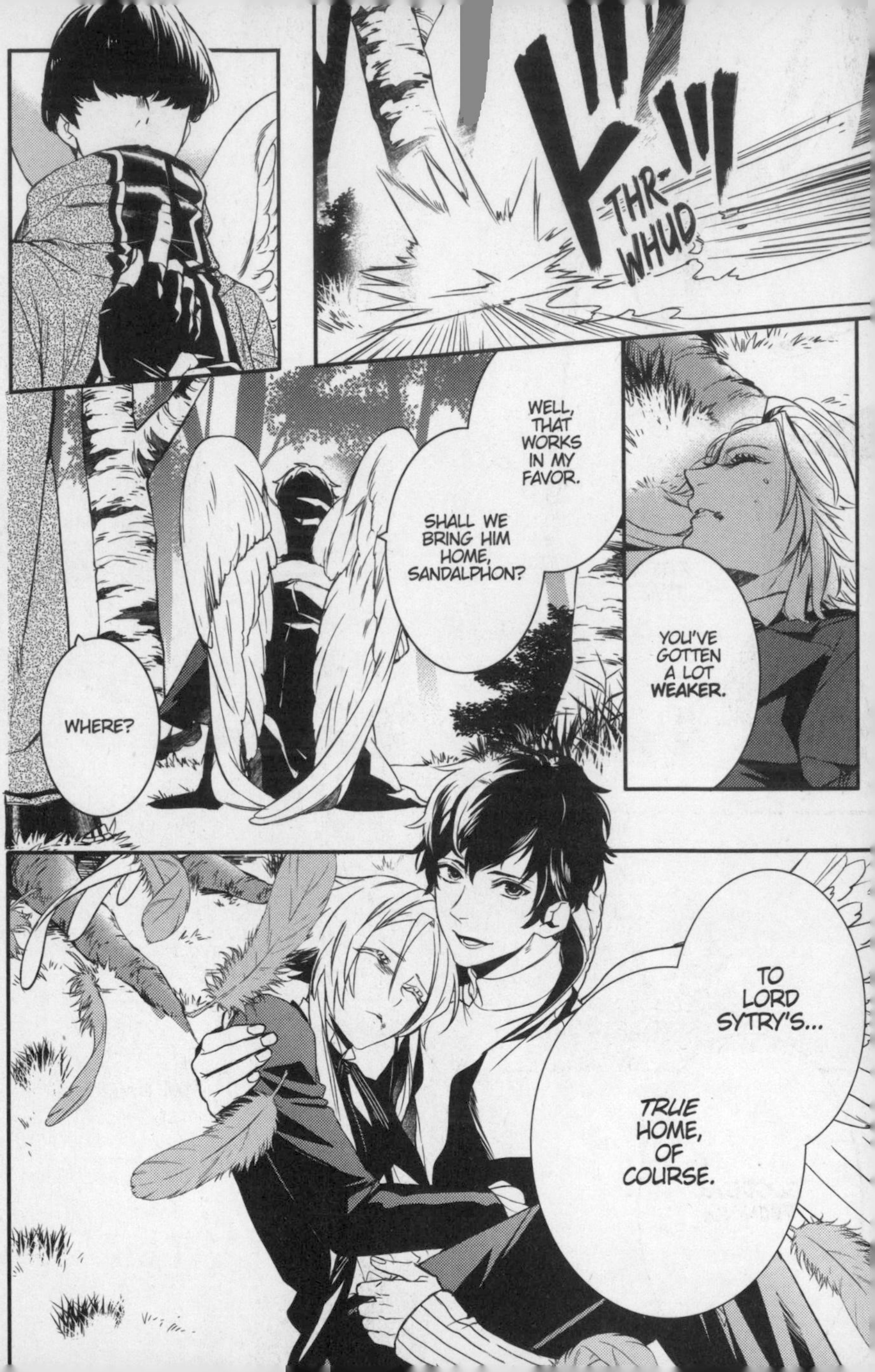
THR-WHUD
YOU'VE GOTTEN A LOT WEAKER.
WELL, THAT WORKS IN MY FAVOR.
SHALL WE BRING HIM HOME, SANDALPHON?
WHERE?
TO LORD SYTRY'S...
TRUE HOME, OF COURSE.

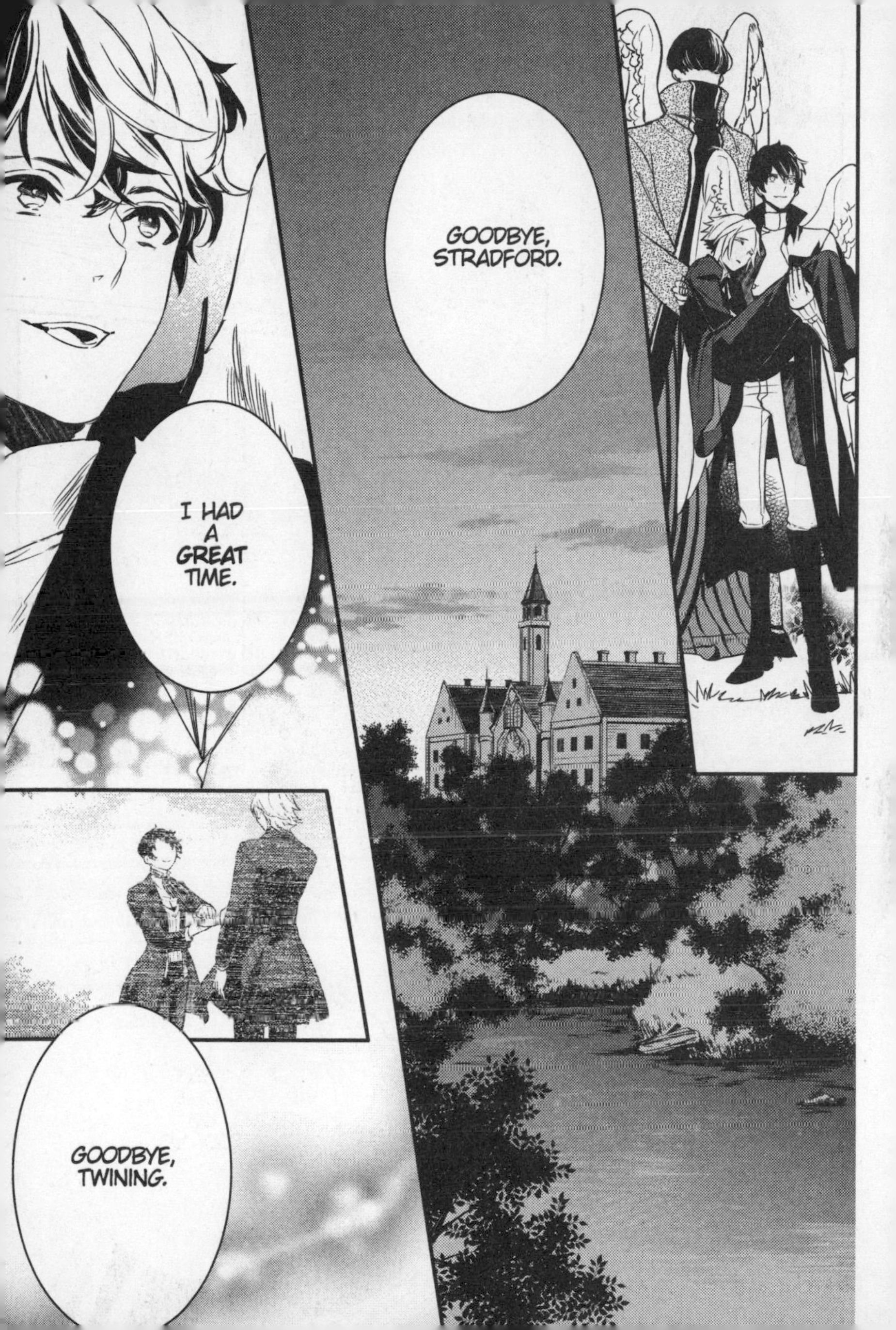
GOODBYE, STRADFORD.
I HAD A GREAT TIME.
GOODBYE, TWINING.

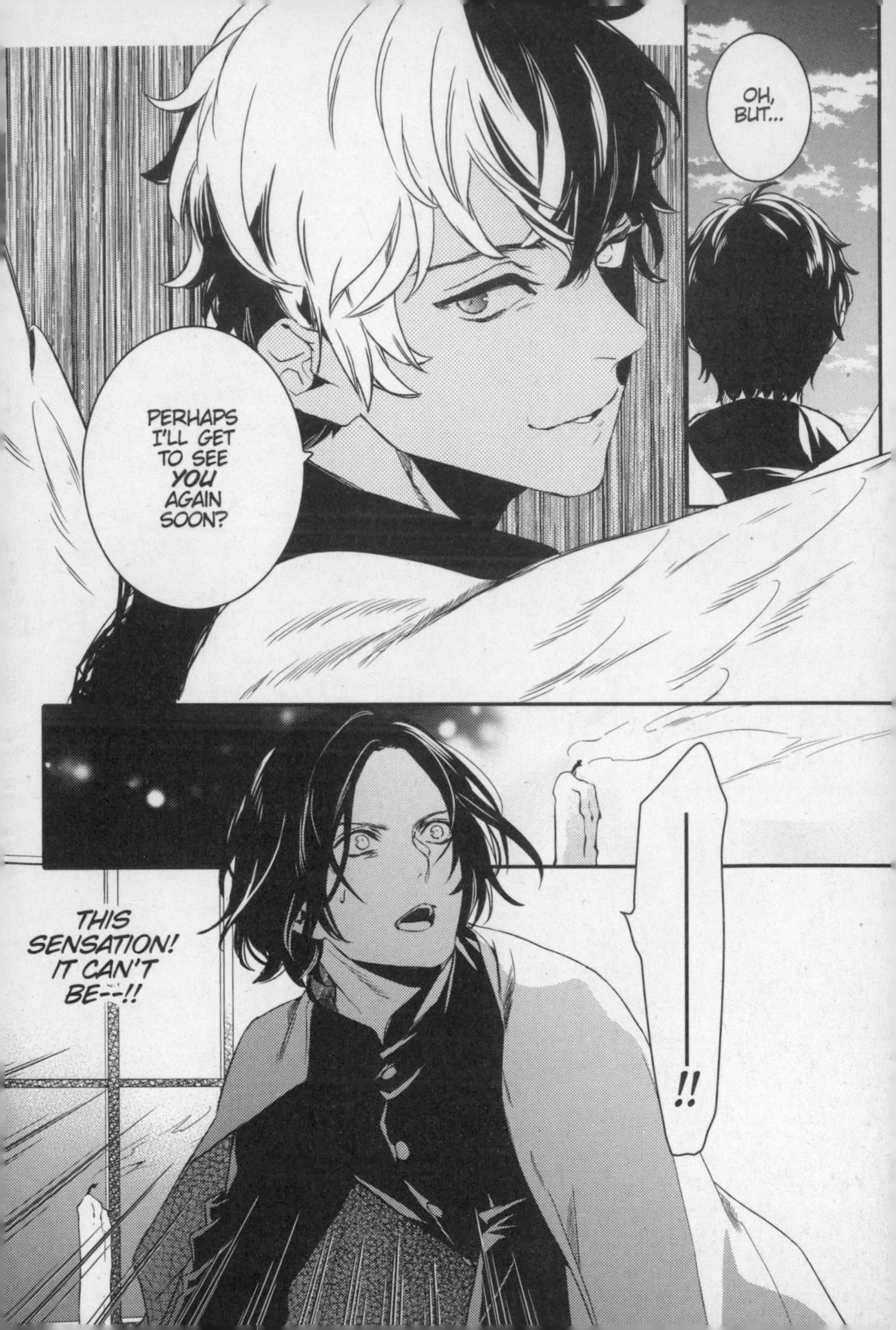

OH, BUT...
PERHAPS I'LL GET TO SEE *YOU* AGAIN SOON?
——!!
THIS SENSATION! IT CAN'T BE--!!

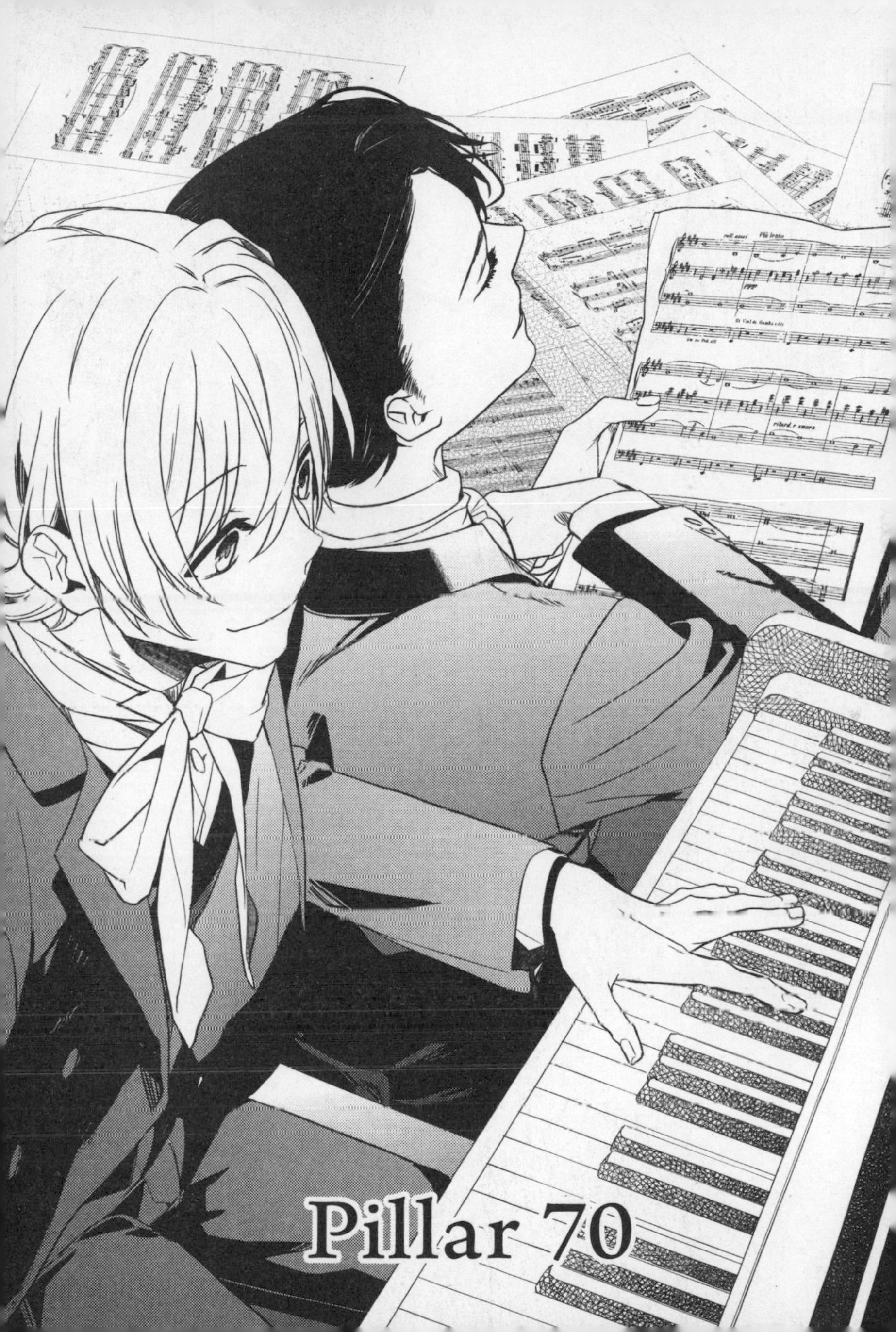
Pillar 70

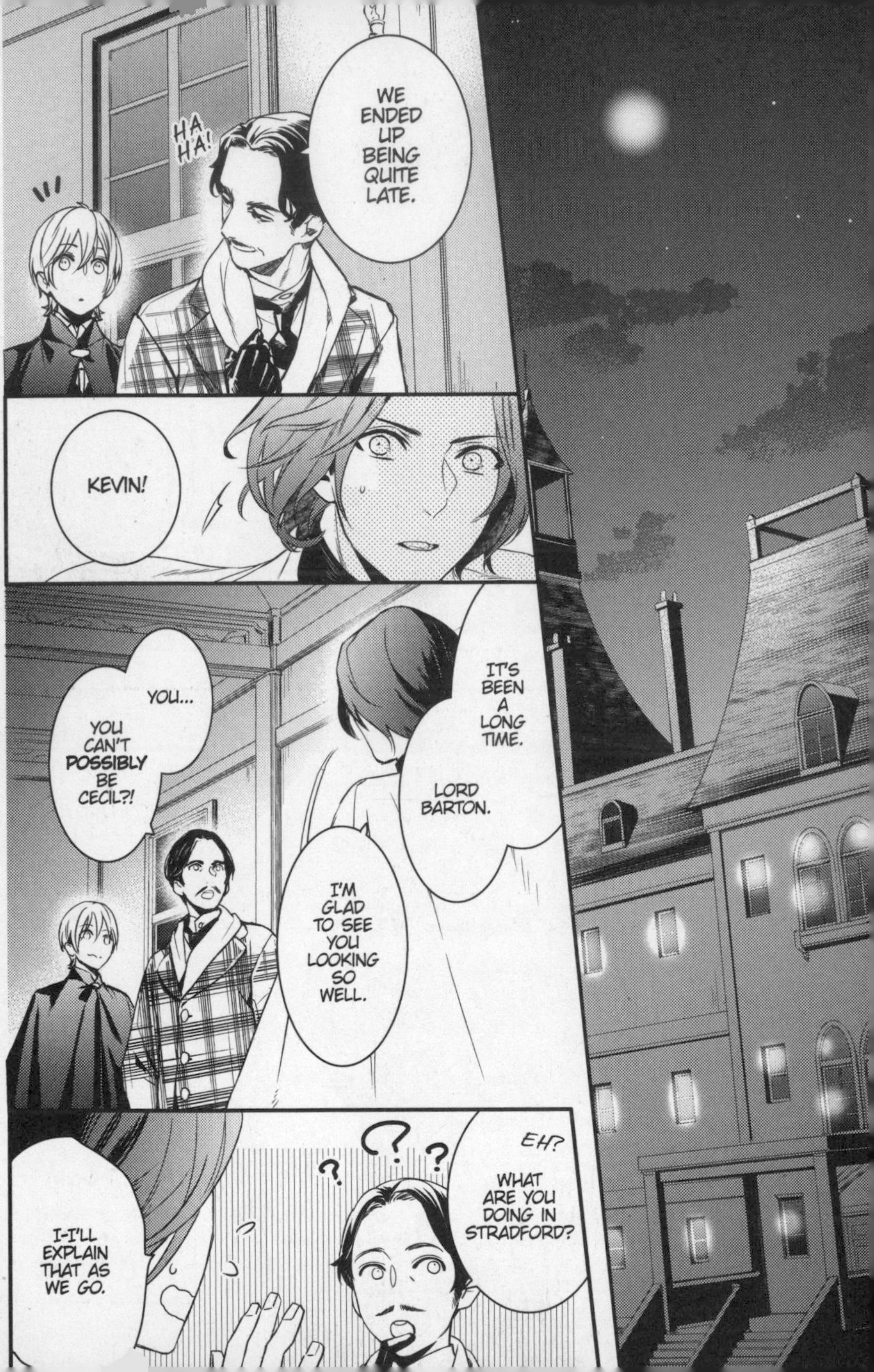
WE ENDED UP BEING QUITE LATE.
HA HA!
KEVIN!
IT'S BEEN A LONG TIME.
LORD BARTON.
I'M GLAD TO SEE YOU LOOKING SO WELL.
YOU...
YOU CAN'T POSSIBLY BE CECIL?!
EH?
WHAT ARE YOU DOING IN STRADFORD?
I-I'LL EXPLAIN THAT AS WE GO.

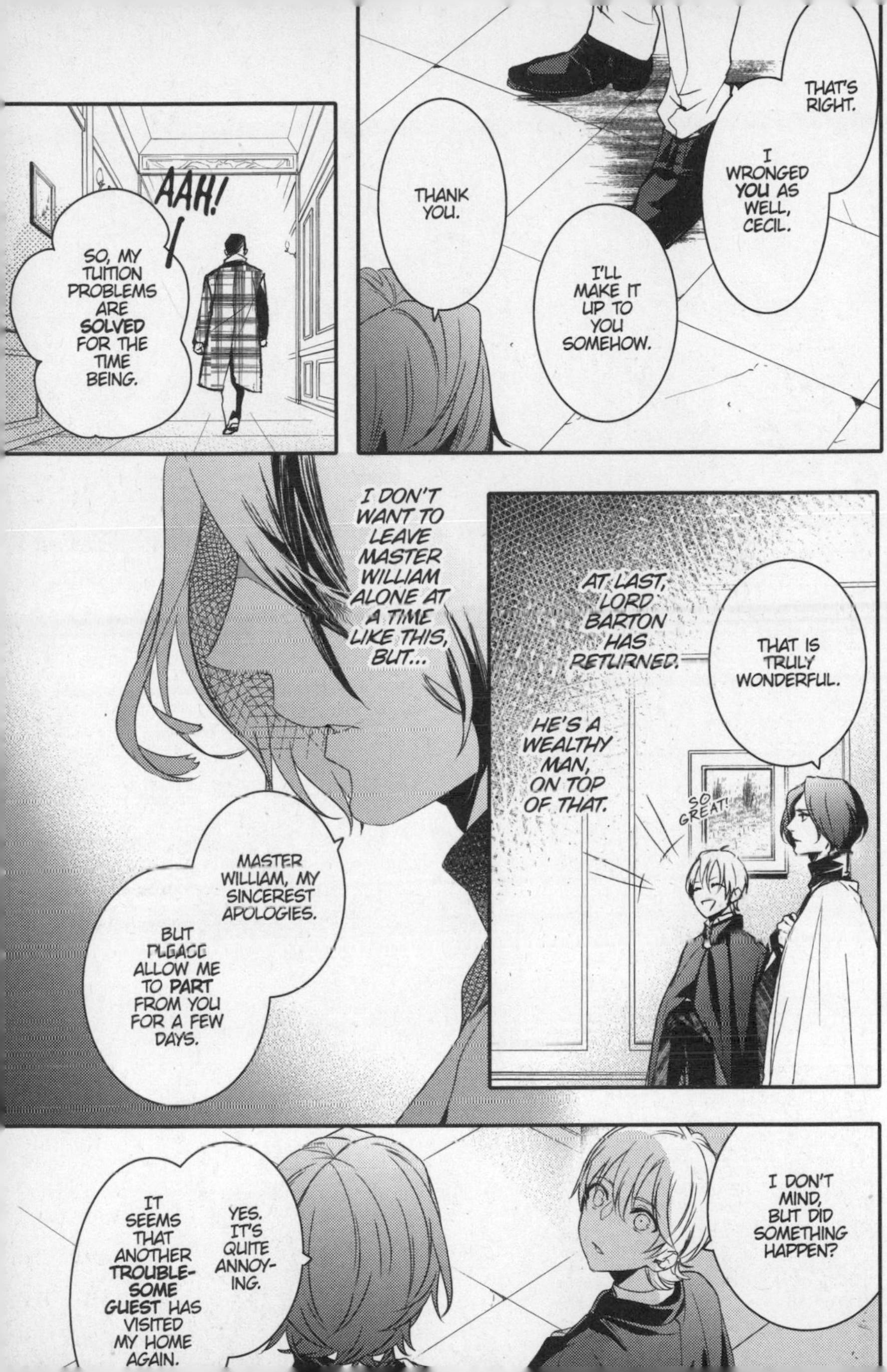
THAT'S RIGHT.
I WRONGED YOU AS WELL, CECIL.
I'LL MAKE IT UP TO YOU SOMEHOW.
THANK YOU.
AAH!
SO, MY TUITION PROBLEMS ARE SOLVED FOR THE TIME BEING.
AT LAST, LORD BARTON HAS RETURNED.
THAT IS TRULY WONDERFUL.
HE'S A WEALTHY MAN, ON TOP OF THAT.
SO GREAT!
I DON'T WANT TO LEAVE MASTER WILLIAM ALONE AT A TIME LIKE THIS, BUT...
MASTER WILLIAM, MY SINCEREST APOLOGIES.
BUT PLEASE ALLOW ME TO PART FROM YOU FOR A FEW DAYS.
I DON'T MIND, BUT DID SOMETHING HAPPEN?
YES. IT'S QUITE ANNOYING.
IT SEEMS THAT ANOTHER TROUBLESOME GUEST HAS VISITED MY HOME AGAIN.

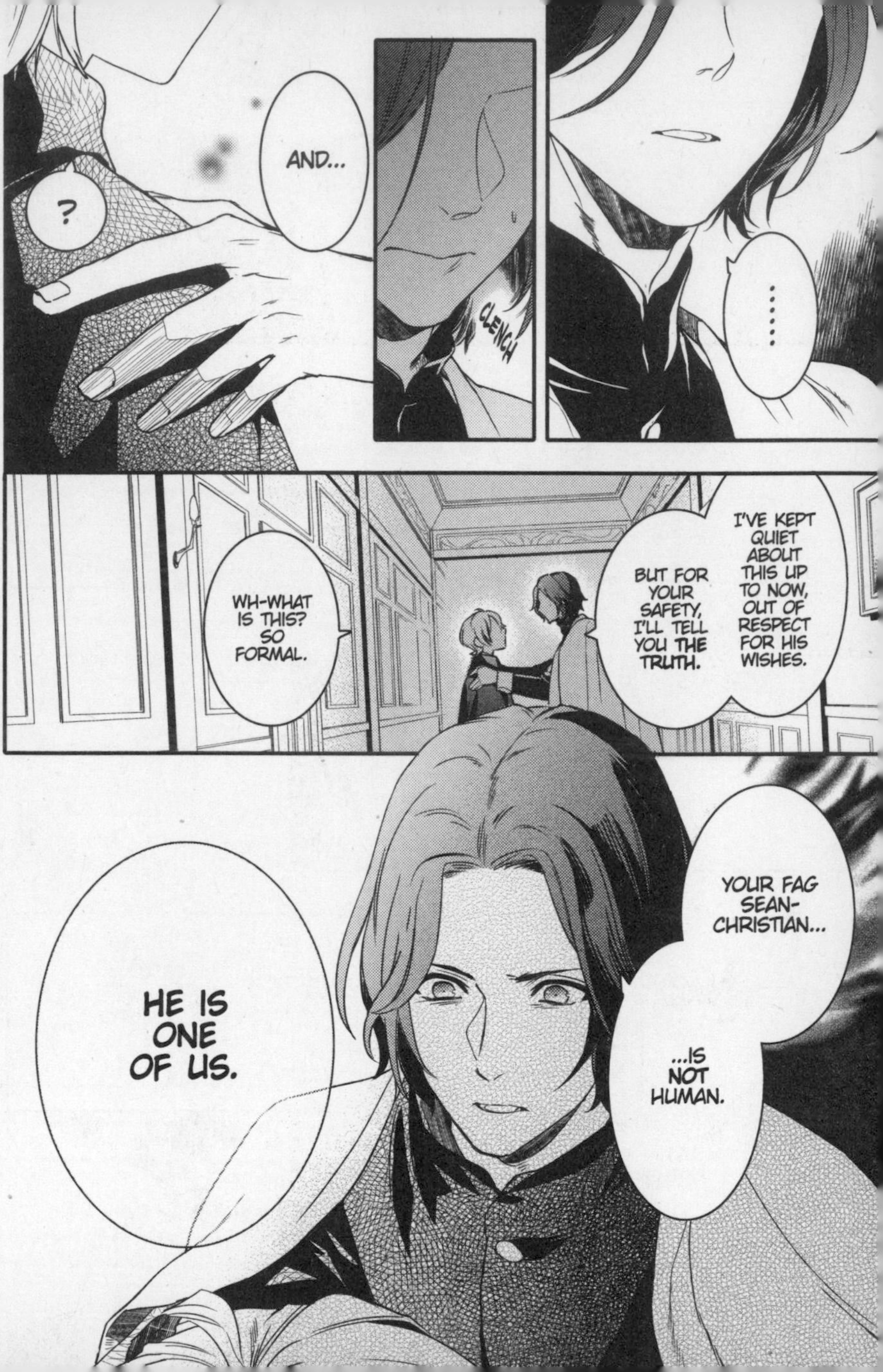
......
CLENCH
AND...
?
I'VE KEPT QUIET ABOUT THIS UP TO NOW, OUT OF RESPECT FOR HIS WISHES.
BUT FOR YOUR SAFETY, I'LL TELL YOU THE TRUTH.
WH-WHAT IS THIS? SO FORMAL.
YOUR FAG SEAN-CHRISTIAN...
...IS NOT HUMAN.
HE IS ONE OF US.

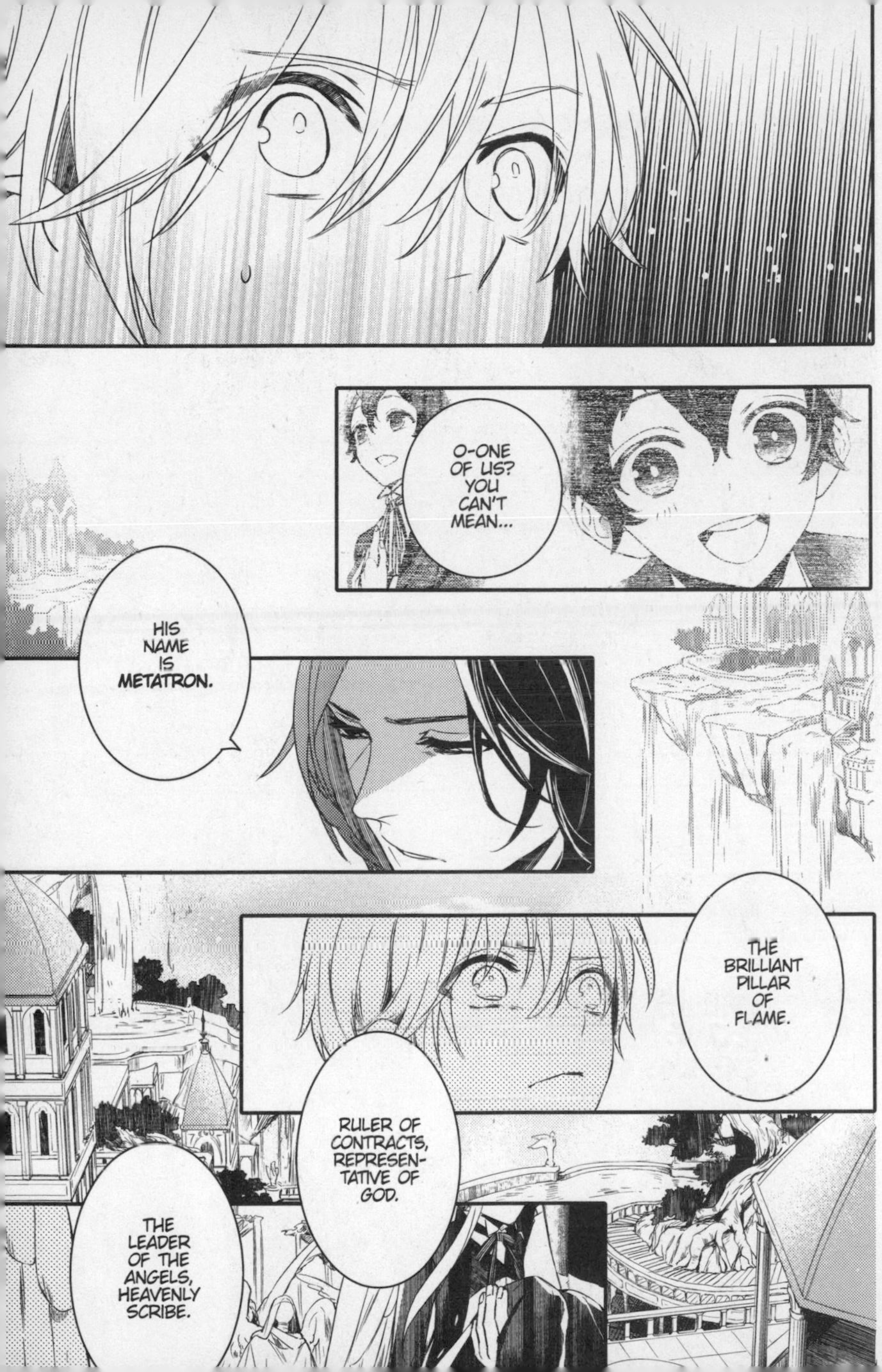
O-ONE OF US? YOU CAN'T MEAN...
HIS NAME IS METATRON.
THE BRILLIANT PILLAR OF FLAME.
RULER OF CONTRACTS, REPRESEN-TATIVE OF GOD.
THE LEADER OF THE ANGELS, HEAVENLY SCRIBE.

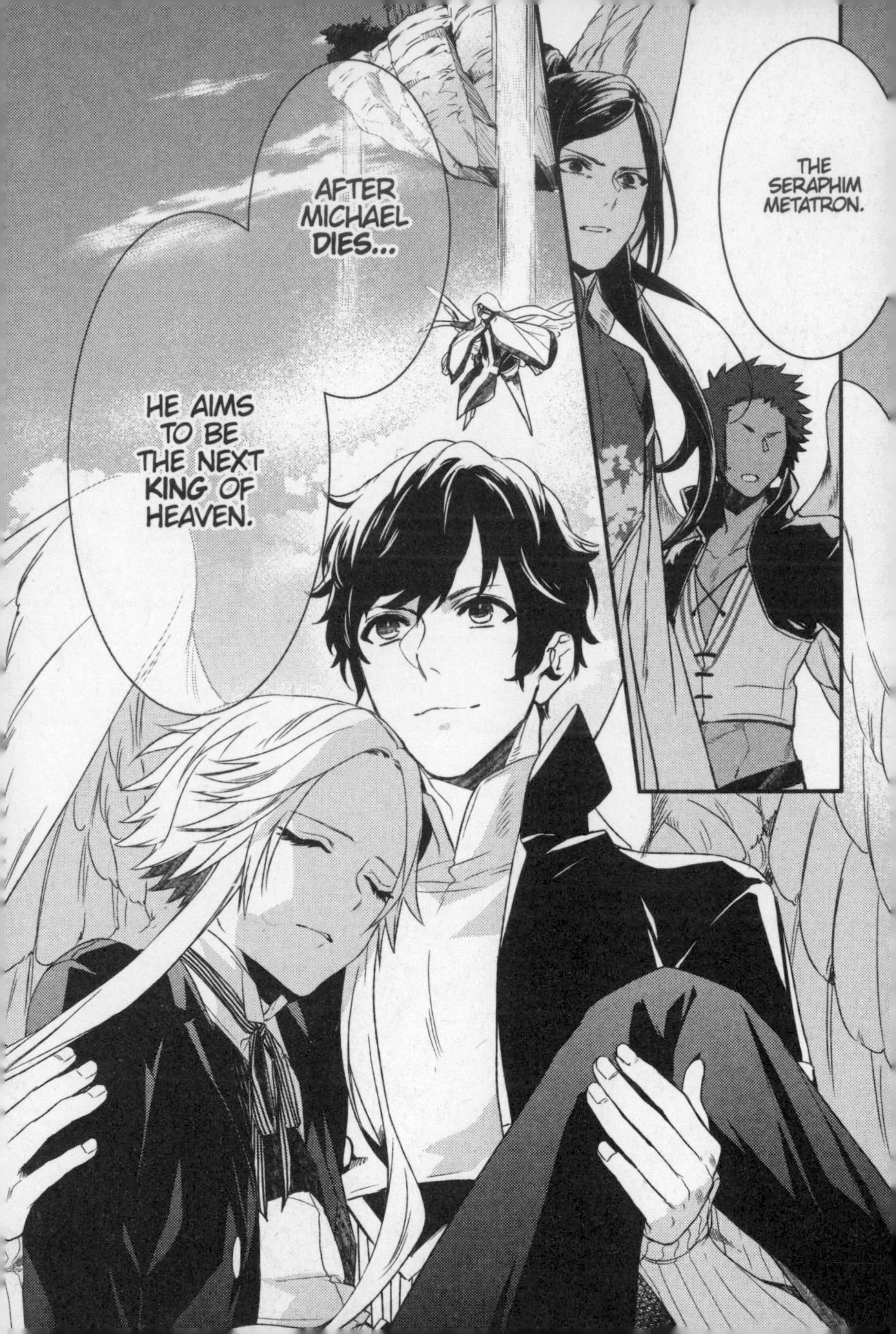
THE SERAPHIM METATRON.
AFTER MICHAEL DIES...
HE AIMS TO BE THE NEXT KING OF HEAVEN.

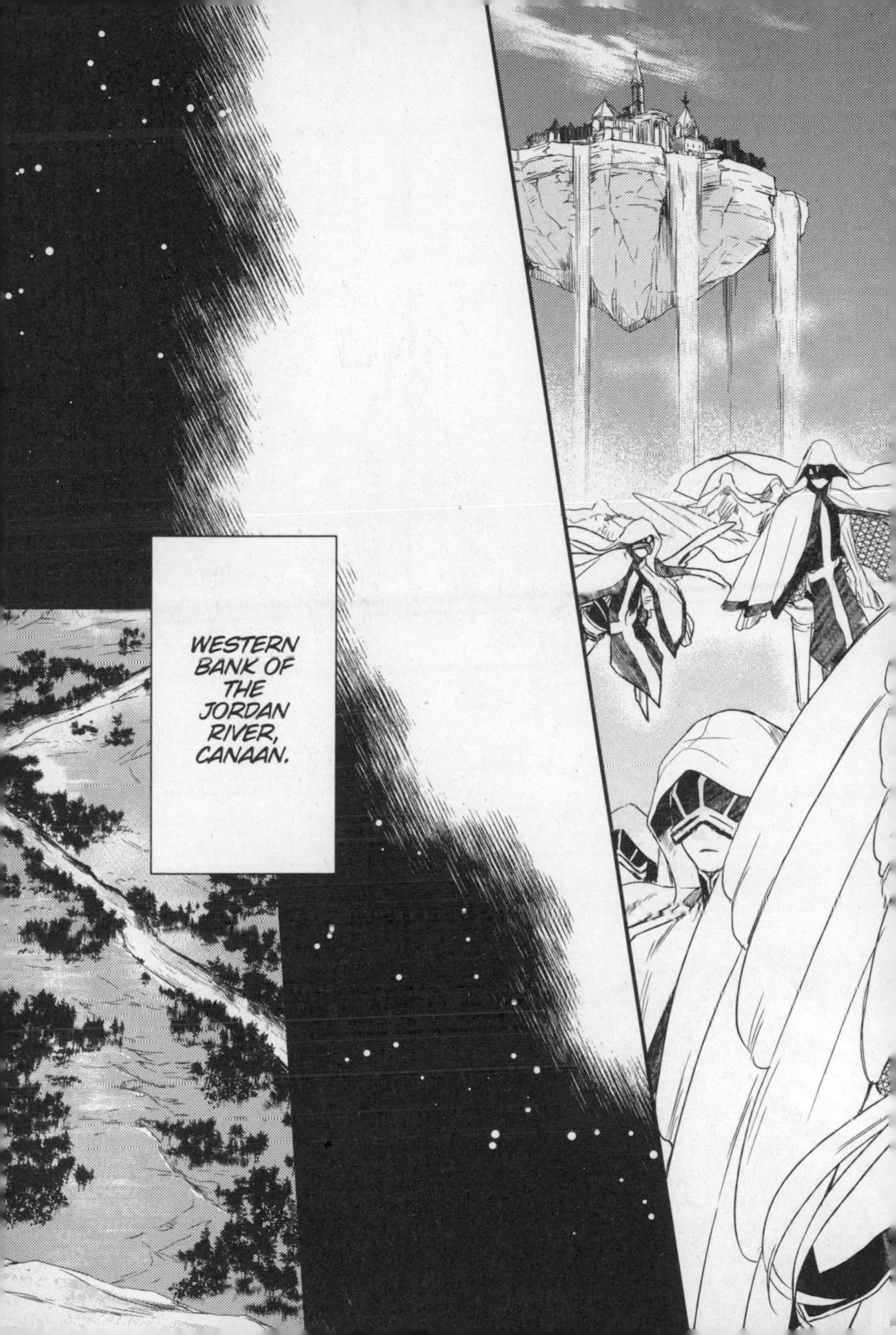
WESTERN BANK OF THE JORDAN RIVER, CANAAN.

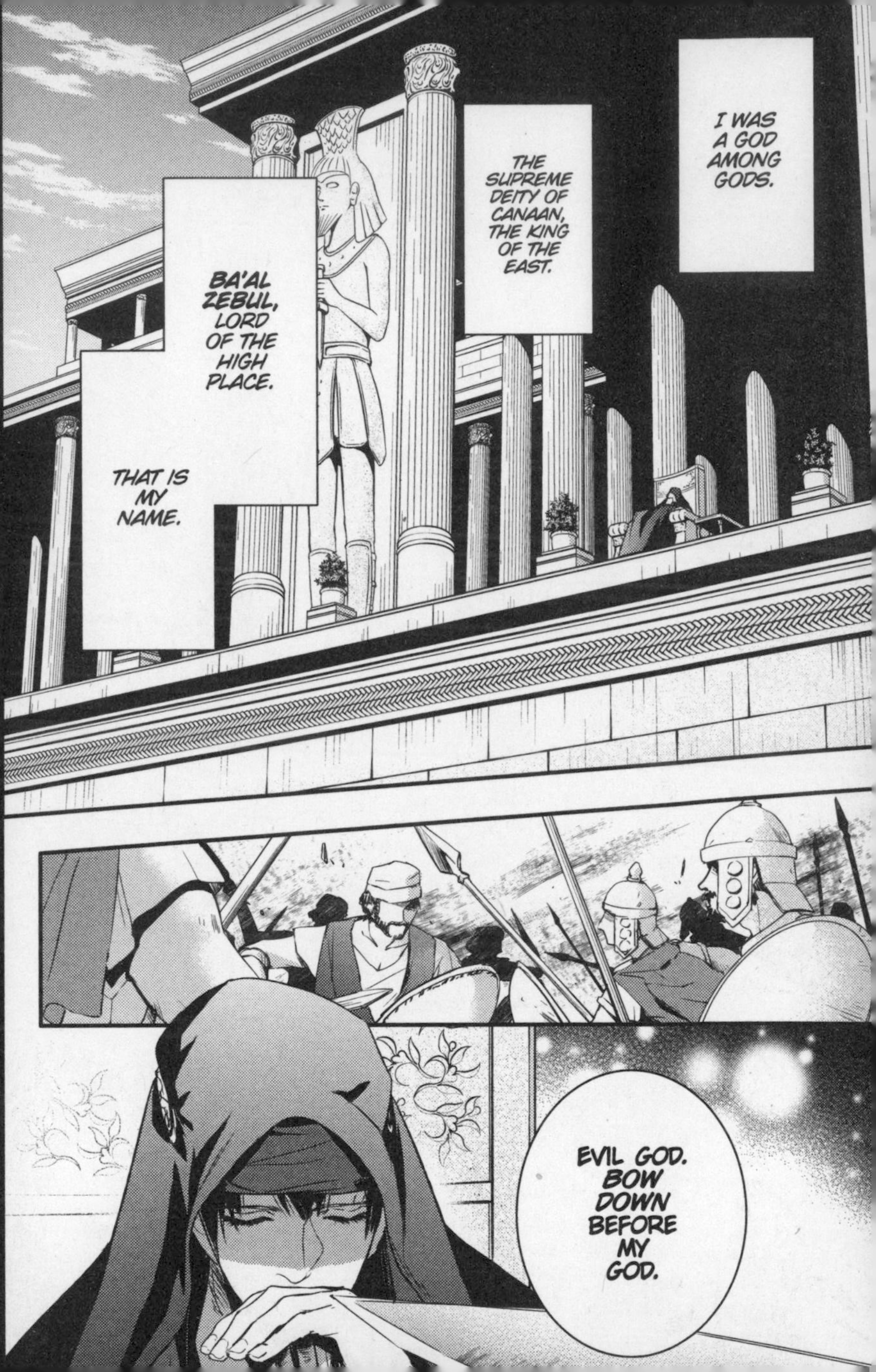
I WAS A GOD AMONG GODS.
THE SUPREME DEITY OF CANAAN, THE KING OF THE EAST.
BA'AL ZEBUL, LORD OF THE HIGH PLACE.
THAT IS MY NAME.
EVIL GOD. BOW DOWN BEFORE MY GOD.

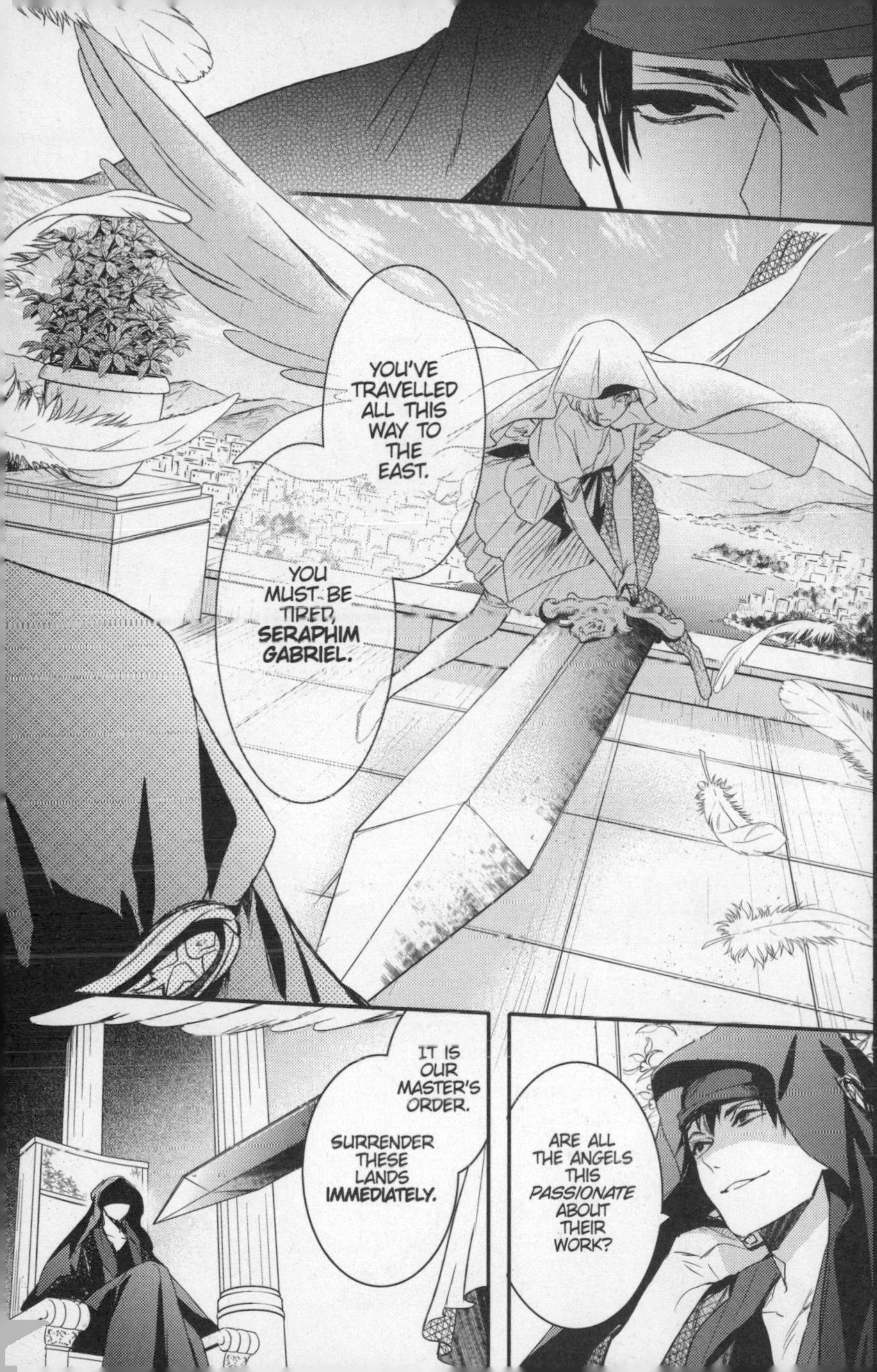
YOU'VE TRAVELLED ALL THIS WAY TO THE EAST.
YOU MUST BE TIRED, **SERAPHIM GABRIEL.**
ARE ALL THE ANGELS THIS *PASSIONATE* ABOUT THEIR WORK?
IT IS OUR MASTER'S ORDER.
SURRENDER THESE LANDS **IMMEDIATELY.**

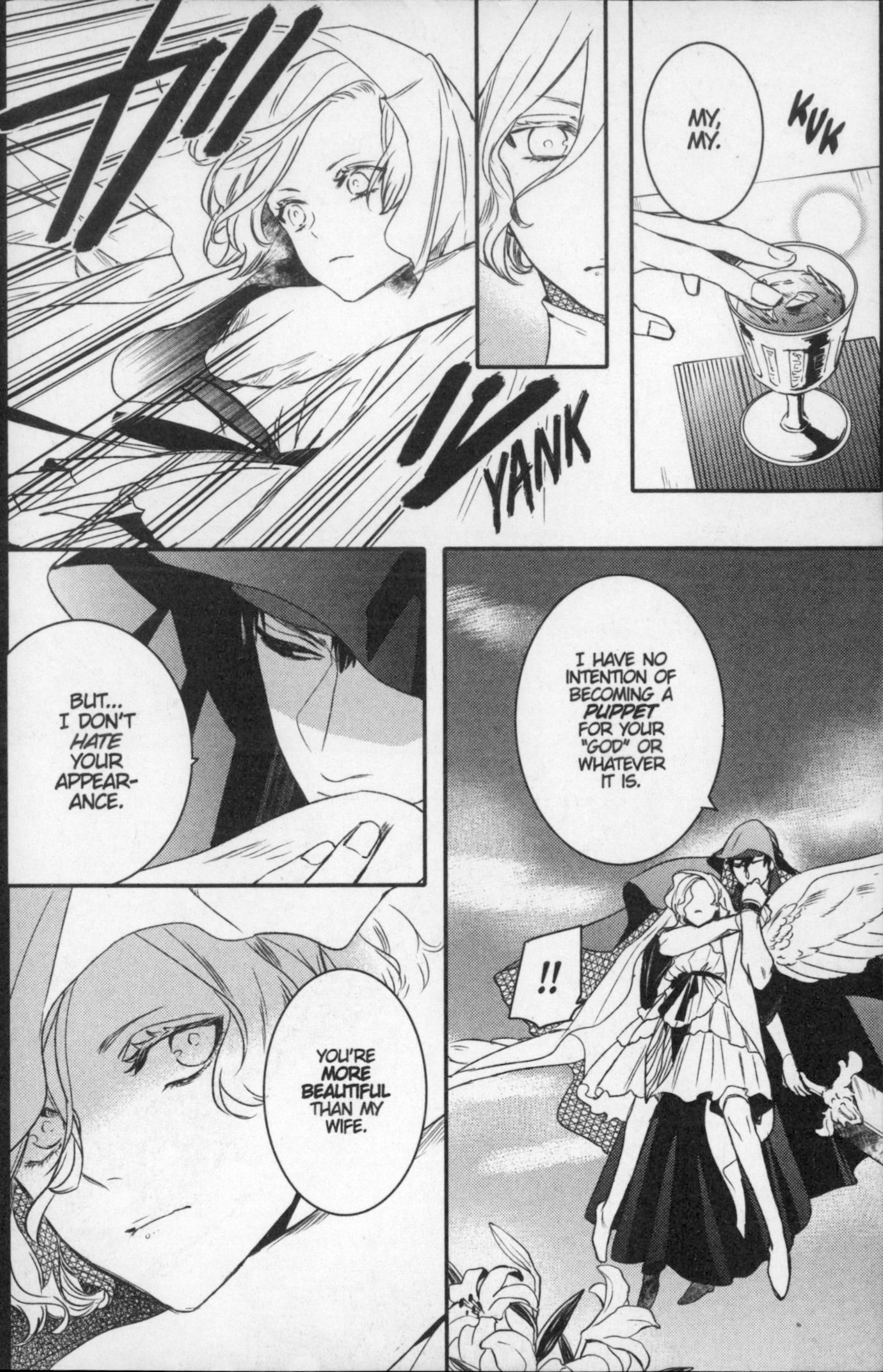
MY, MY.
KUK
YANK
I HAVE NO INTENTION OF BECOMING A PUPPET FOR YOUR "GOD" OR WHATEVER IT IS.
!!
BUT... I DON'T HATE YOUR APPEARANCE.
YOU'RE MORE BEAUTIFUL THAN MY WIFE.

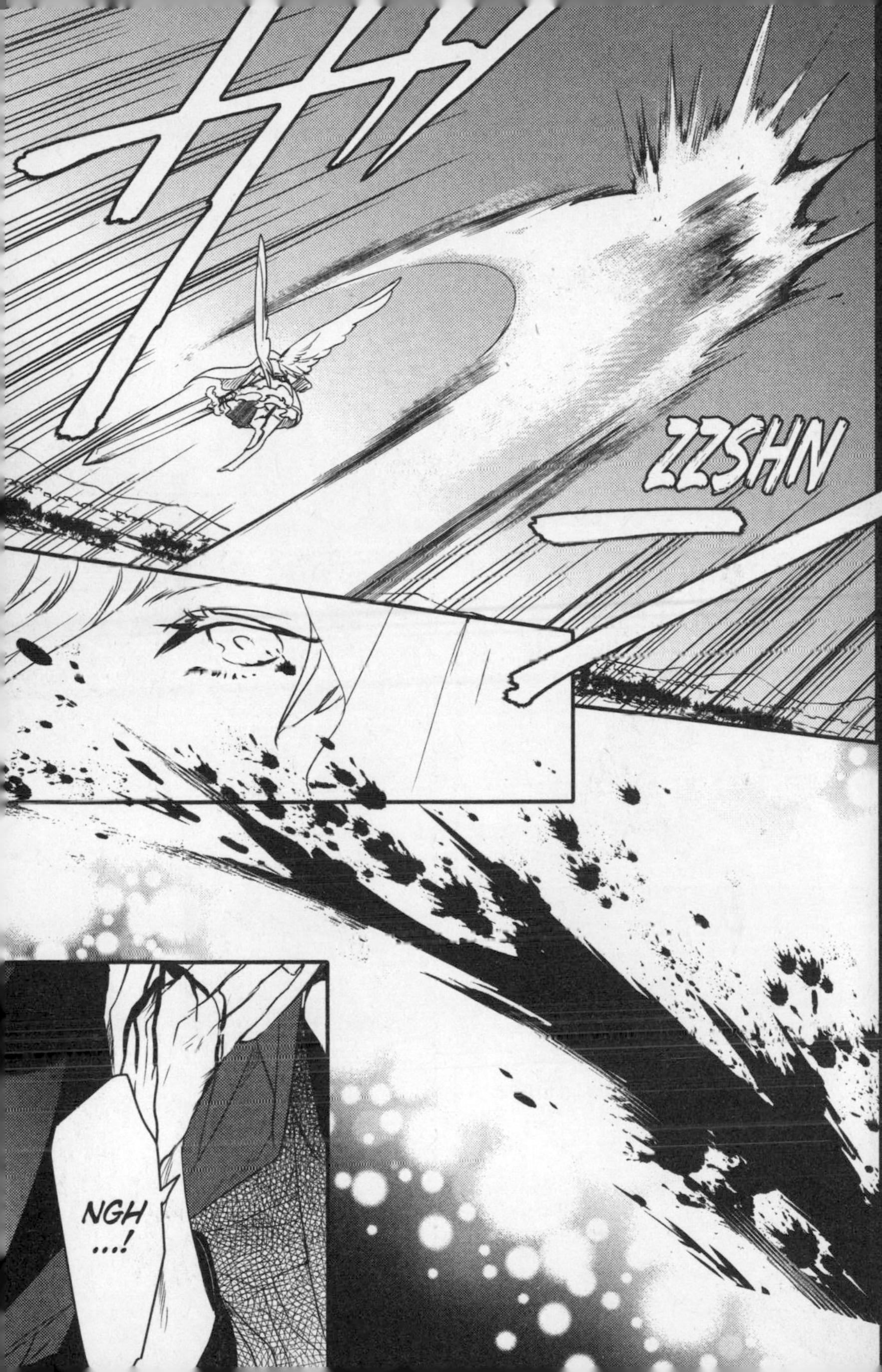
ZZSHN
NGH ...!

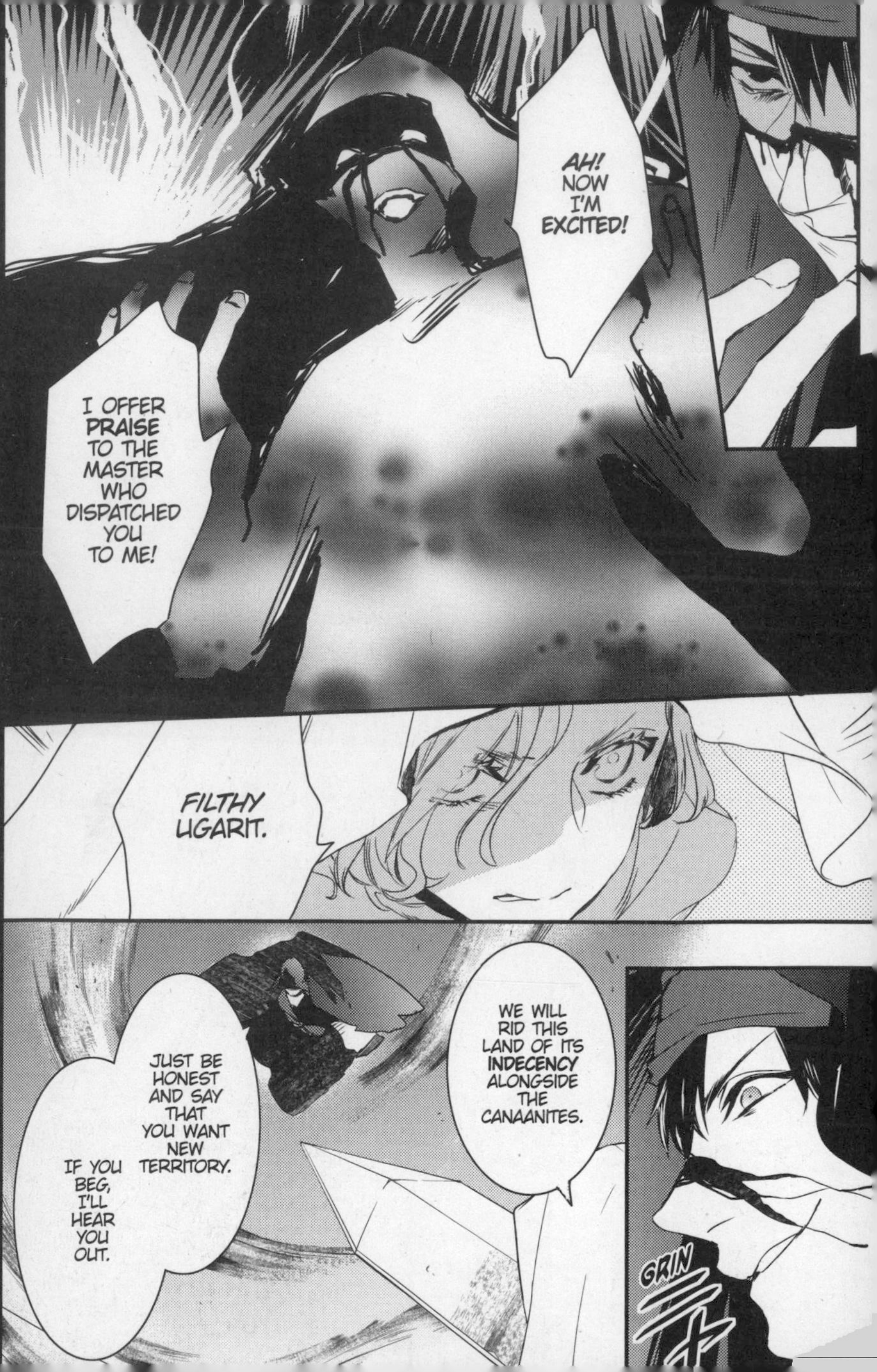
AH! NOW I'M EXCITED!
I OFFER PRAISE TO THE MASTER WHO DISPATCHED YOU TO ME!
FILTHY UGARIT.
WE WILL RID THIS LAND OF ITS INDECENCY ALONGSIDE THE CANAANITES.
JUST BE HONEST AND SAY THAT YOU WANT NEW TERRITORY.
IF YOU BEG, I'LL HEAR YOU OUT.
GRIN

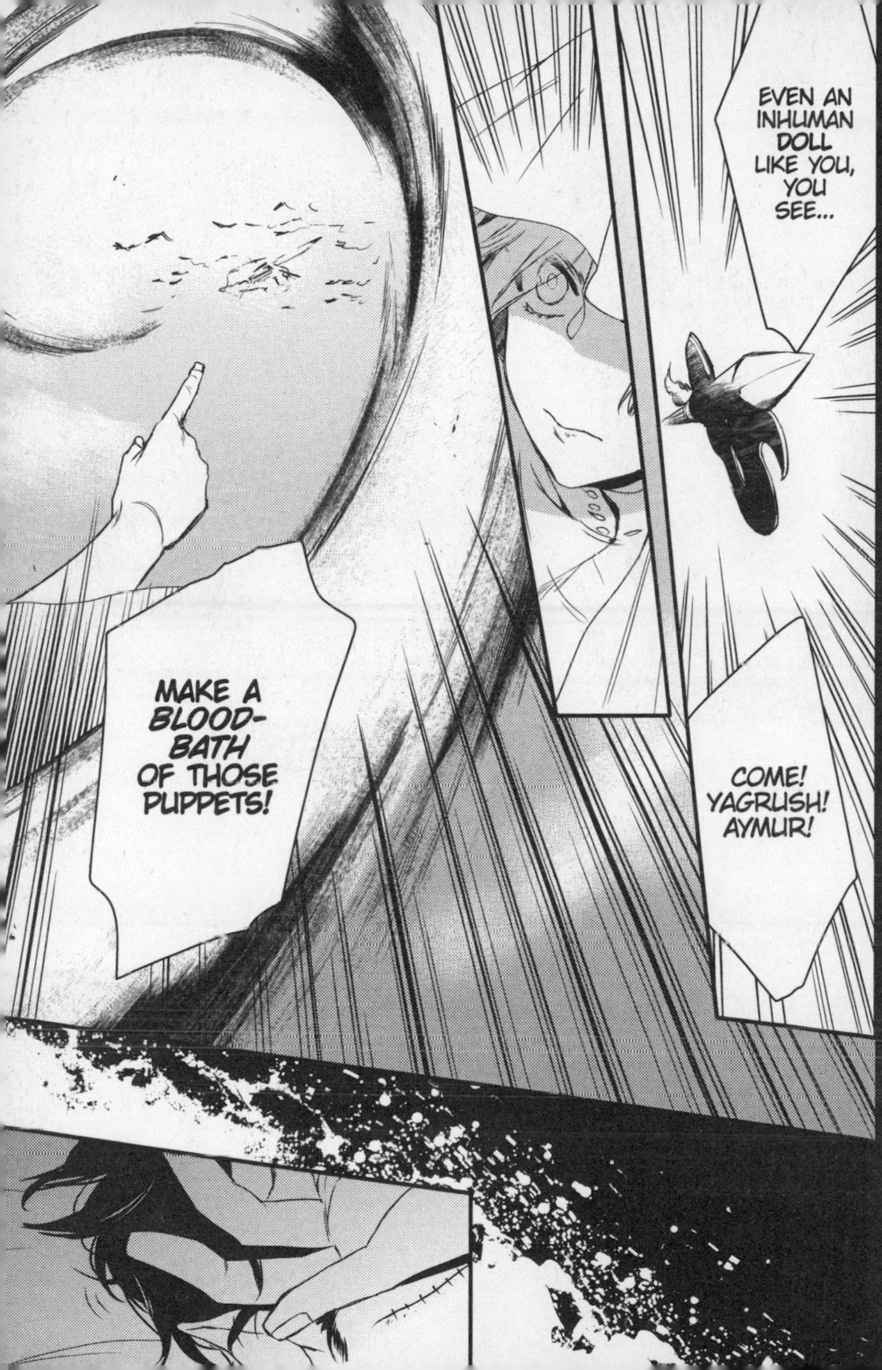
EVEN AN INHUMAN DOLL LIKE YOU, YOU SEE...
COME! YAGRUSH! AYMUR!
MAKE A BLOOD-BATH OF THOSE PUPPETS!

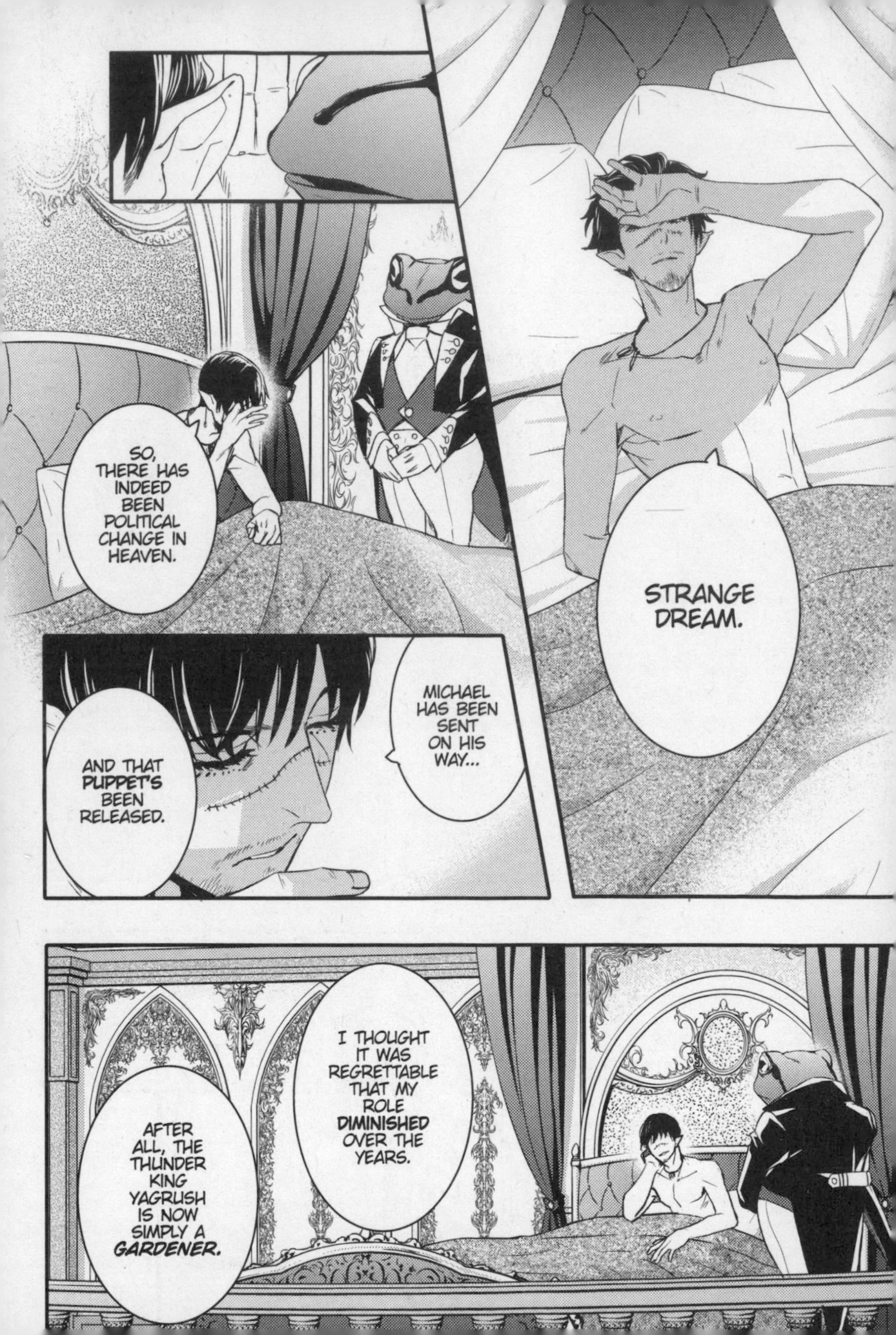
STRANGE DREAM.
SO, THERE HAS INDEED BEEN POLITICAL CHANGE IN HEAVEN.
MICHAEL HAS BEEN SENT ON HIS WAY...
AND THAT PUPPET'S BEEN RELEASED.
I THOUGHT IT WAS REGRETTABLE THAT MY ROLE DIMINISHED OVER THE YEARS.
AFTER ALL, THE THUNDER KING YAGRUSH IS NOW SIMPLY A GARDENER.

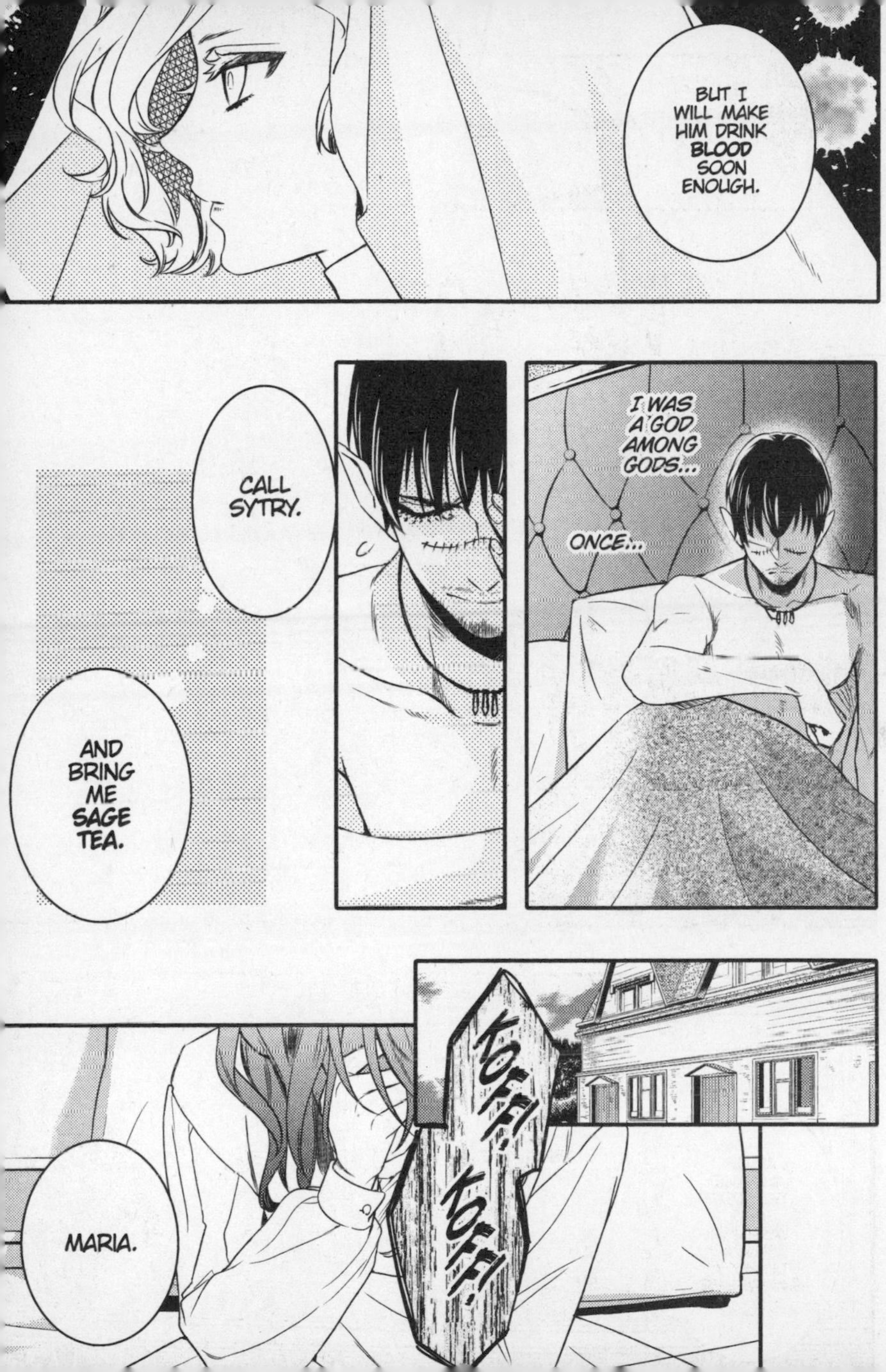
BUT I WILL MAKE HIM DRINK BLOOD SOON ENOUGH.
I WAS A GOD AMONG GODS...
ONCE...
CALL SYTRY.
AND BRING ME SAGE TEA.
KOFF! KOFF!
MARIA.

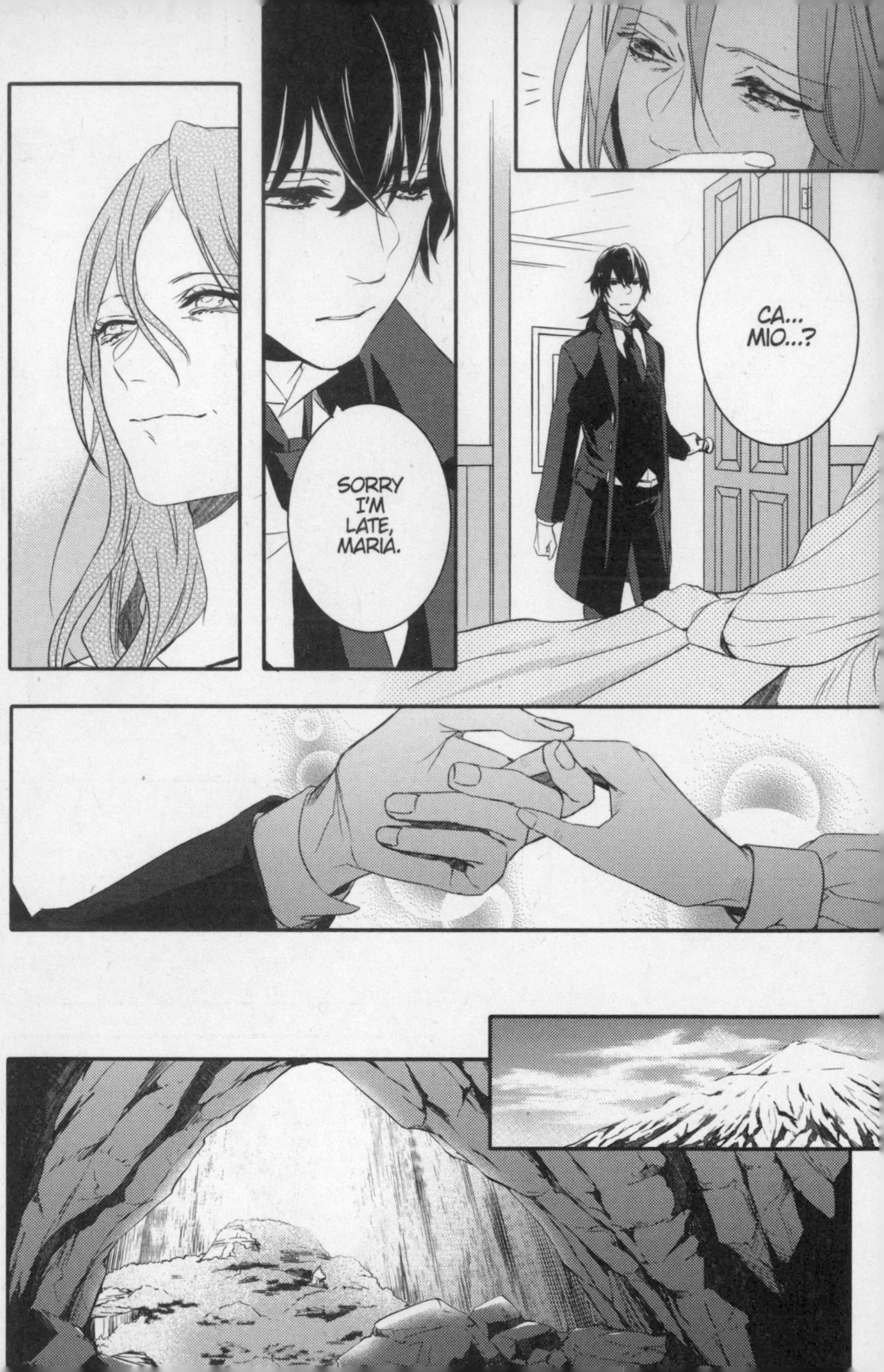
CA... MIO...?
SORRY I'M LATE, MARIA.

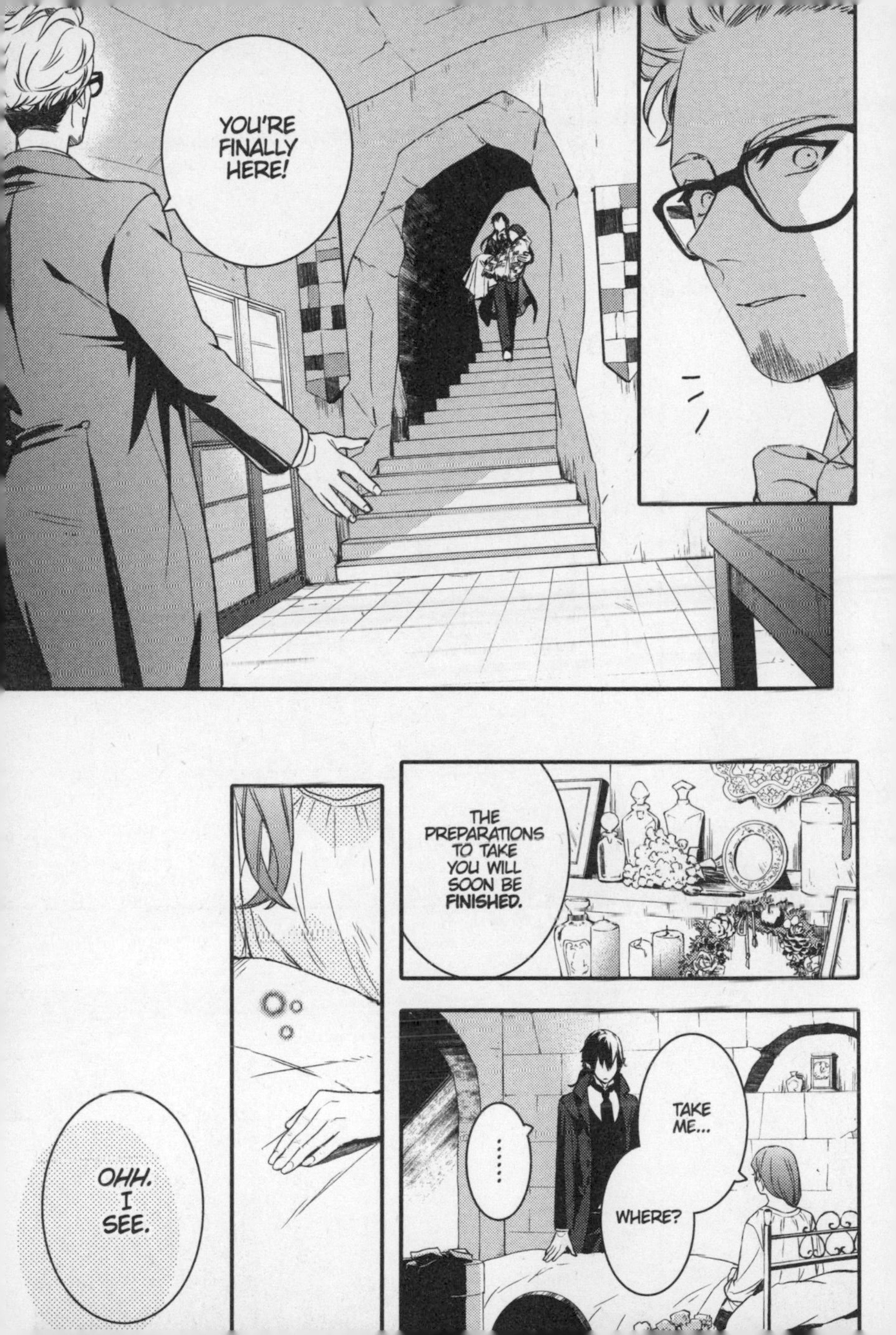
YOU'RE FINALLY HERE!
THE PREPARATIONS TO TAKE YOU WILL SOON BE FINISHED.
TAKE ME...
WHERE?
......
OHH. I SEE.

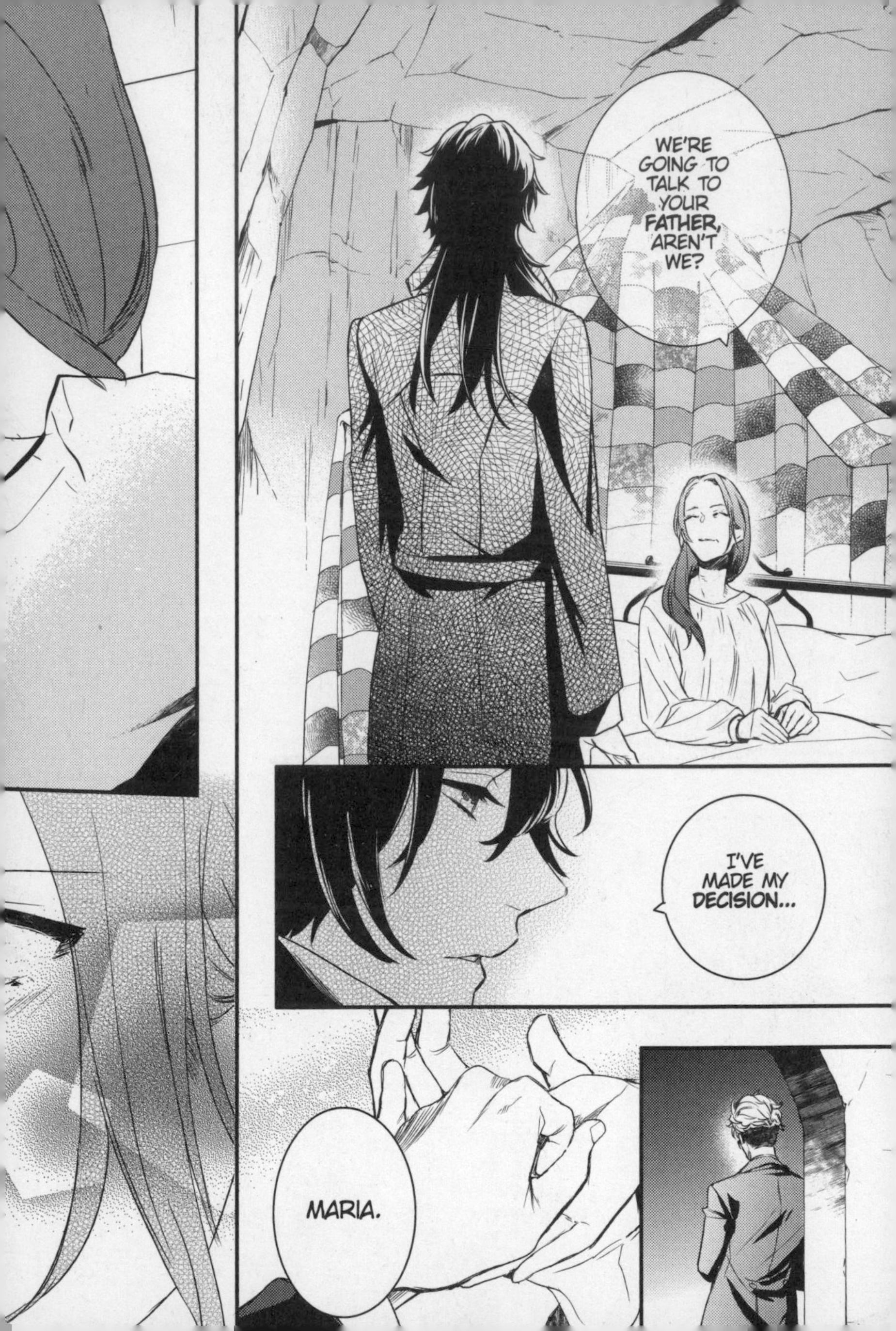
WE'RE GOING TO TALK TO YOUR FATHER, AREN'T WE?
I'VE MADE MY DECISION...
MARIA.

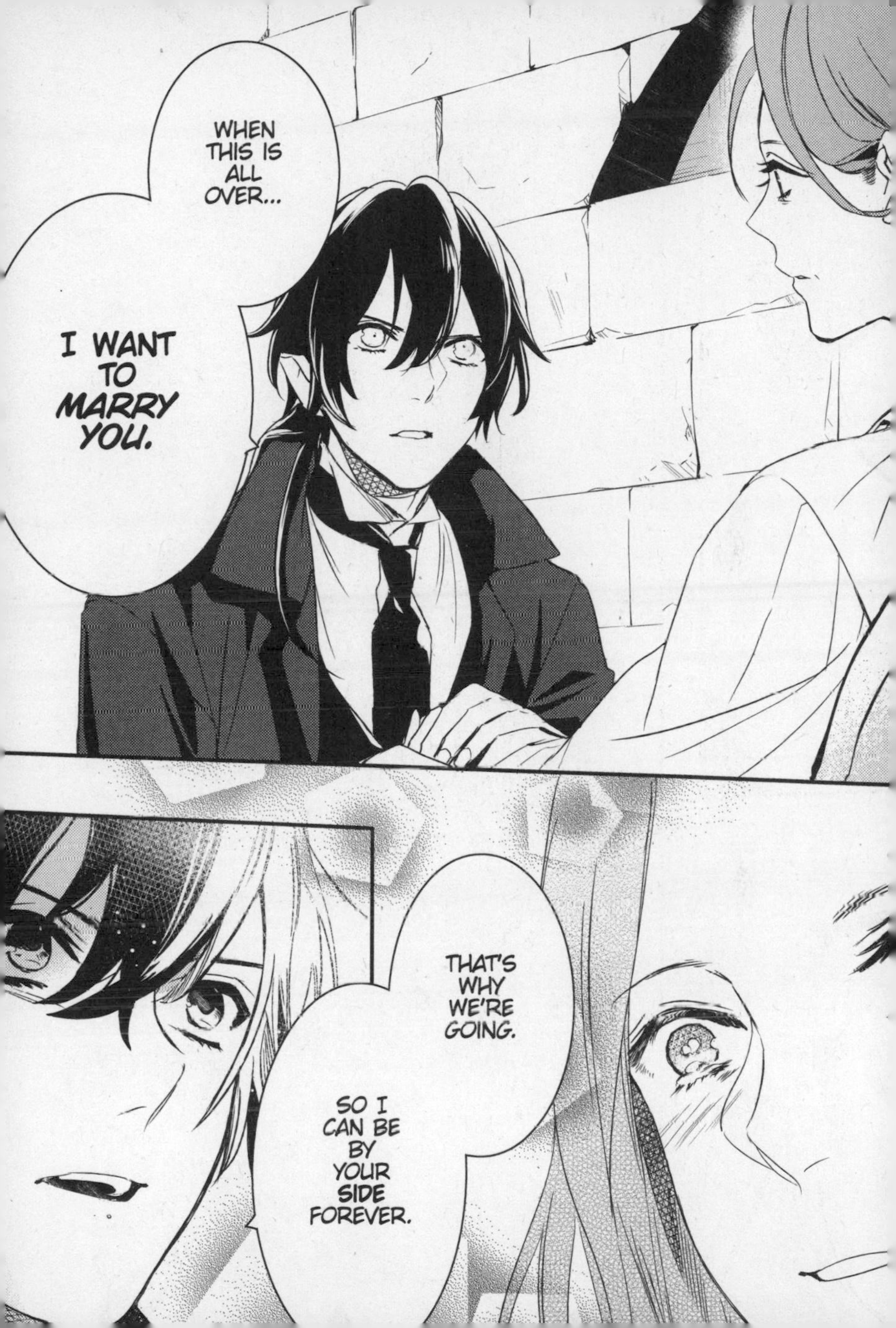
WHEN THIS IS ALL OVER...
I WANT TO MARRY YOU.
THAT'S WHY WE'RE GOING.
SO I CAN BE BY YOUR SIDE FOREVER.

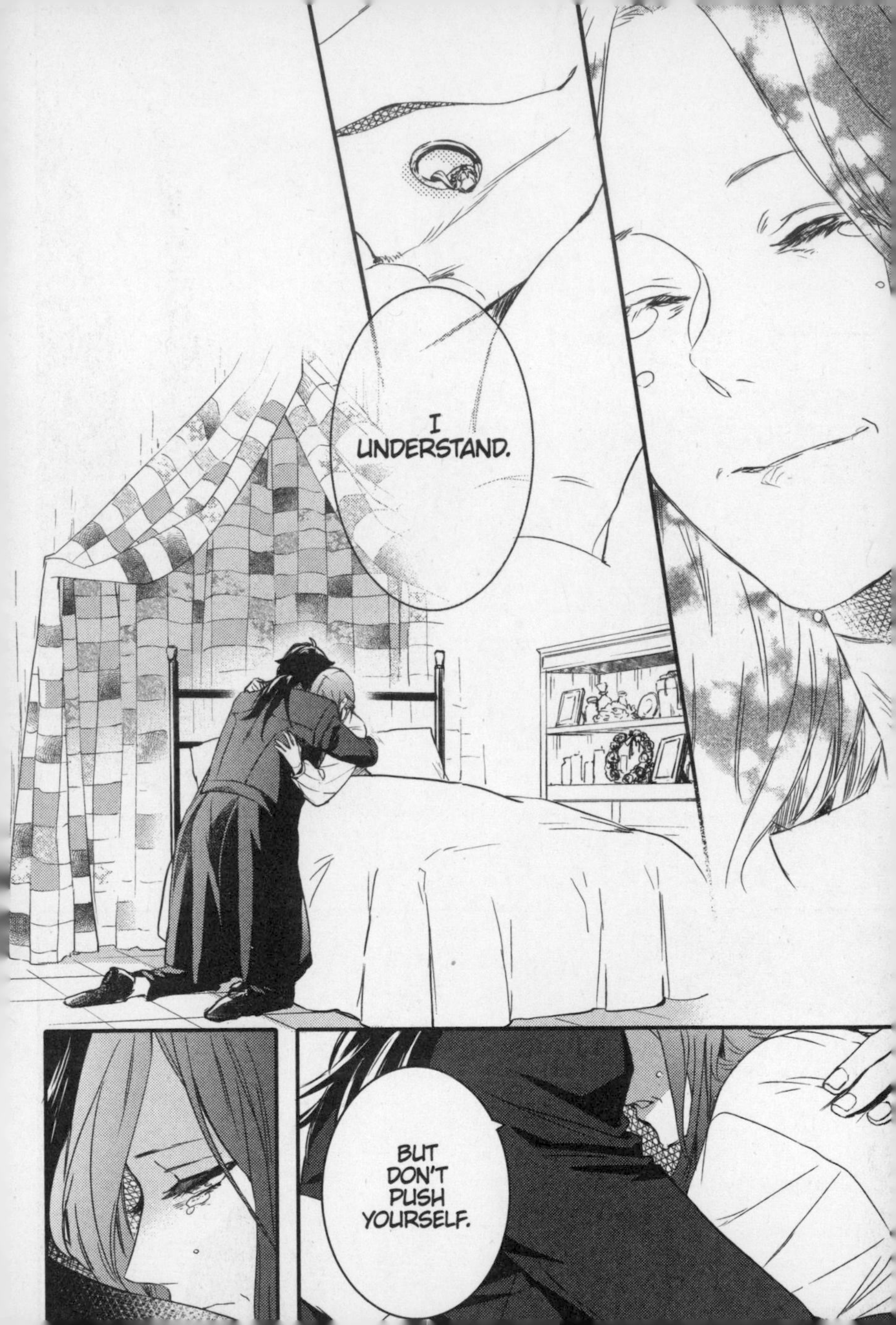
I UNDERSTAND.
BUT DON'T PUSH YOURSELF.

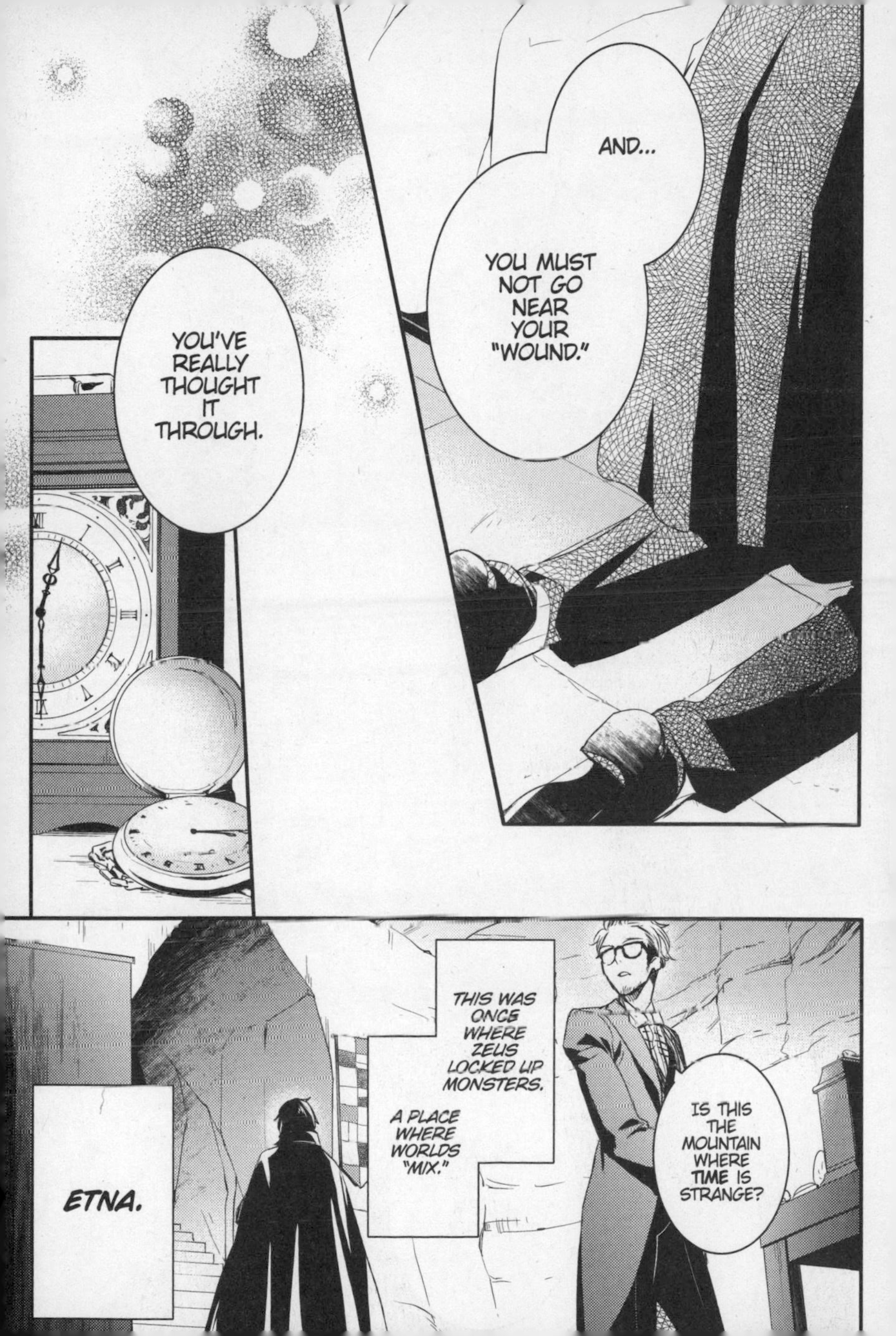
AND...
YOU MUST NOT GO NEAR YOUR "WOUND."
YOU'VE REALLY THOUGHT IT THROUGH.
IS THIS THE MOUNTAIN WHERE TIME IS STRANGE?
THIS WAS ONCE WHERE ZEUS LOCKED UP MONSTERS.
A PLACE WHERE WORLDS "MIX."
ETNA.

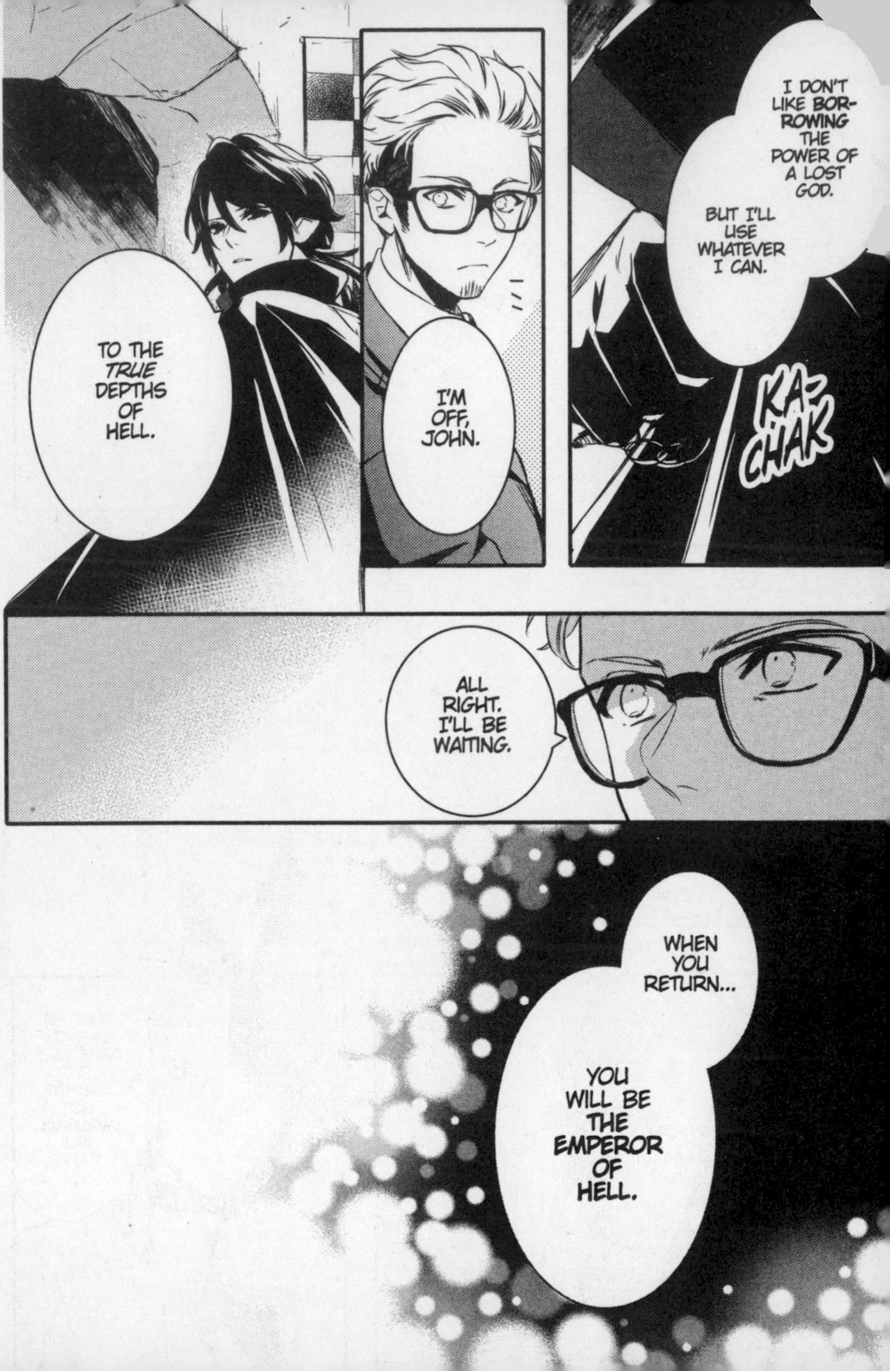
I DON'T LIKE BOR-ROWING THE POWER OF A LOST GOD.
BUT I'LL USE WHATEVER I CAN.
KA-CHAK
I'M OFF, JOHN.
TO THE *TRUE* DEPTHS OF HELL.
ALL RIGHT. I'LL BE WAITING.
WHEN YOU RETURN...
YOU WILL BE THE EMPEROR OF HELL.

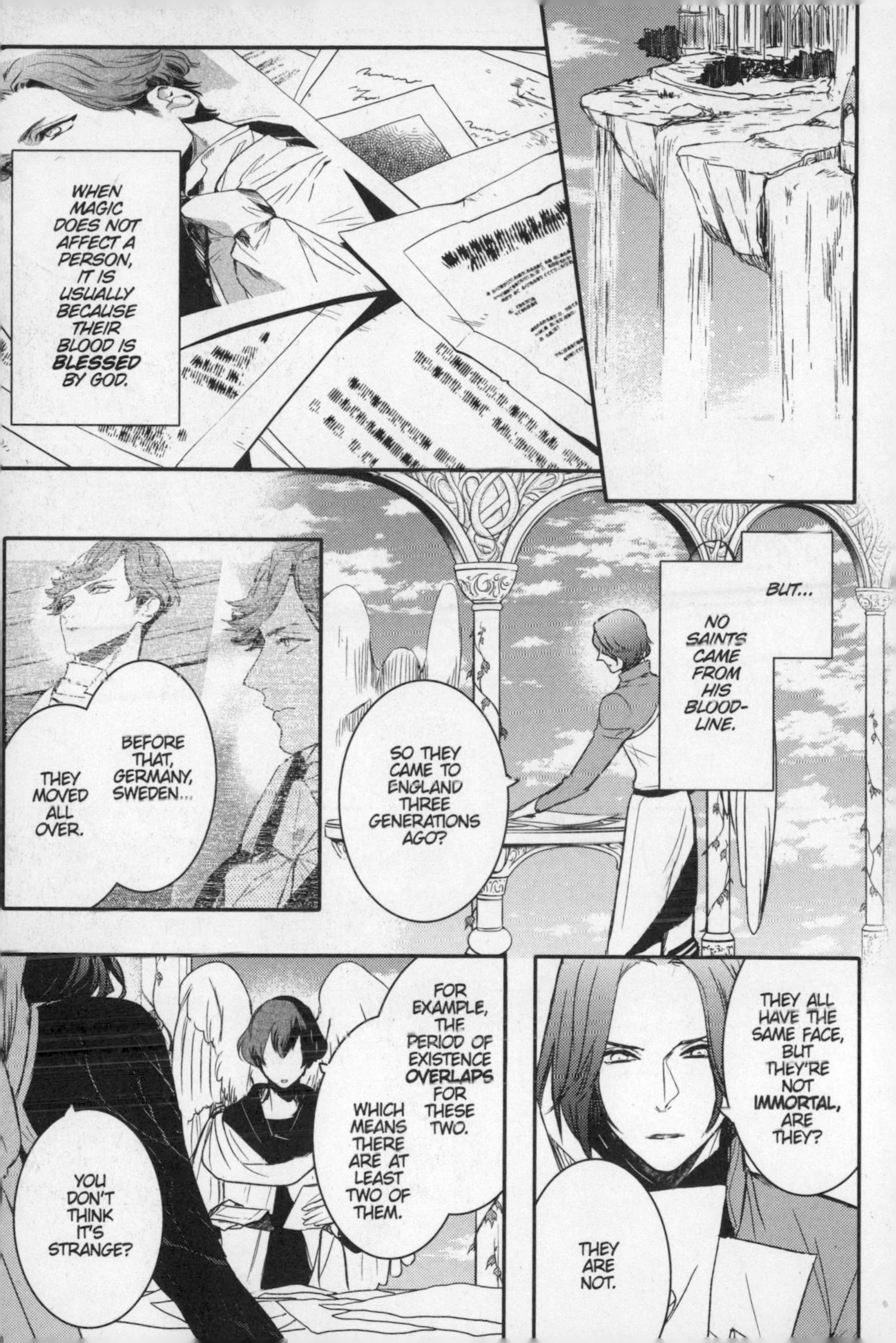

WHEN MAGIC DOES NOT AFFECT A PERSON, IT IS USUALLY BECAUSE THEIR BLOOD IS **BLESSED** BY GOD.
BUT...
NO SAINTS CAME FROM HIS BLOODLINE.
SO THEY CAME TO ENGLAND THREE GENERATIONS AGO?
BEFORE THAT, GERMANY, SWEDEN...
THEY MOVED ALL OVER.
THEY ALL HAVE THE SAME FACE, BUT THEY'RE NOT **IMMORTAL**, ARE THEY?
THEY ARE NOT.
FOR EXAMPLE, THE PERIOD OF EXISTENCE **OVERLAPS** FOR THESE TWO.
WHICH MEANS THERE ARE AT LEAST TWO OF THEM.
YOU DON'T THINK IT'S STRANGE?

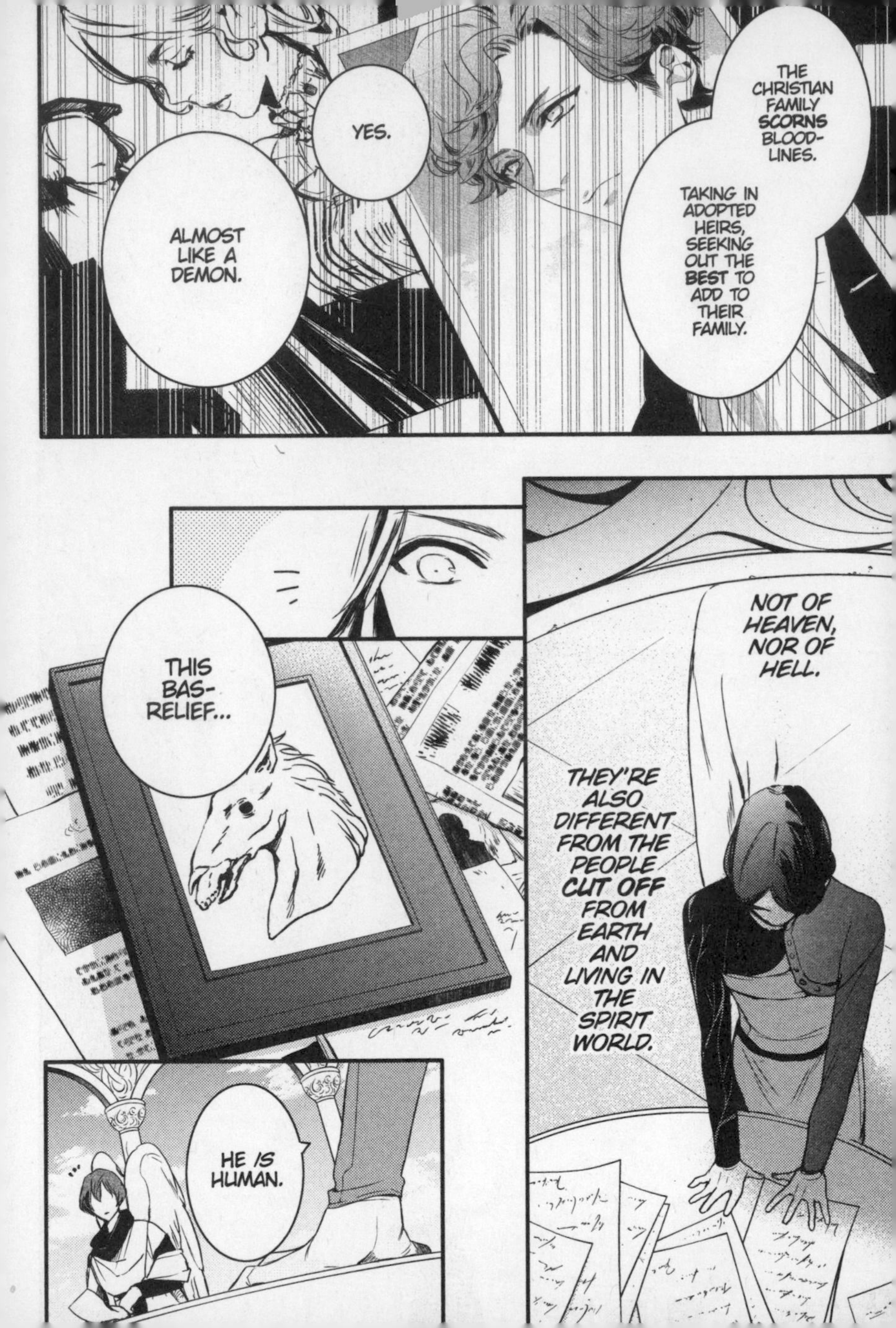
THE CHRISTIAN FAMILY SCORNS BLOOD-LINES.
TAKING IN ADOPTED HEIRS, SEEKING OUT THE BEST TO ADD TO THEIR FAMILY.
YES.
ALMOST LIKE A DEMON.
NOT OF HEAVEN, NOR OF HELL.
THEY'RE ALSO DIFFERENT FROM THE PEOPLE CUT OFF FROM EARTH AND LIVING IN THE SPIRIT WORLD.
THIS BAS-RELIEF...
HE IS HUMAN.

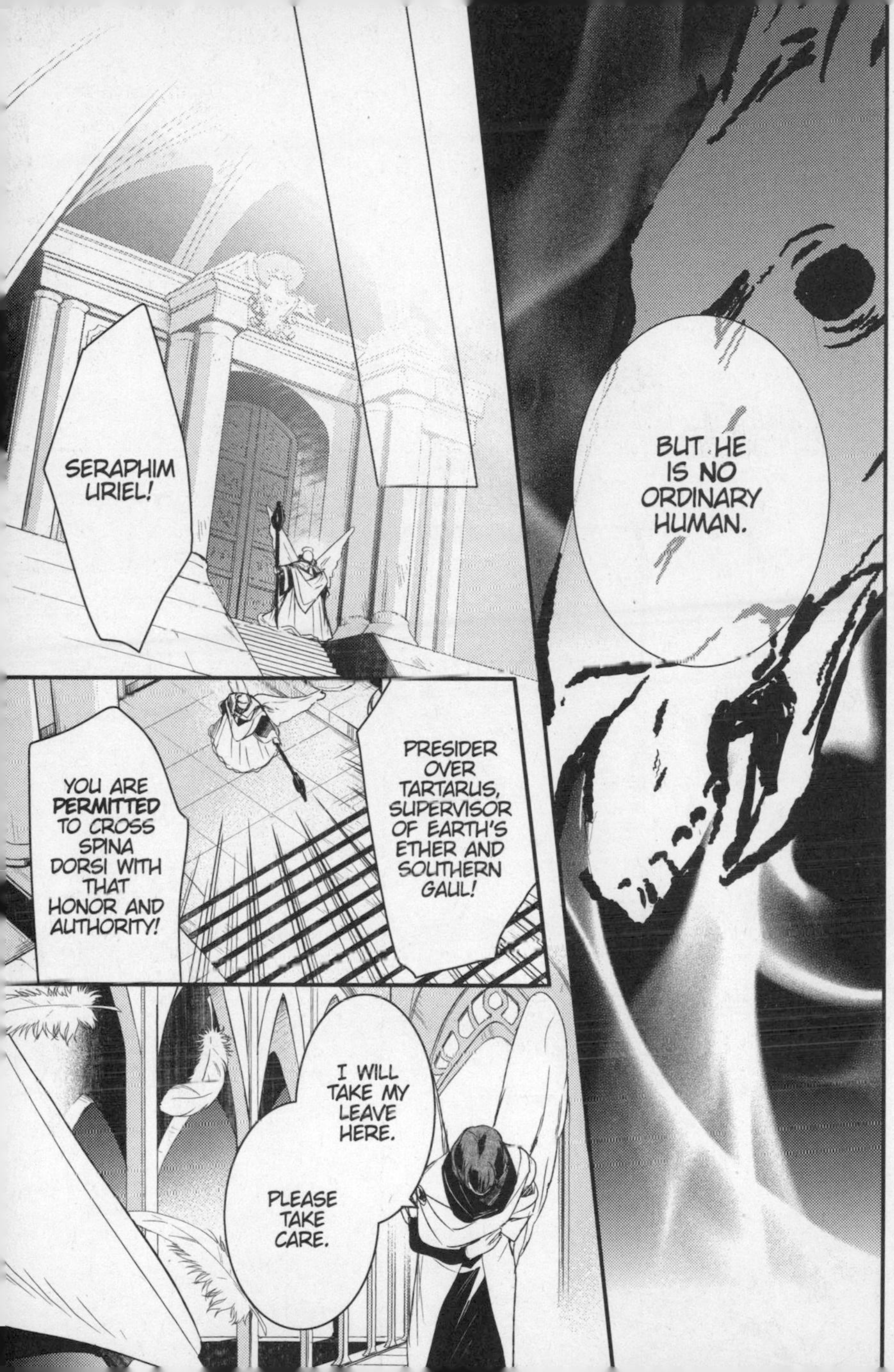
BUT HE IS NO ORDINARY HUMAN.
SERAPHIM URIEL!
PRESIDER OVER TARTARUS, SUPERVISOR OF EARTH'S ETHER AND SOUTHERN GAUL!
YOU ARE PERMITTED TO CROSS SPINA DORSI WITH THAT HONOR AND AUTHORITY!
I WILL TAKE MY LEAVE HERE.
PLEASE TAKE CARE.

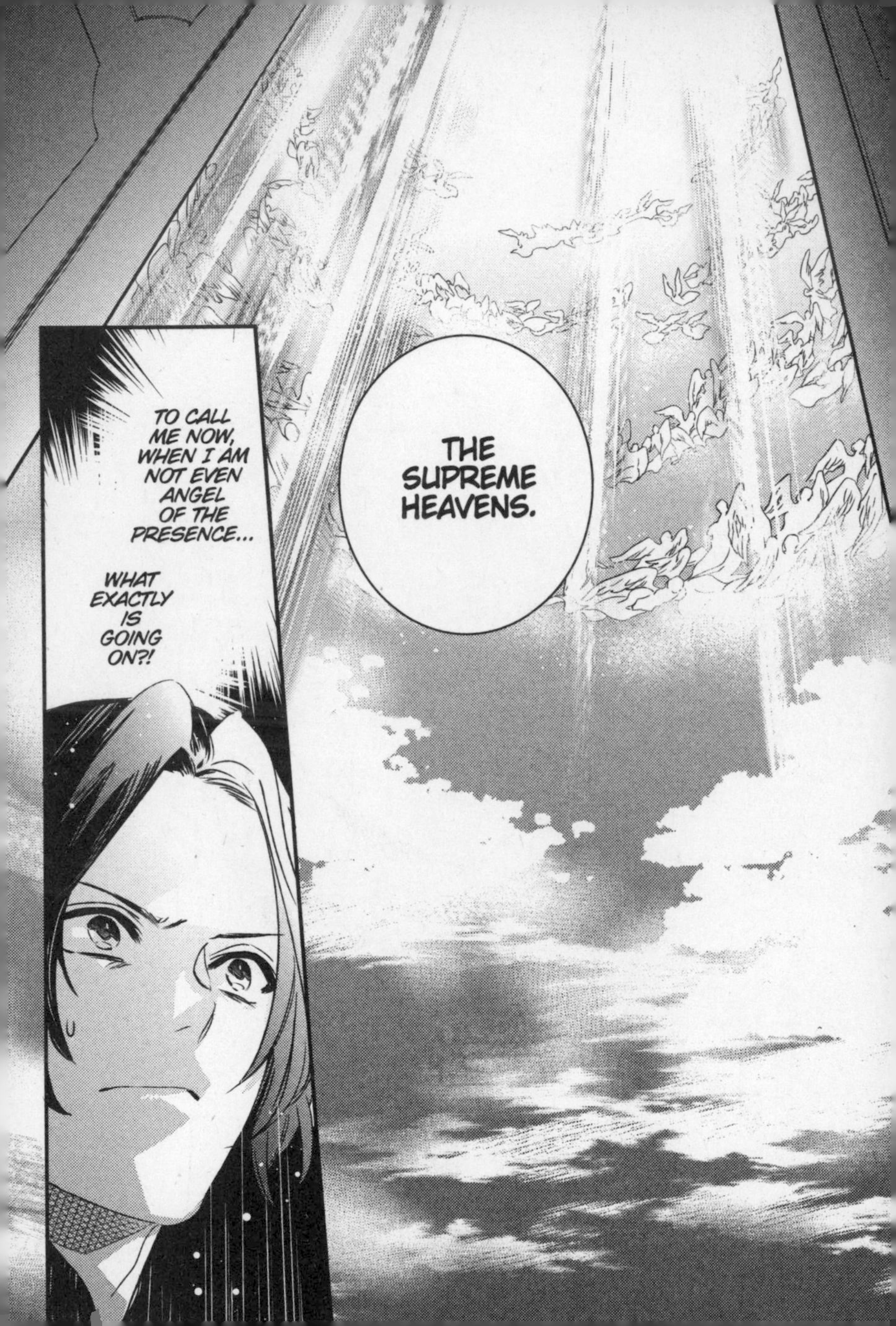
THE SUPREME HEAVENS.
TO CALL ME NOW, WHEN I AM NOT EVEN ANGEL OF THE PRESENCE...
WHAT EXACTLY IS GOING ON?!

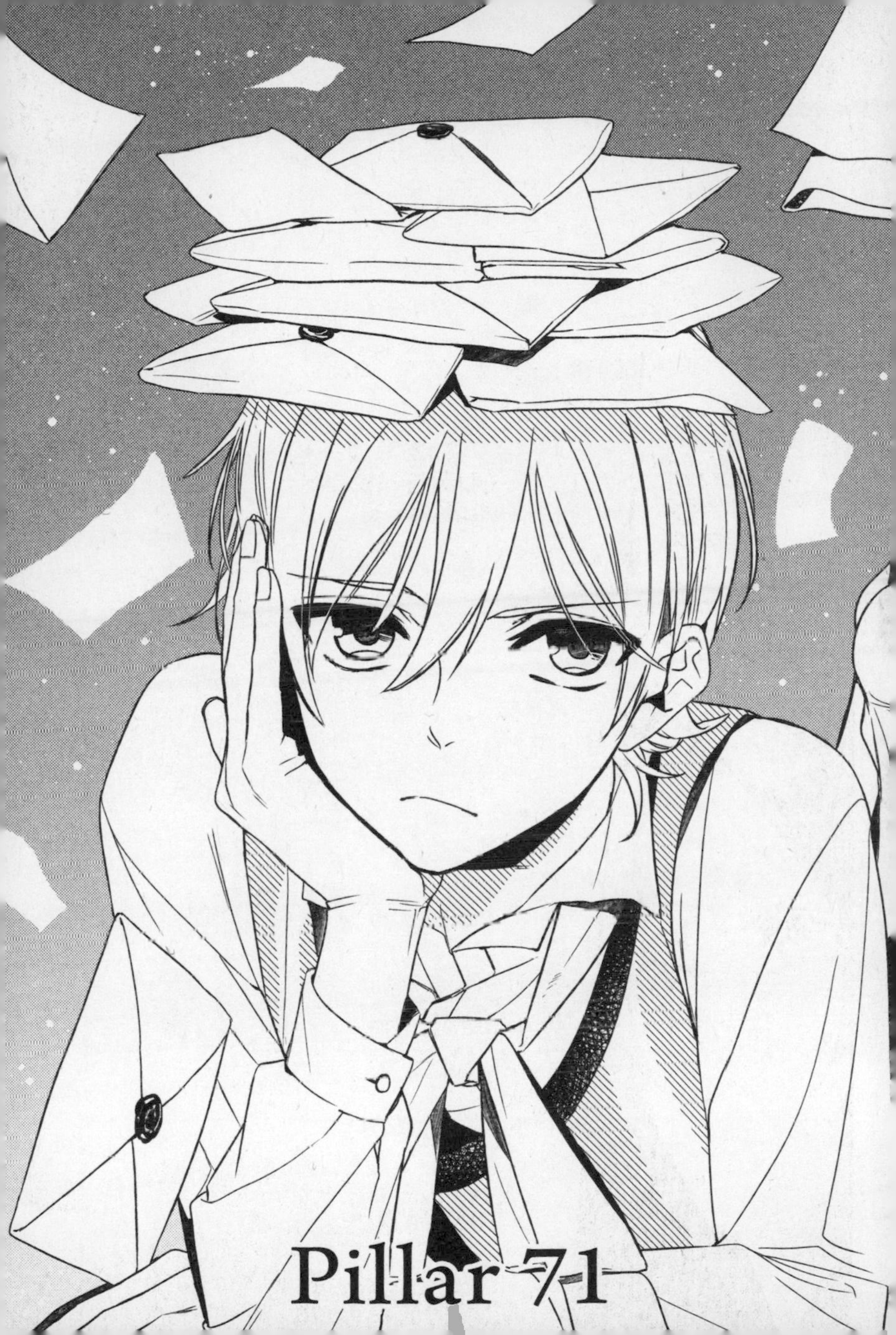
Pillar 71

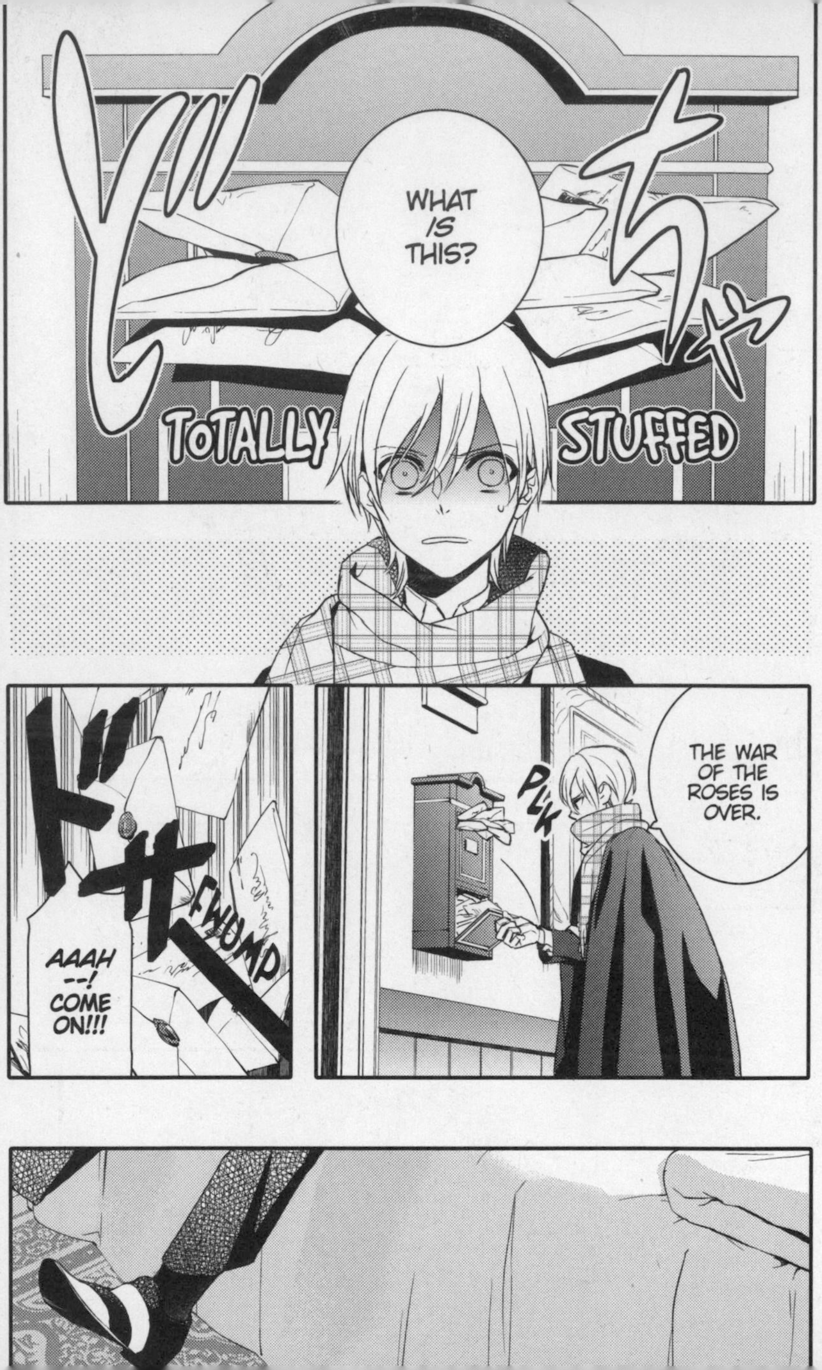
WHAT IS THIS?
TOTALLY STUFFED
THE WAR OF THE ROSES IS OVER.
PLIK
FWUMP
AAAH--! COME ON!!!

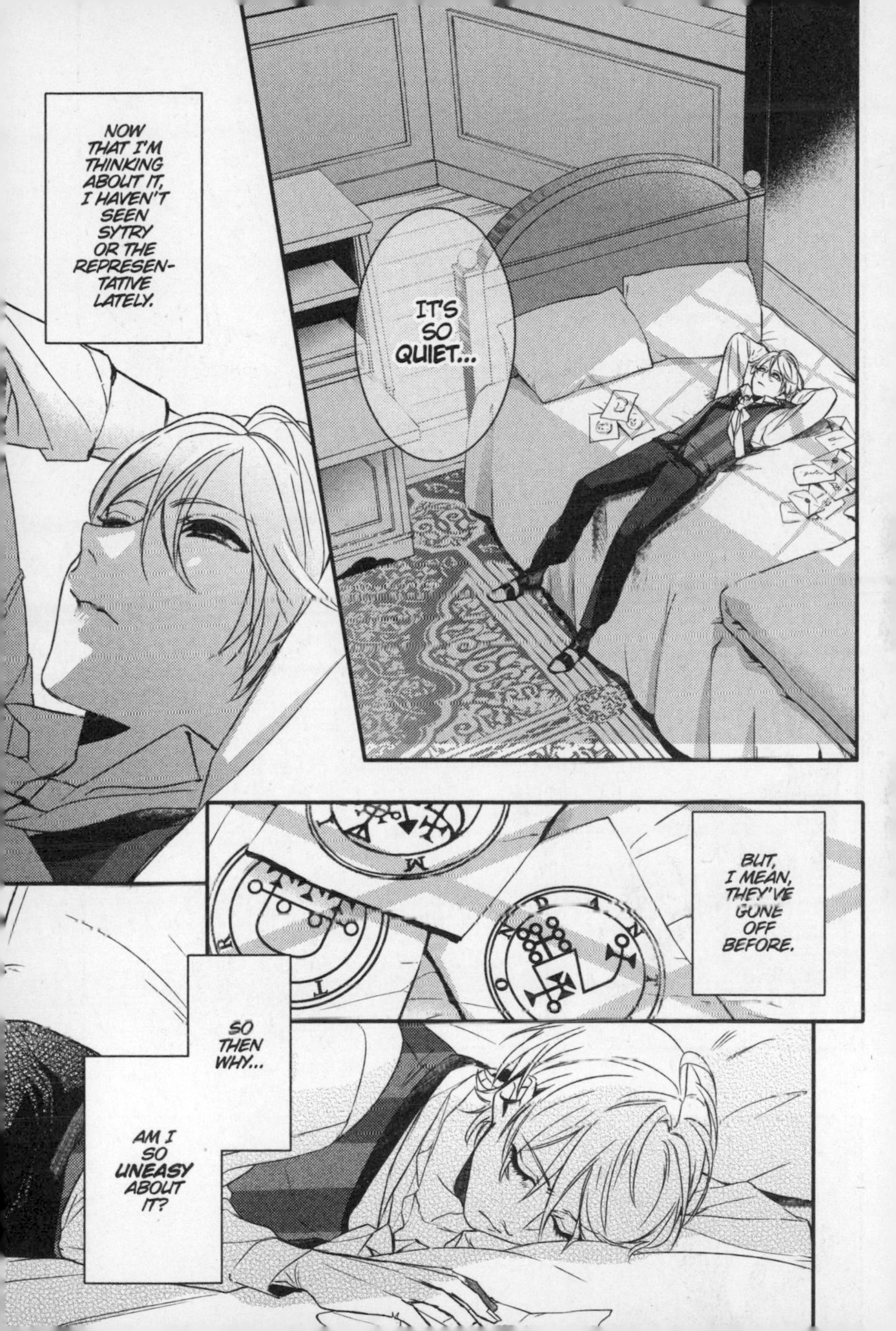
IT'S SO QUIET...
NOW THAT I'M THINKING ABOUT IT, I HAVEN'T SEEN SYTRY OR THE REPRESEN-TATIVE LATELY.
BUT, I MEAN, THEY'VE GONE OFF BEFORE.
SO THEN WHY...
AM I SO UNEASY ABOUT IT?

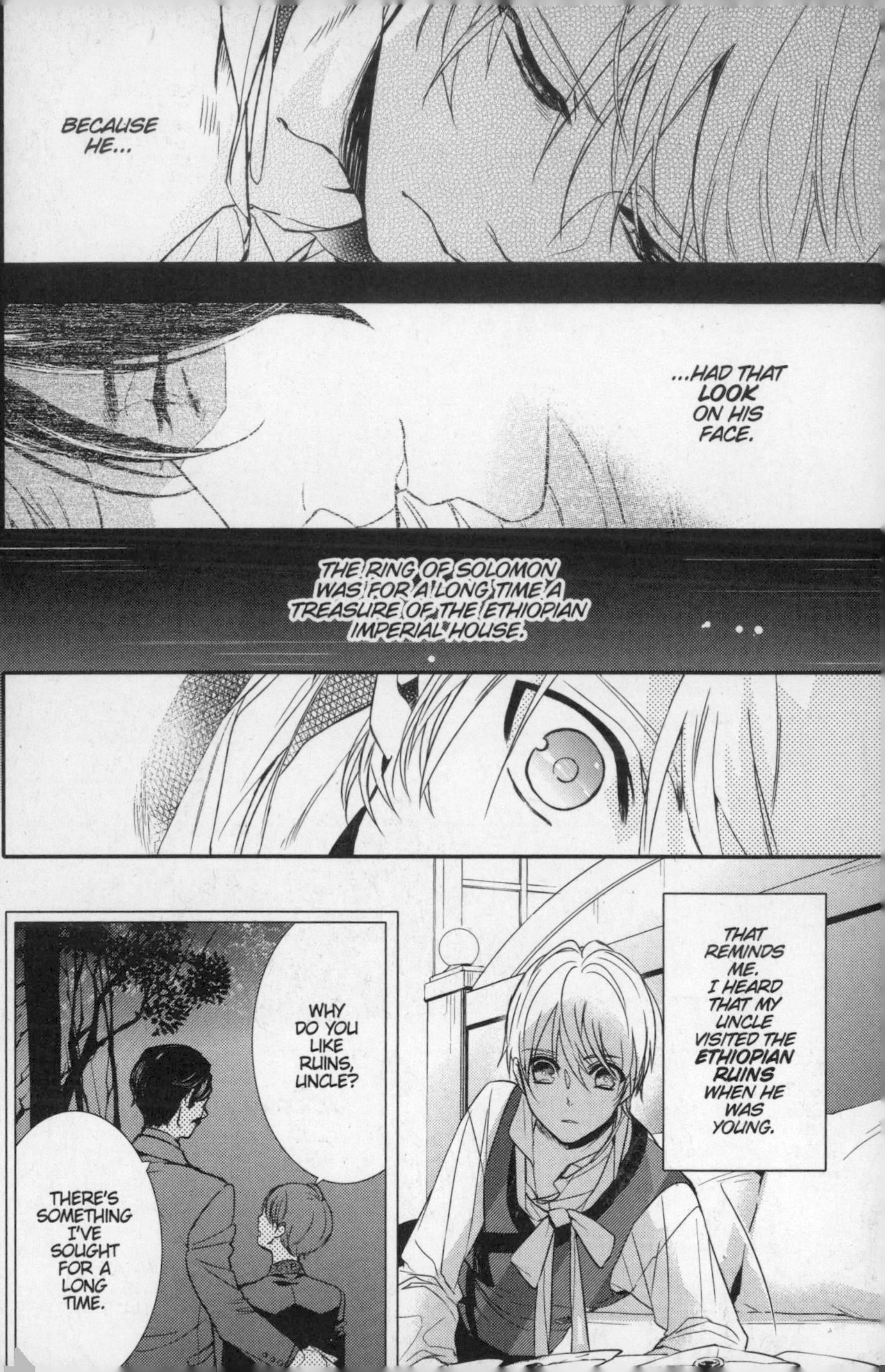
BECAUSE HE...
...HAD THAT LOOK ON HIS FACE.
THE RING OF SOLOMON WAS FOR A LONG TIME A TREASURE OF THE ETHIOPIAN IMPERIAL HOUSE.
THAT REMINDS ME. I HEARD THAT MY UNCLE VISITED THE ETHIOPIAN RUINS WHEN HE WAS YOUNG.
WHY DO YOU LIKE RUINS, UNCLE?
THERE'S SOMETHING I'VE SOUGHT FOR A LONG TIME.

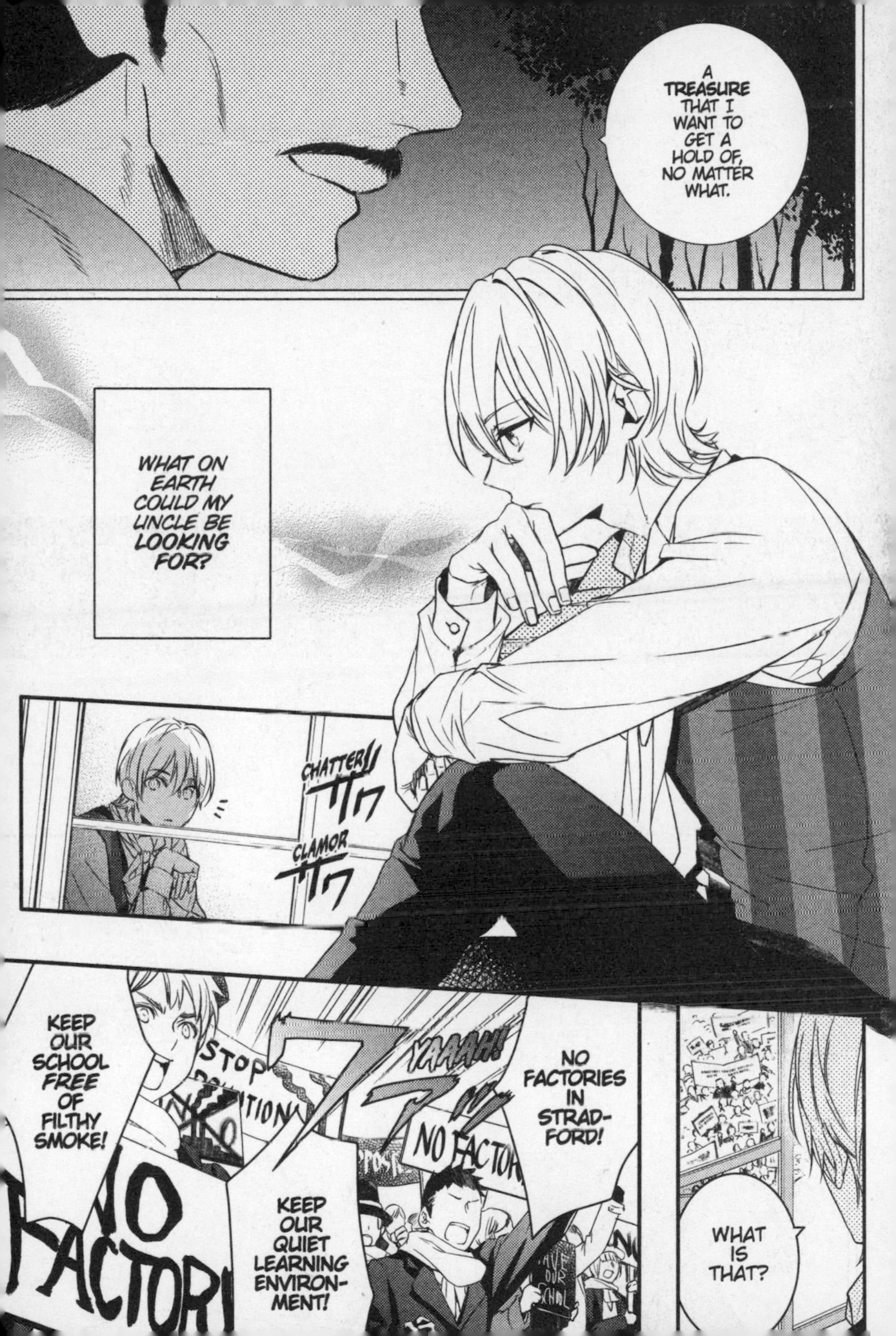
A TREASURE THAT I WANT TO GET A HOLD OF, NO MATTER WHAT.
WHAT ON EARTH COULD MY UNCLE BE LOOKING FOR?
CHATTER
CLAMOR
WHAT IS THAT?
NO FACTORIES IN STRAD-FORD!
NO FACTOR
YAAAH!!
KEEP OUR QUIET LEARNING ENVIRONMENT!
STOP
KEEP OUR SCHOOL FREE OF FILTHY SMOKE!
NO FACTORI

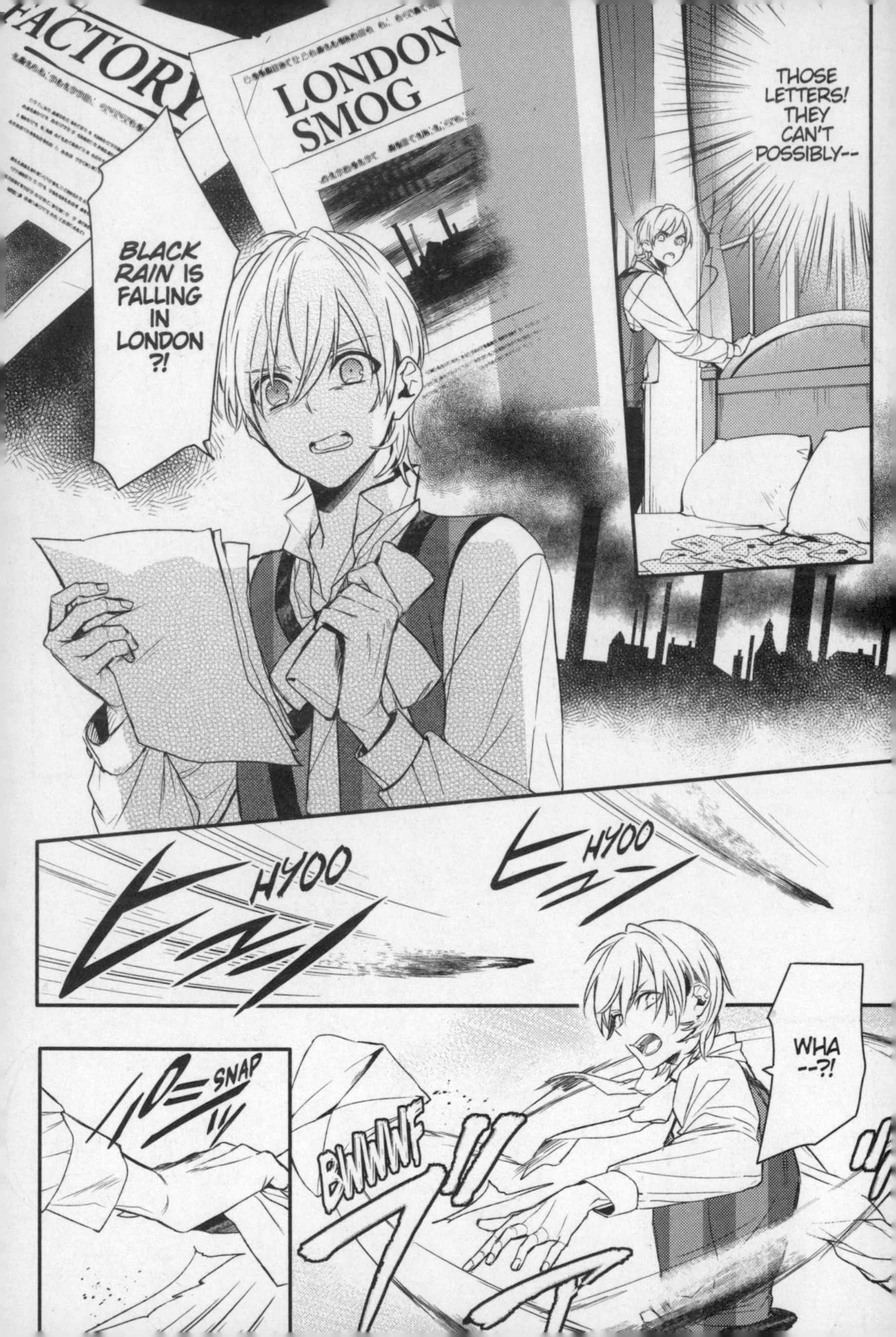
THOSE LETTERS! THEY CAN'T POSSIBLY--
LONDON SMOG
FACTORY
BLACK RAIN IS FALLING IN LONDON?!
HYOO
HYOO
WHA--?!
BWWWF
SNAP

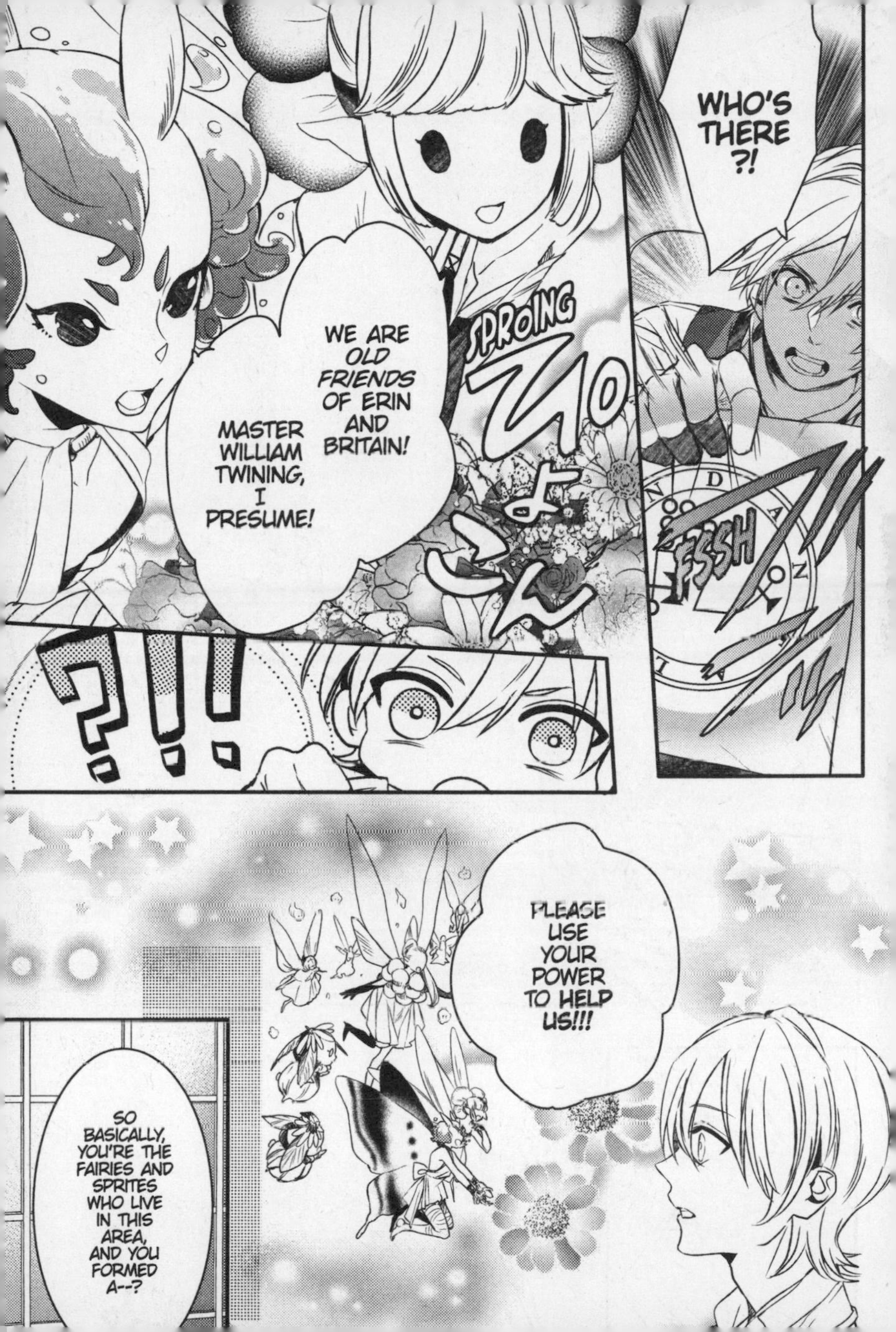
WHO'S THERE ?!
FSSH
SPROING
WE ARE OLD FRIENDS OF ERIN AND BRITAIN!
MASTER WILLIAM TWINING, I PRESUME!
?!!
PLEASE USE YOUR POWER TO HELP US!!!
SO BASICALLY, YOU'RE THE FAIRIES AND SPRITES WHO LIVE IN THIS AREA, AND YOU FORMED A--?

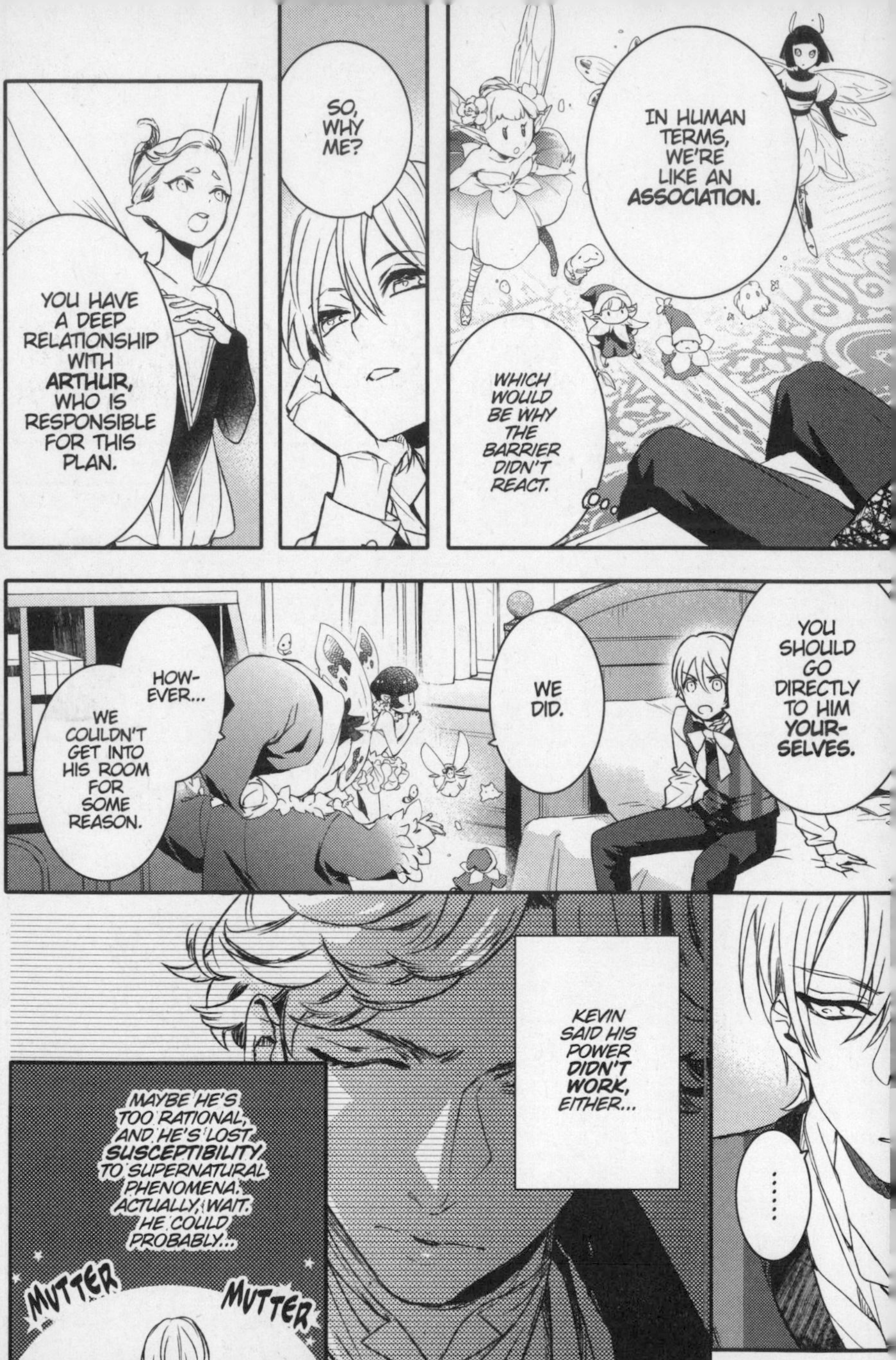
IN HUMAN TERMS, WE'RE LIKE AN ASSOCIATION.
WHICH WOULD BE WHY THE BARRIER DIDN'T REACT.
SO, WHY ME?
YOU HAVE A DEEP RELATIONSHIP WITH ARTHUR, WHO IS RESPONSIBLE FOR THIS PLAN.
YOU SHOULD GO DIRECTLY TO HIM YOURSELVES.
WE DID.
HOWEVER... WE COULDN'T GET INTO HIS ROOM FOR SOME REASON.
......
KEVIN SAID HIS POWER DIDN'T WORK, EITHER...
MAYBE HE'S TOO RATIONAL, AND HE'S LOST SUSCEPTIBILITY TO SUPERNATURAL PHENOMENA. ACTUALLY, WAIT. HE COULD PROBABLY...
MUTTER
MUTTER

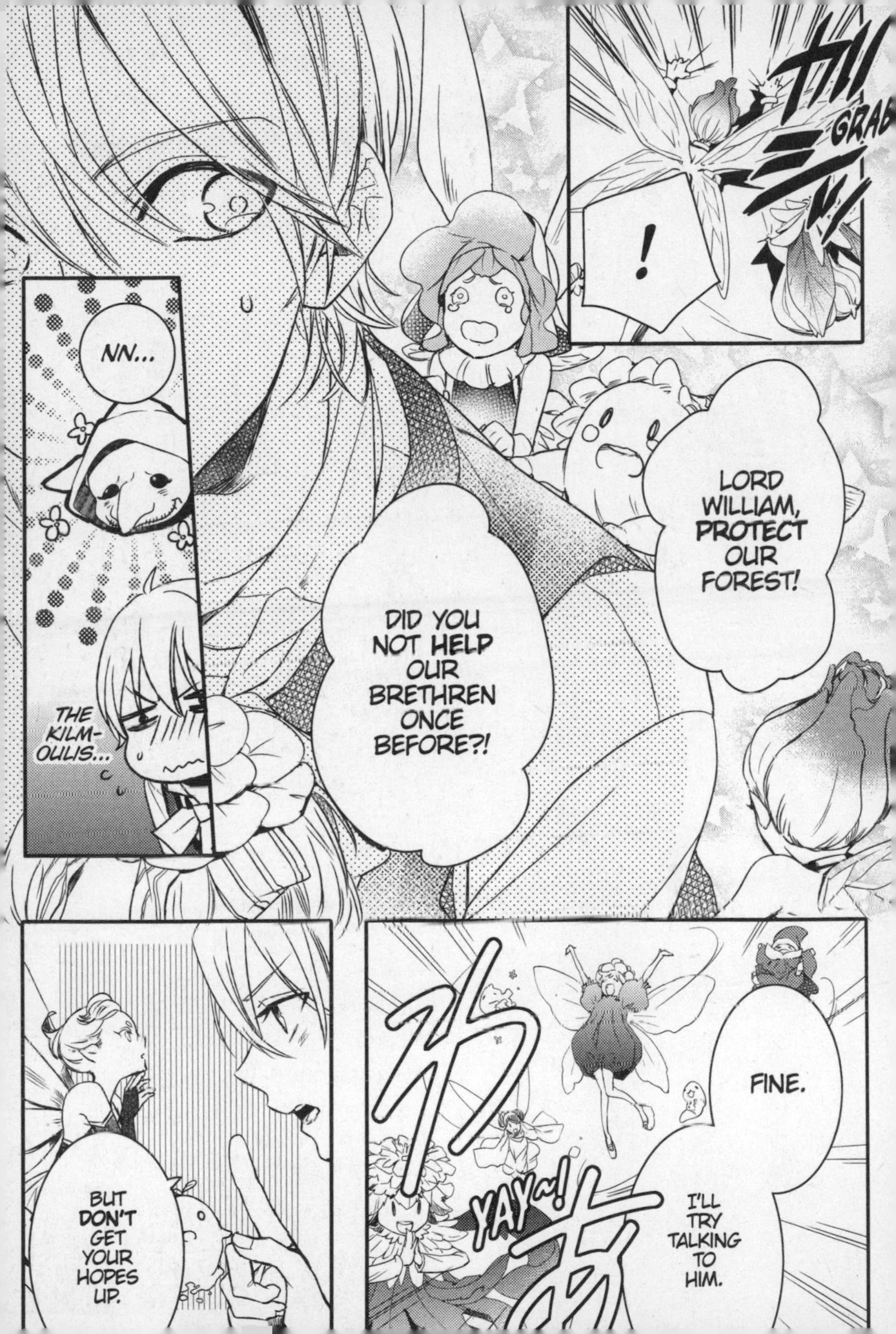
GRAB
!
LORD WILLIAM, PROTECT OUR FOREST!
DID YOU NOT HELP OUR BRETHREN ONCE BEFORE?!
NN...
THE KILM-OULIS...
FINE.
I'LL TRY TALKING TO HIM.
YAY~!
BUT DON'T GET YOUR HOPES UP.

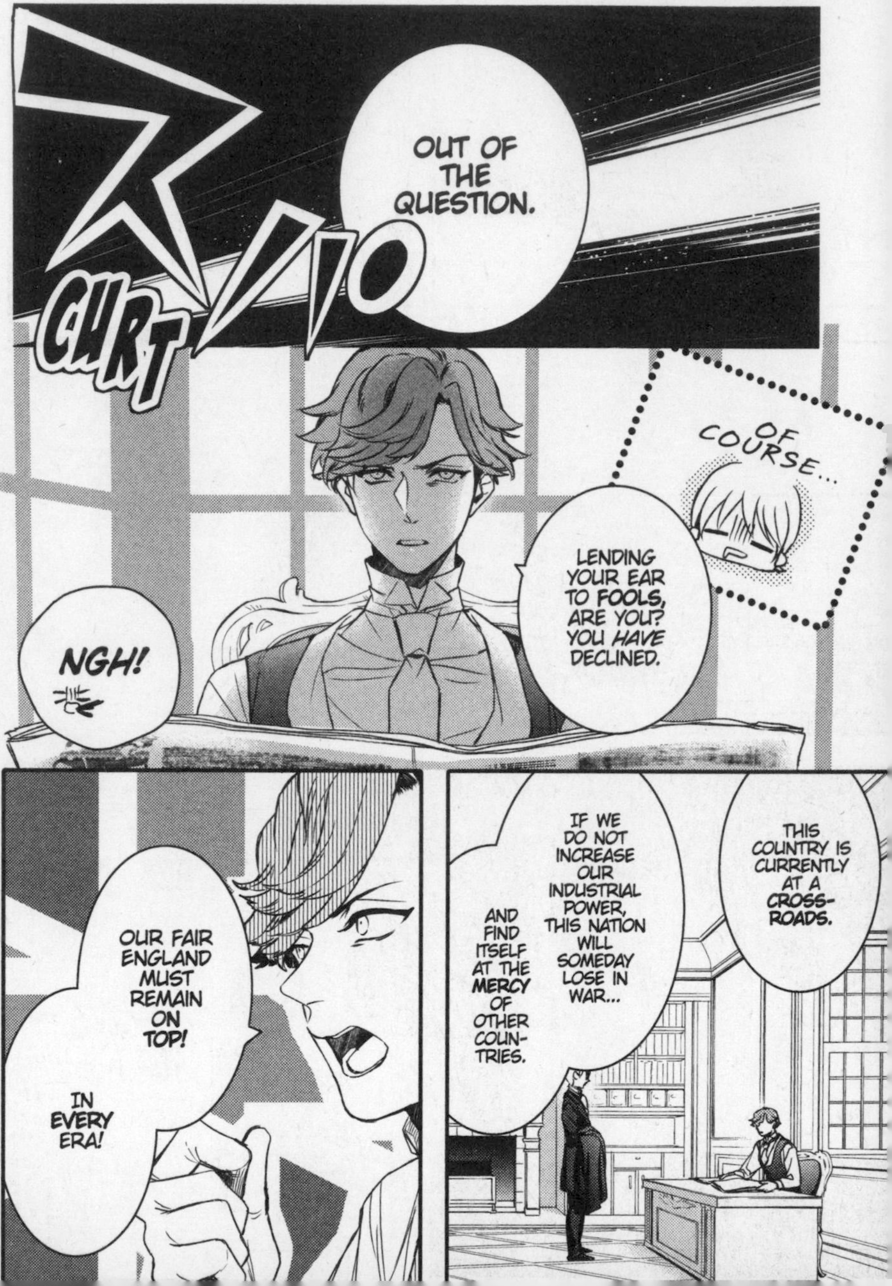
NO
CURT
OUT OF THE QUESTION.
OF COURSE...
LENDING YOUR EAR TO FOOLS, ARE YOU? YOU *HAVE* DECLINED.
NGH!
THIS COUNTRY IS CURRENTLY AT A CROSS-ROADS.
IF WE DO NOT INCREASE OUR INDUSTRIAL POWER, THIS NATION WILL SOMEDAY LOSE IN WAR...
AND FIND ITSELF AT THE **MERCY** OF OTHER COUN-TRIES.
OUR FAIR ENGLAND MUST REMAIN ON **TOP!**
IN EVERY ERA!

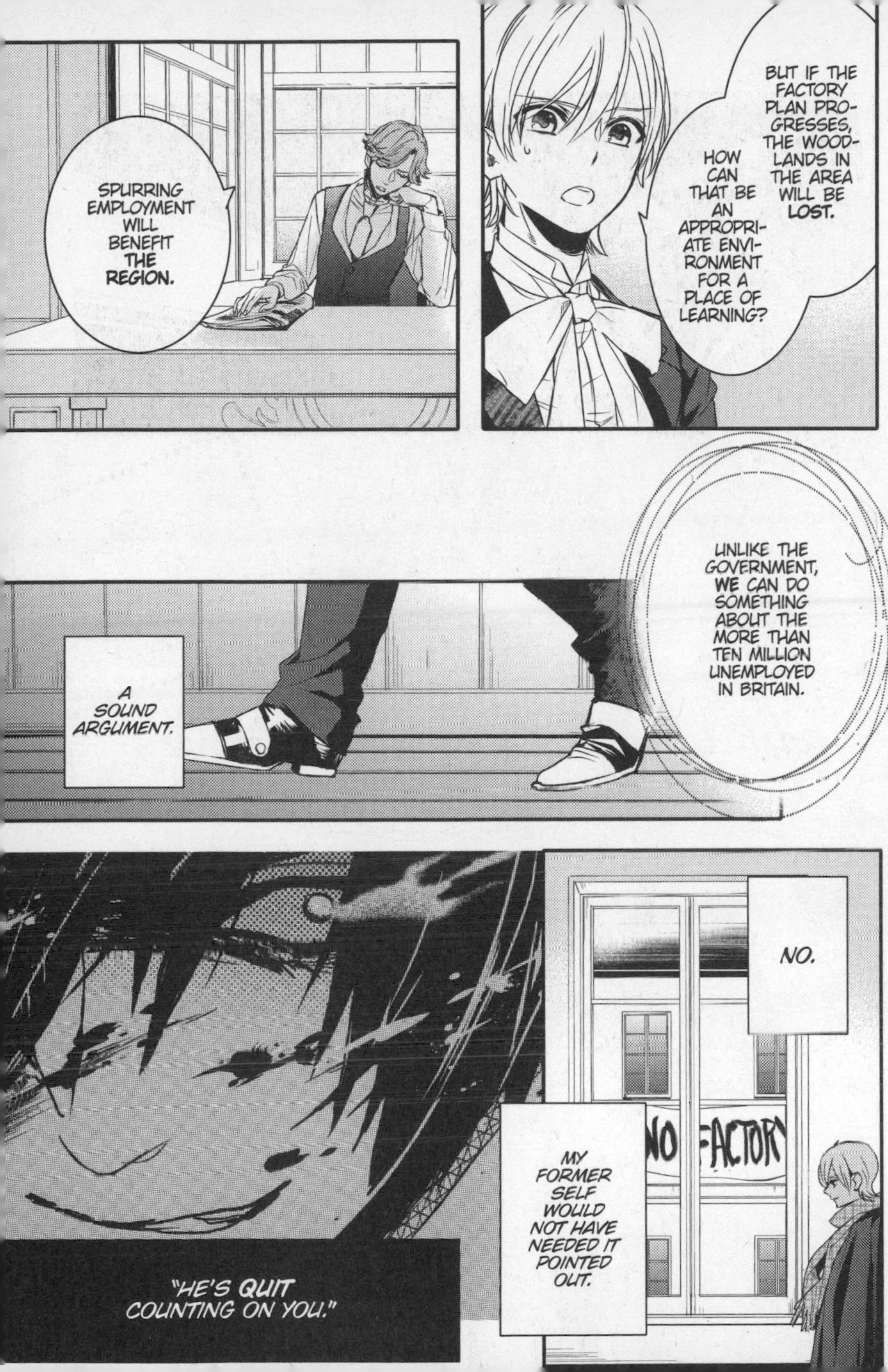
BUT IF THE FACTORY PLAN PROGRESSES, THE WOODLANDS IN THE AREA WILL BE LOST.
HOW CAN THAT BE AN APPROPRIATE ENVIRONMENT FOR A PLACE OF LEARNING?
SPURRING EMPLOYMENT WILL BENEFIT THE REGION.
UNLIKE THE GOVERNMENT, WE CAN DO SOMETHING ABOUT THE MORE THAN TEN MILLION UNEMPLOYED IN BRITAIN.
A SOUND ARGUMENT.
NO.
NO FACTORY
MY FORMER SELF WOULD NOT HAVE NEEDED IT POINTED OUT.
"HE'S QUIT COUNTING ON YOU."

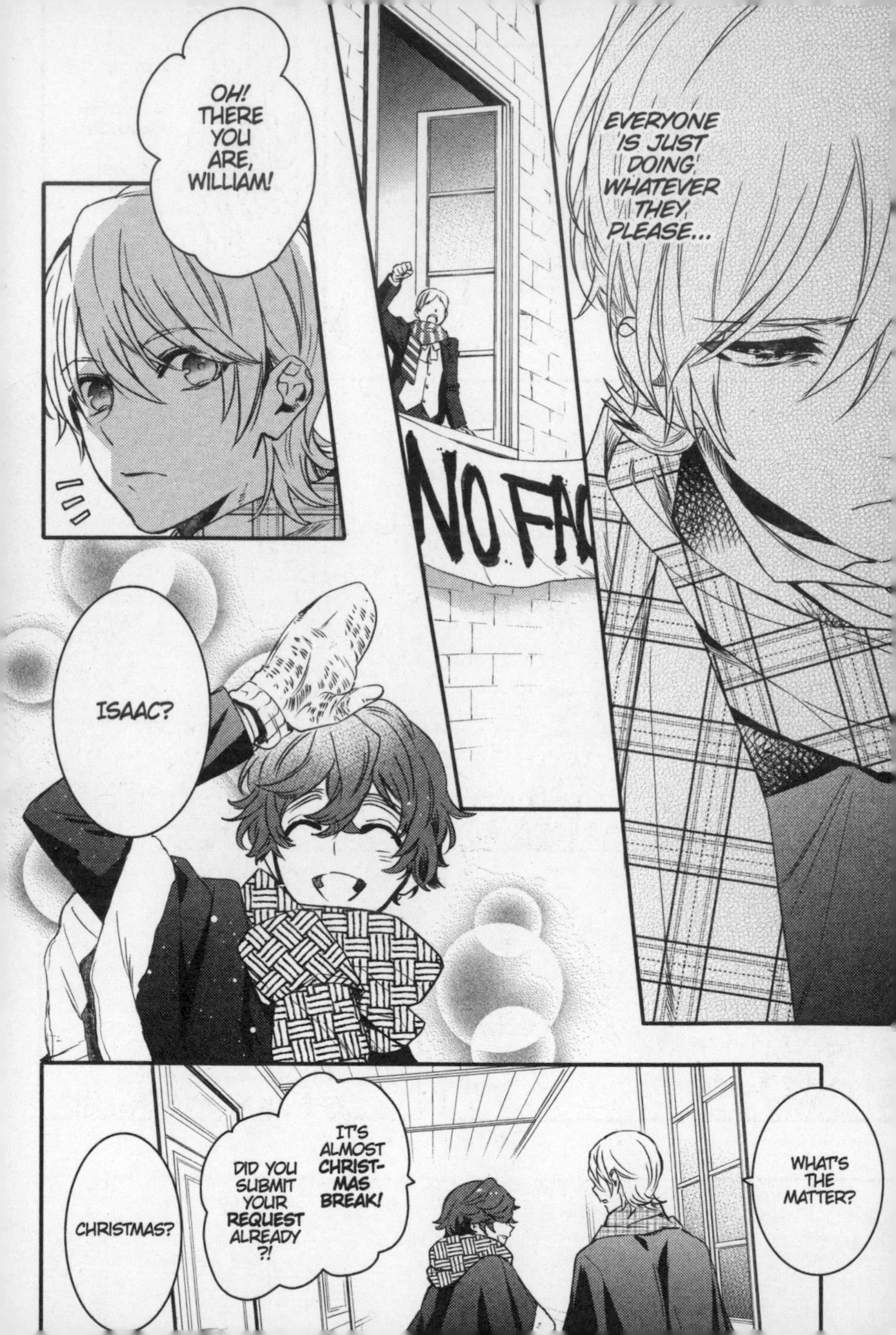
EVERYONE IS JUST DOING WHATEVER THEY PLEASE...
OH! THERE YOU ARE, WILLIAM!
NO FAC
ISAAC?
WHAT'S THE MATTER?
IT'S ALMOST CHRIST-MAS BREAK!
DID YOU SUBMIT YOUR REQUEST ALREADY ?!
CHRISTMAS?

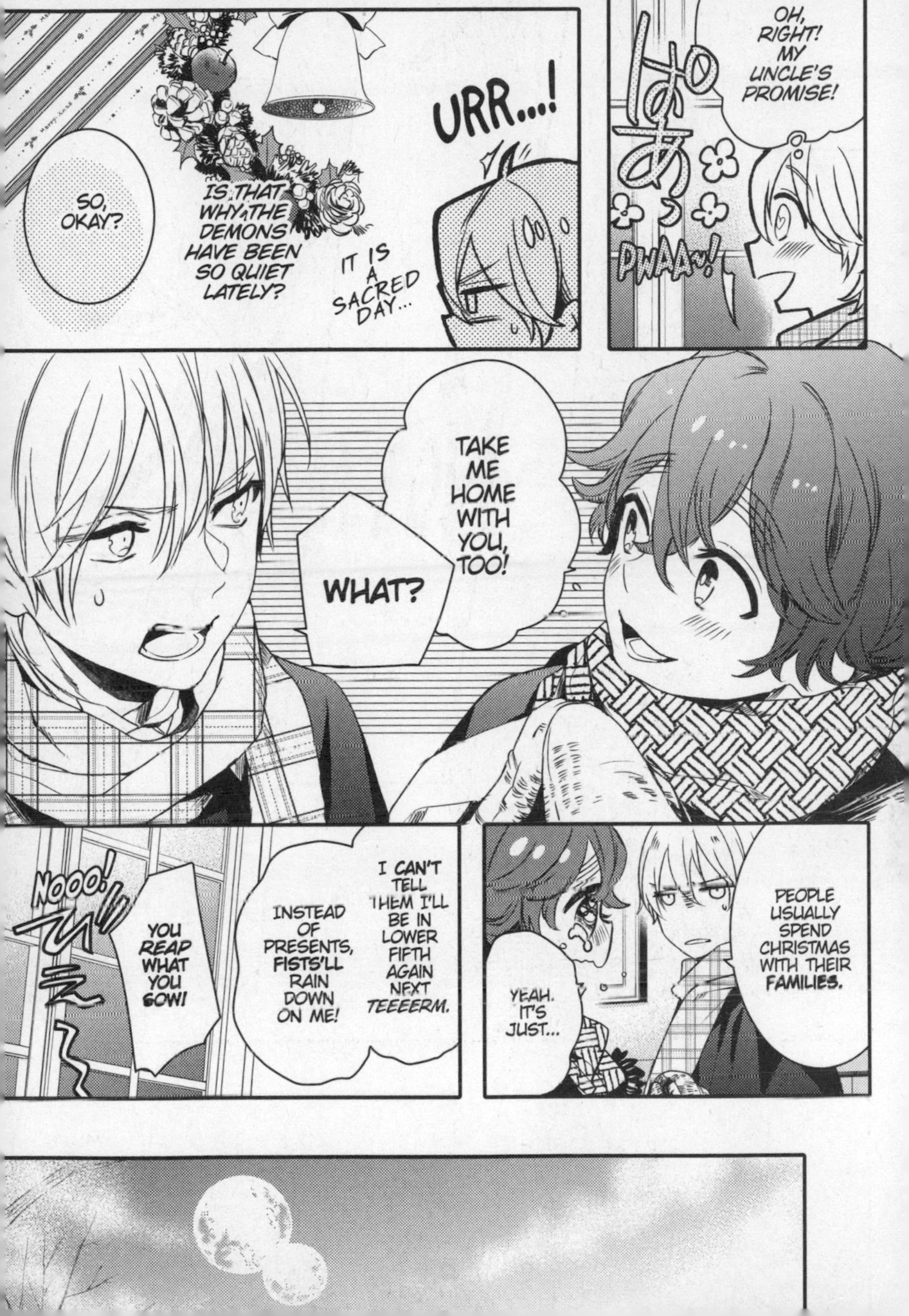
OH, RIGHT! MY UNCLE'S PROMISE!
PWAA♥!
URR...!
IT IS A SACRED DAY...
IS THAT WHY THE DEMONS HAVE BEEN SO QUIET LATELY?
SO, OKAY?
TAKE ME HOME WITH YOU, TOO!
WHAT?
PEOPLE USUALLY SPEND CHRISTMAS WITH THEIR FAMILIES.
YEAH. IT'S JUST...
I CAN'T TELL THEM I'LL BE IN LOWER FIFTH AGAIN NEXT TEEEERM.
INSTEAD OF PRESENTS, FISTS'LL RAIN DOWN ON ME!
YOU REAP WHAT YOU SOW!
NOOO!

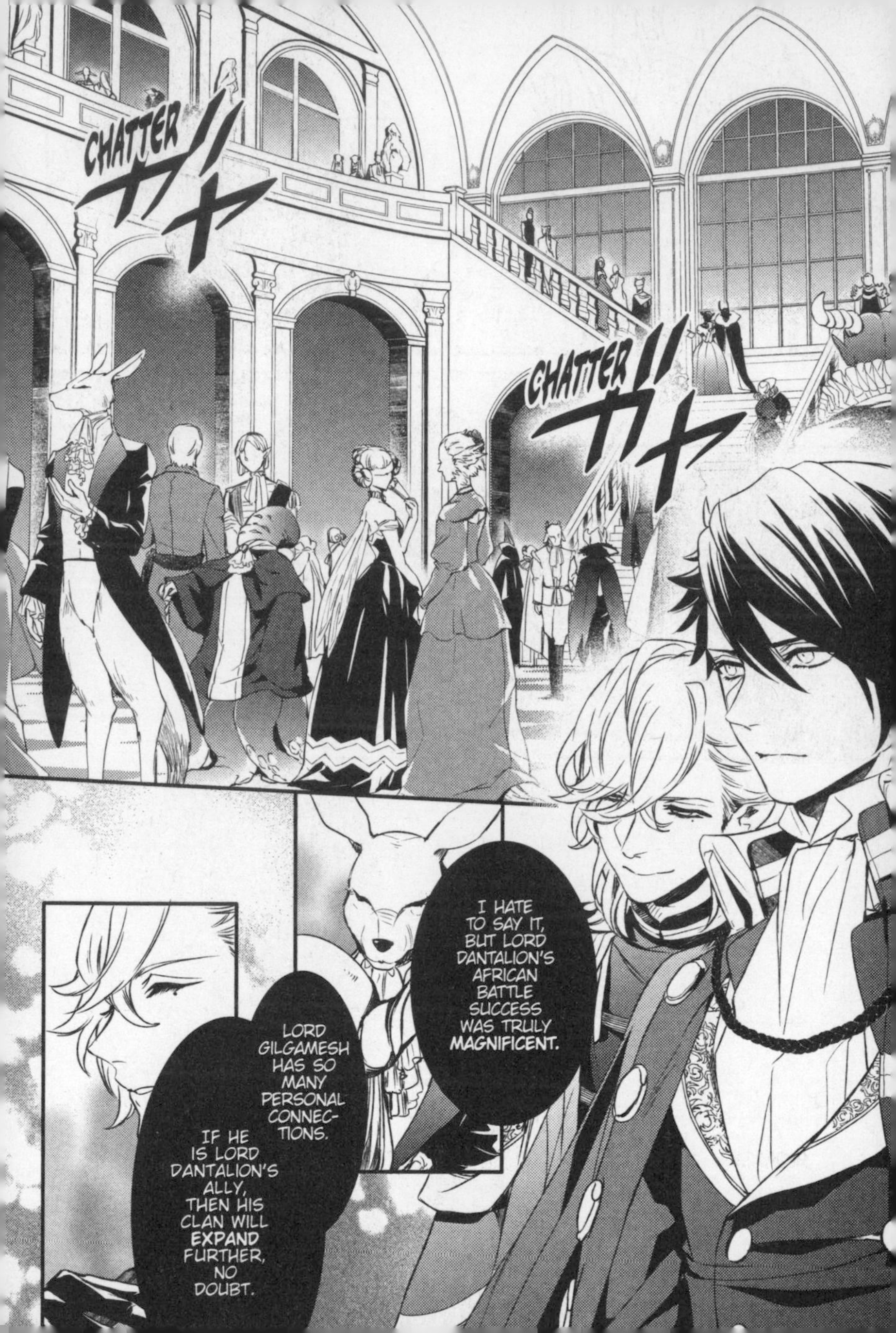
CHATTER
CHATTER
I HATE TO SAY IT, BUT LORD DANTALION'S AFRICAN BATTLE SUCCESS WAS TRULY **MAGNIFICENT.**
LORD GILGAMESH HAS SO MANY PERSONAL CONNEC- TIONS.
IF HE IS LORD DANTALION'S ALLY, THEN HIS CLAN WILL **EXPAND** FURTHER, NO DOUBT.

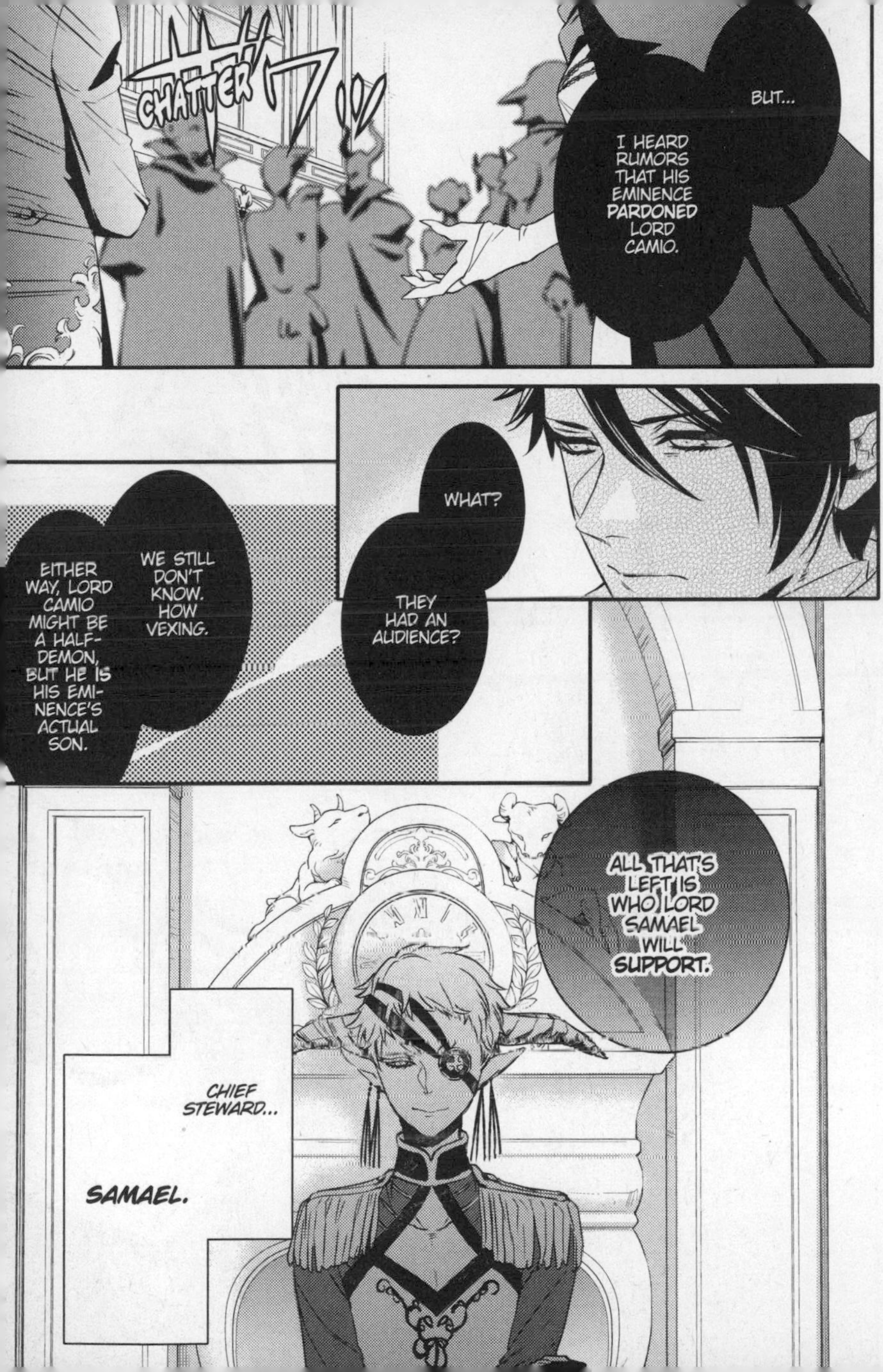
BUT...
I HEARD RUMORS THAT HIS EMINENCE PARDONED LORD CAMIO.
CHATTER
WHAT?
THEY HAD AN AUDIENCE?
WE STILL DON'T KNOW. HOW VEXING.
EITHER WAY, LORD CAMIO MIGHT BE A HALF-DEMON, BUT HE IS HIS EMINENCE'S ACTUAL SON.
ALL THAT'S LEFT IS WHO LORD SAMAEL WILL SUPPORT.
CHIEF STEWARD...
SAMAEL.

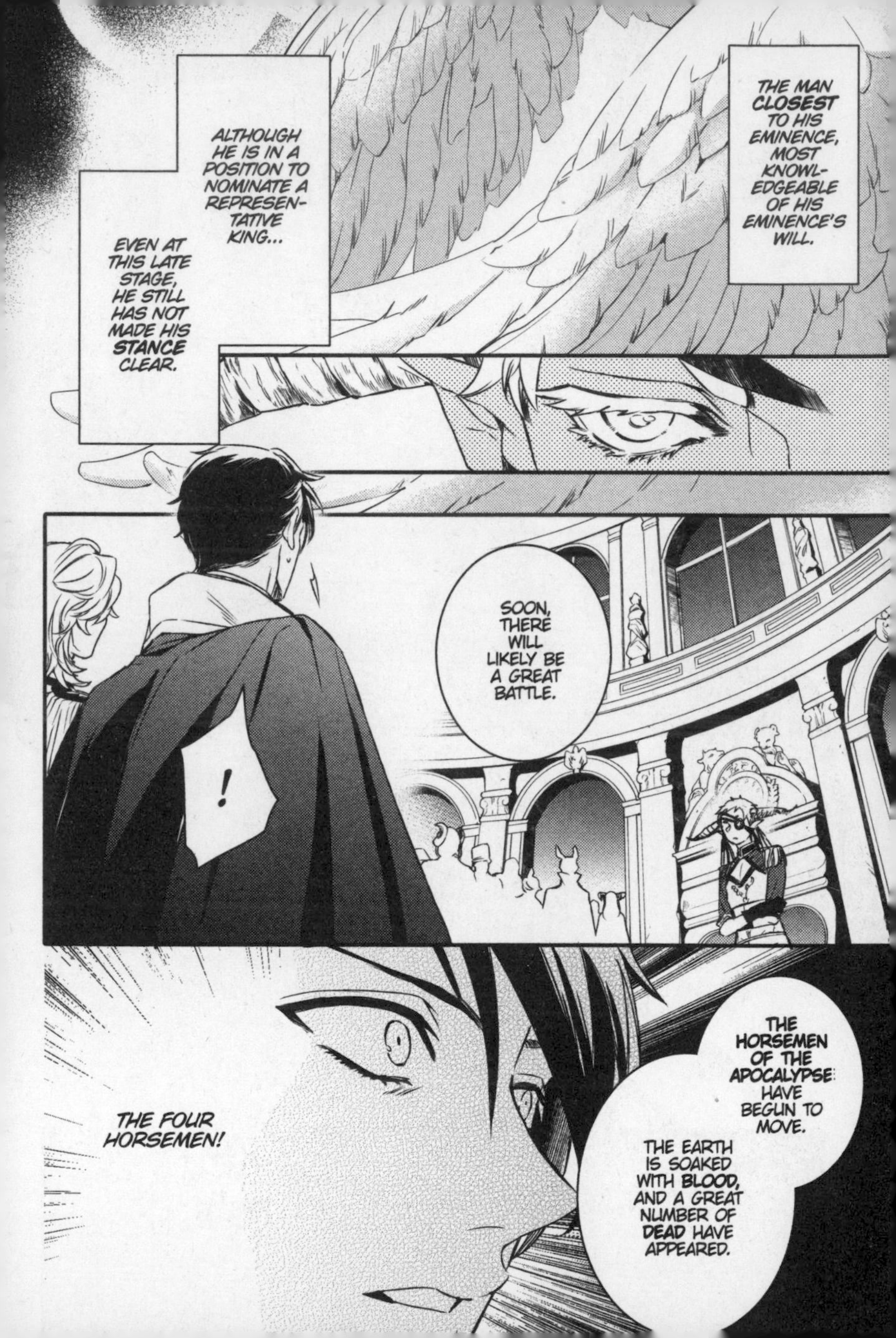
THE MAN CLOSEST TO HIS EMINENCE, MOST KNOWL-EDGEABLE OF HIS EMINENCE'S WILL.
ALTHOUGH HE IS IN A POSITION TO NOMINATE A REPRESEN-TATIVE KING...
EVEN AT THIS LATE STAGE, HE STILL HAS NOT MADE HIS STANCE CLEAR.
SOON, THERE WILL LIKELY BE A GREAT BATTLE.
!
THE HORSEMEN OF THE APOCALYPSE HAVE BEGUN TO MOVE.
THE EARTH IS SOAKED WITH BLOOD, AND A GREAT NUMBER OF DEAD HAVE APPEARED.
THE FOUR HORSEMEN!

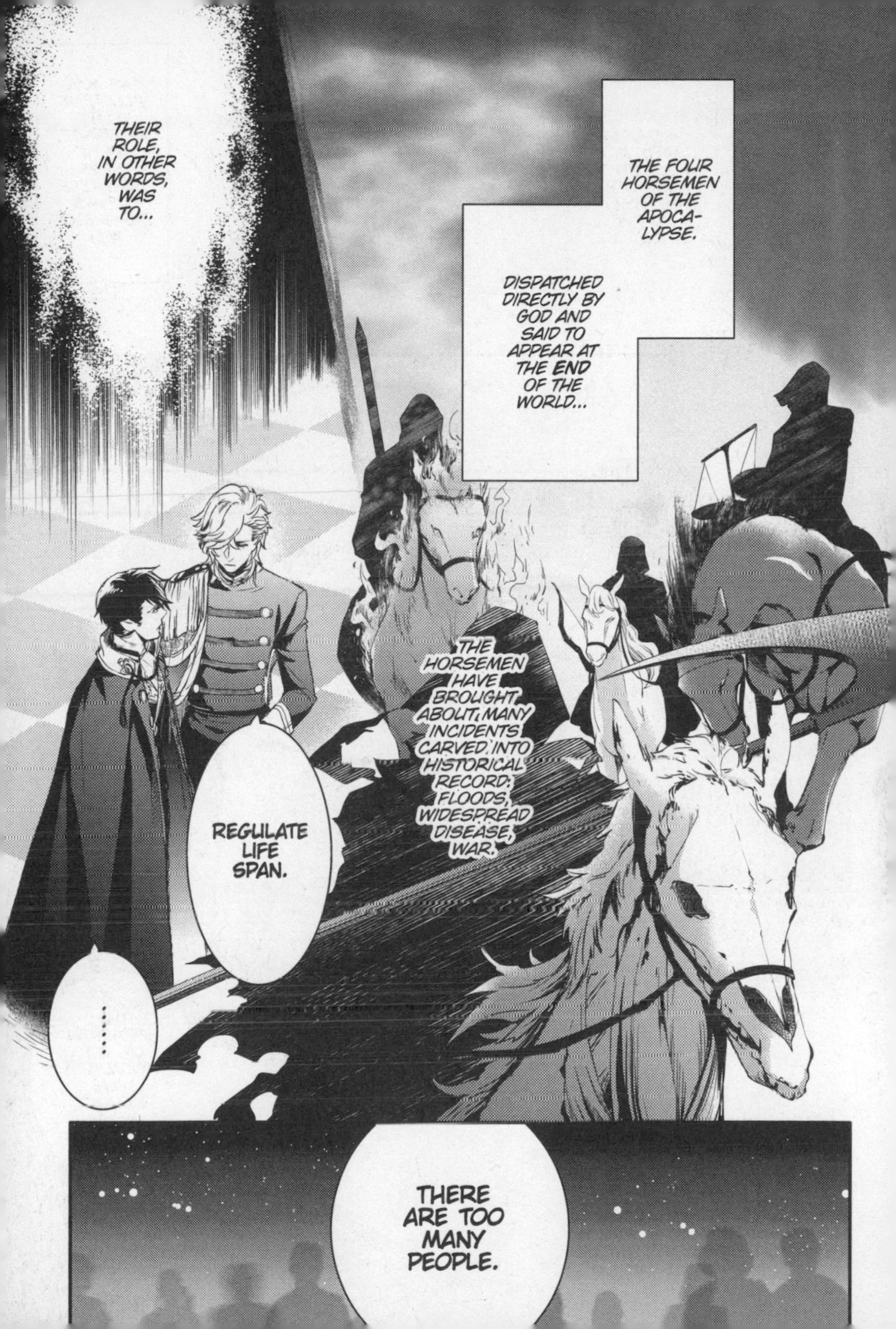
THE FOUR HORSEMEN OF THE APOCA-LYPSE.
DISPATCHED DIRECTLY BY GOD AND SAID TO APPEAR AT THE **END** OF THE WORLD...
THE HORSEMEN HAVE BROUGHT ABOUT MANY INCIDENTS CARVED INTO HISTORICAL RECORD: FLOODS, WIDESPREAD DISEASE, WAR.
THEIR ROLE, IN OTHER WORDS, WAS TO...
REGULATE LIFE SPAN.
......
THERE ARE TOO MANY PEOPLE.

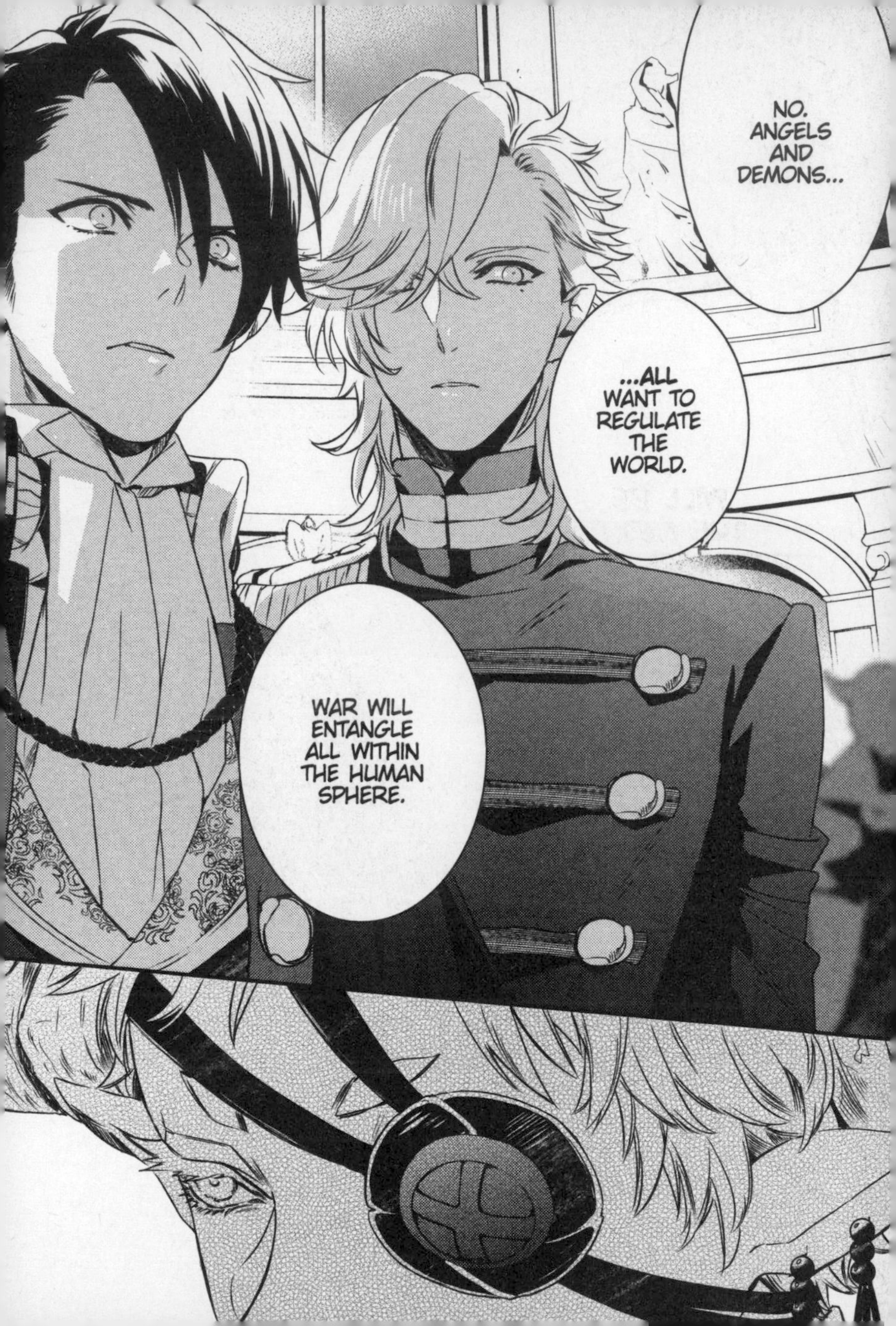
NO. ANGELS AND DEMONS...
...ALL WANT TO REGULATE THE WORLD.
WAR WILL ENTANGLE ALL WITHIN THE HUMAN SPHERE.

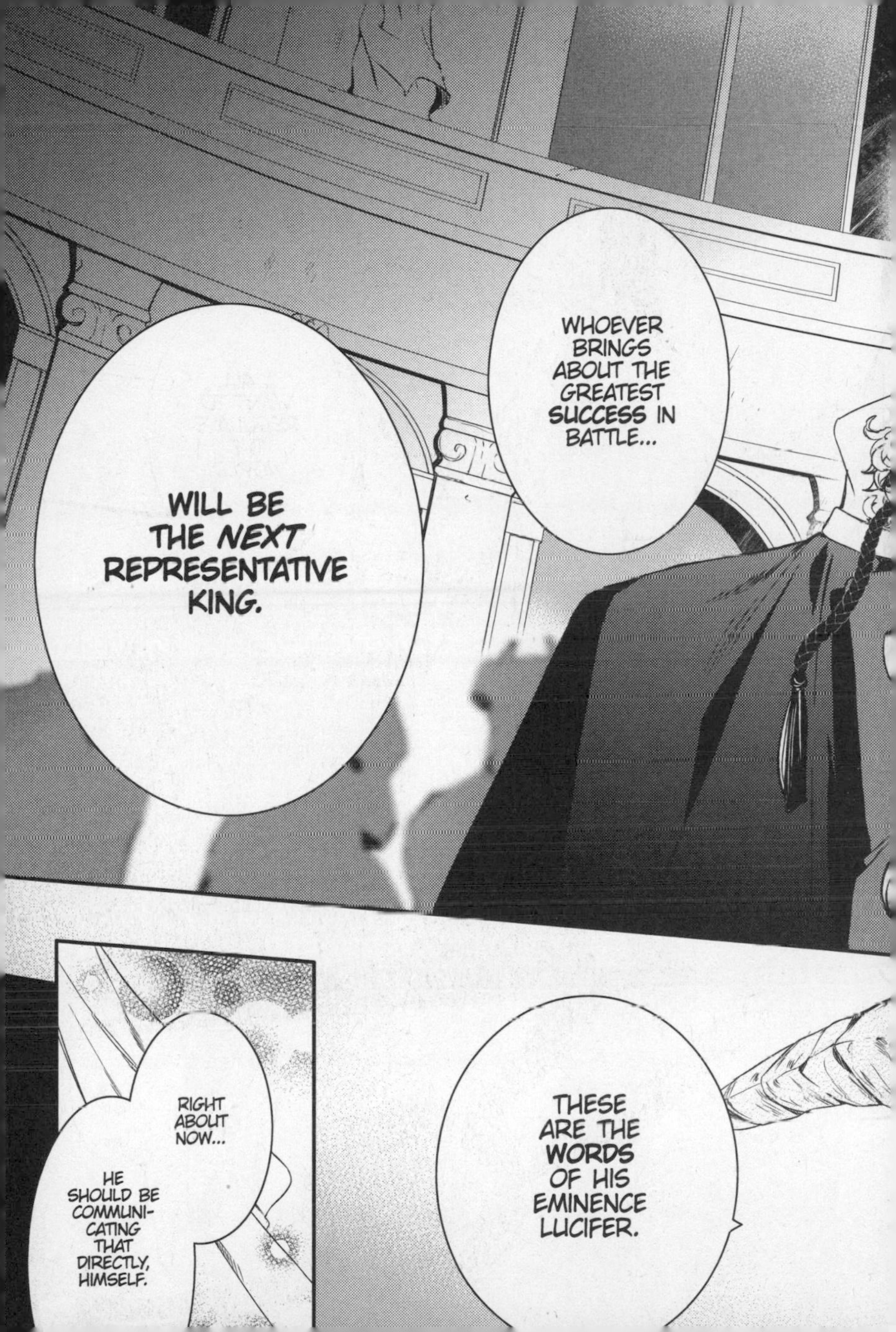
WHOEVER BRINGS ABOUT THE GREATEST SUCCESS IN BATTLE...
WILL BE THE *NEXT* REPRESENTATIVE KING.
THESE ARE THE WORDS OF HIS EMINENCE LUCIFER.
RIGHT ABOUT NOW...
HE SHOULD BE COMMUNI-CATING THAT DIRECTLY, HIMSELF.

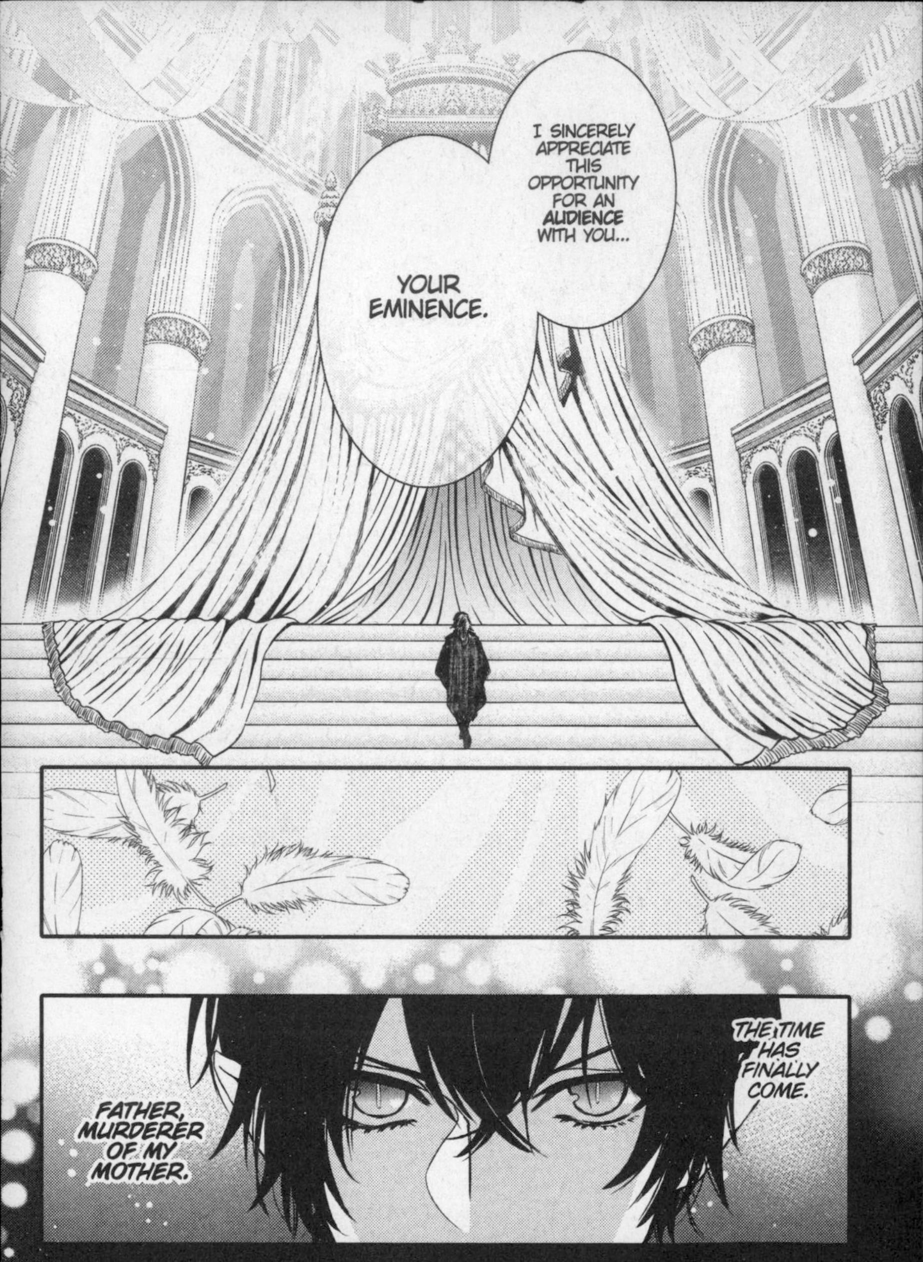
I SINCERELY APPRECIATE THIS OPPORTUNITY FOR AN AUDIENCE WITH YOU...
YOUR EMINENCE.
THE TIME HAS FINALLY COME.
FATHER, MURDERER OF MY MOTHER.

魔界王子
devils and realist

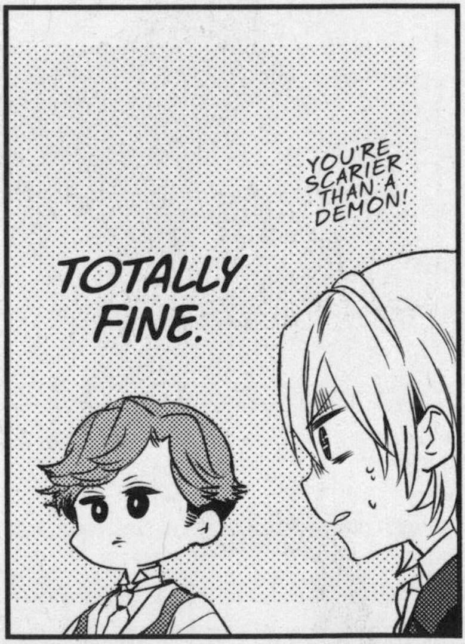
YOU'RE SCARIER THAN A DEMON!
TOTALLY FINE.

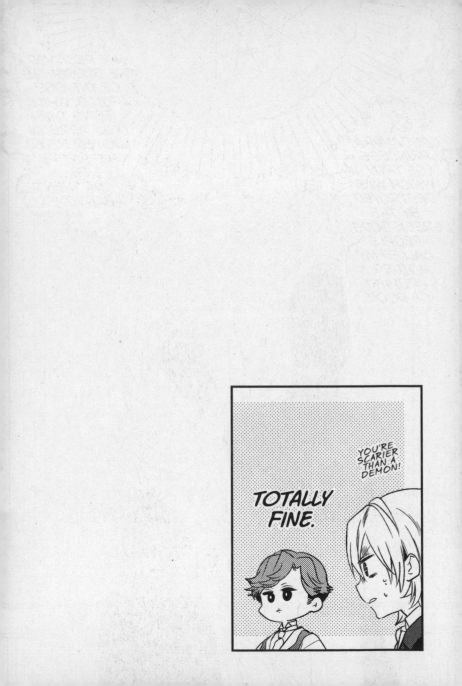

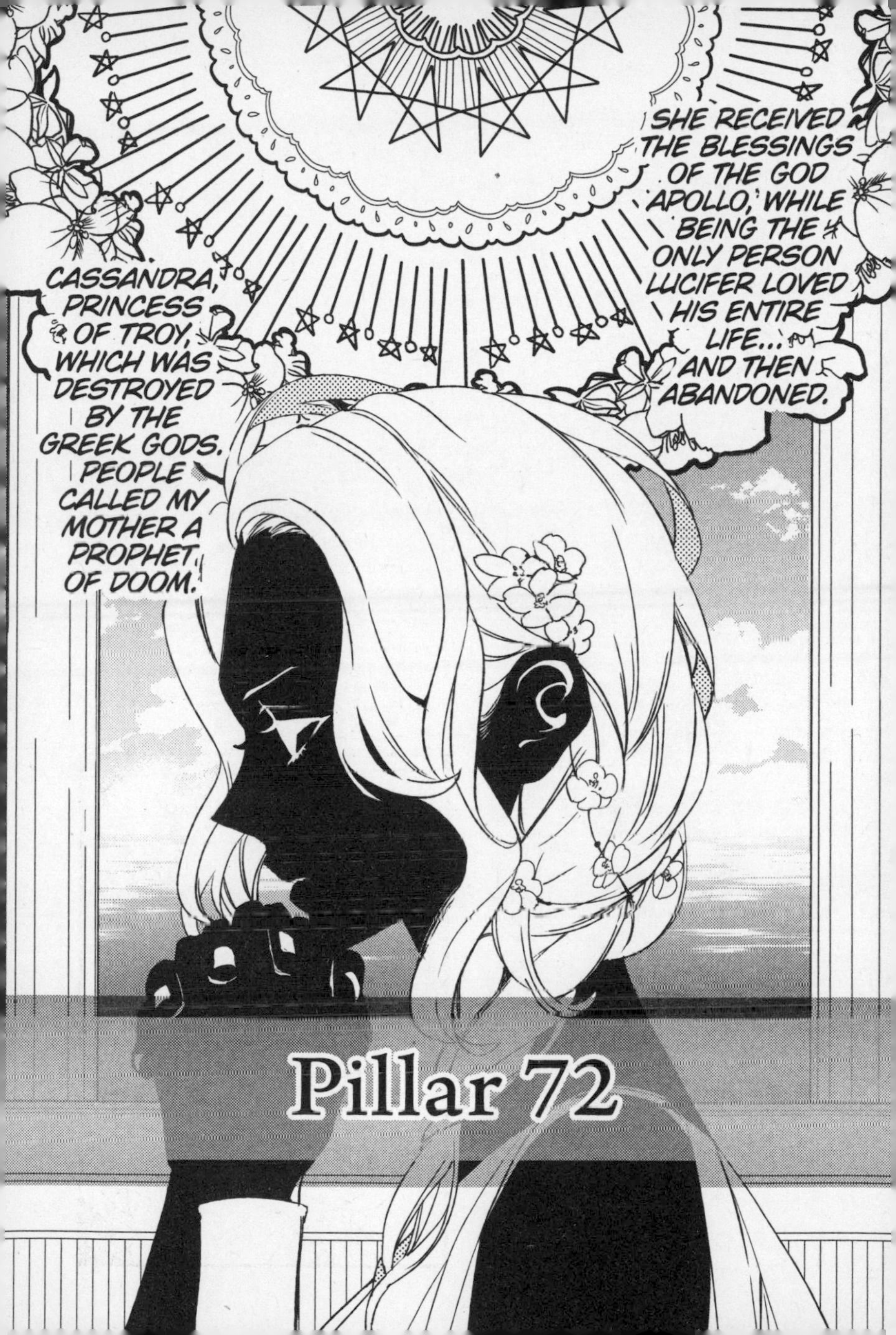
SHE RECEIVED THE BLESSINGS OF THE GOD APOLLO, WHILE BEING THE ONLY PERSON LUCIFER LOVED HIS ENTIRE LIFE... AND THEN ABANDONED.
CASSANDRA, PRINCESS OF TROY, WHICH WAS DESTROYED BY THE GREEK GODS. PEOPLE CALLED MY MOTHER A PROPHET OF DOOM.
Pillar 72

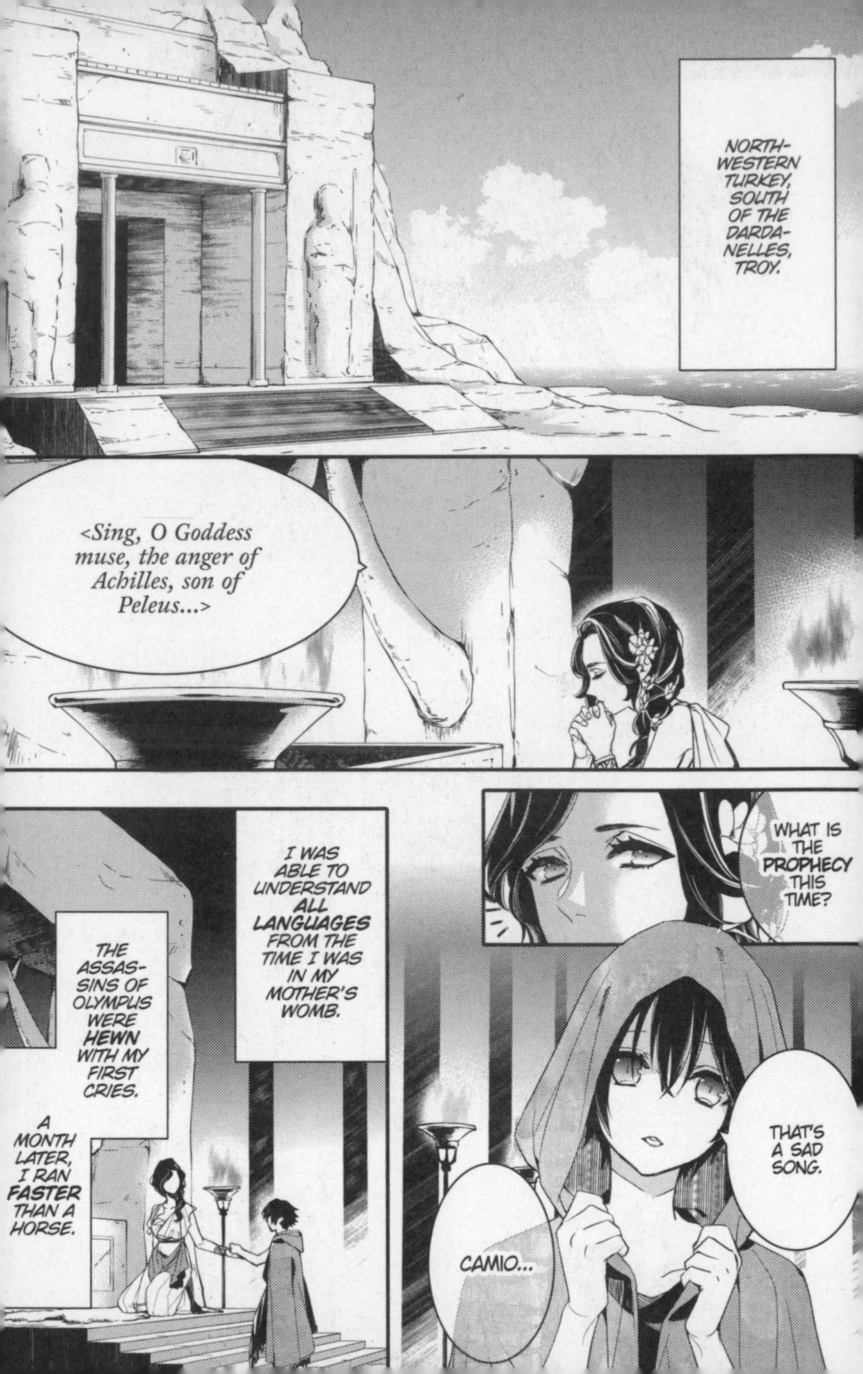
NORTH-WESTERN TURKEY, SOUTH OF THE DARDANELLES, TROY.
<Sing, O Goddess muse, the anger of Achilles, son of Peleus...>
WHAT IS THE **PROPHECY** THIS TIME?
THAT'S A SAD SONG.
CAMIO...
I WAS ABLE TO UNDERSTAND **ALL LANGUAGES** FROM THE TIME I WAS IN MY MOTHER'S WOMB.
THE ASSAS-SINS OF OLYMPUS WERE **HEWN** WITH MY FIRST CRIES.
A MONTH LATER, I RAN **FASTER** THAN A HORSE.

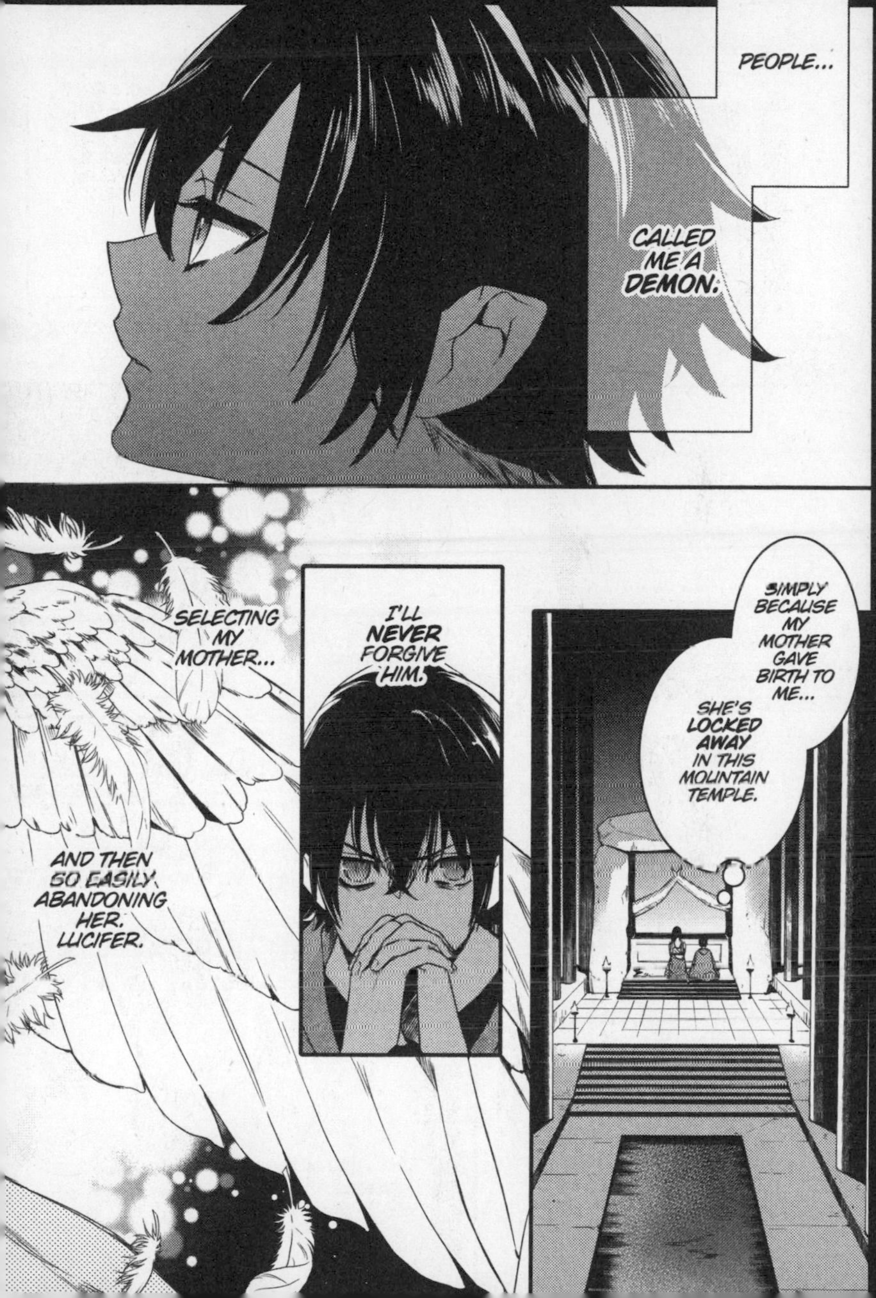
PEOPLE...
CALLED ME A DEMON.
SIMPLY BECAUSE MY MOTHER GAVE BIRTH TO ME...
SHE'S LOCKED AWAY IN THIS MOUNTAIN TEMPLE.
I'LL NEVER FORGIVE HIM.
SELECTING MY MOTHER...
AND THEN SO EASILY ABANDONING HER. LUCIFER.

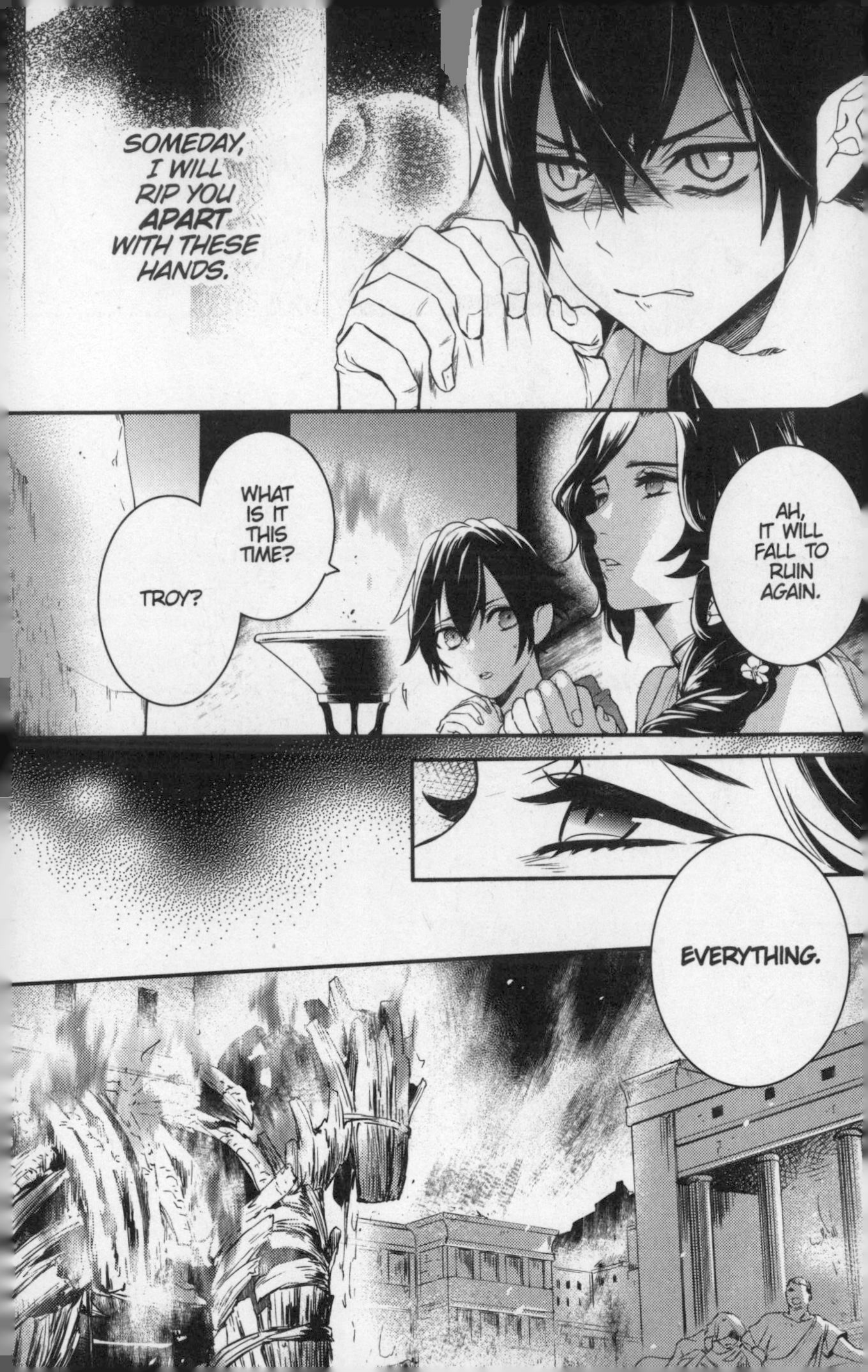
SOMEDAY, I WILL RIP YOU APART WITH THESE HANDS.
AH, IT WILL FALL TO RUIN AGAIN.
WHAT IS IT THIS TIME?
TROY?
EVERYTHING.

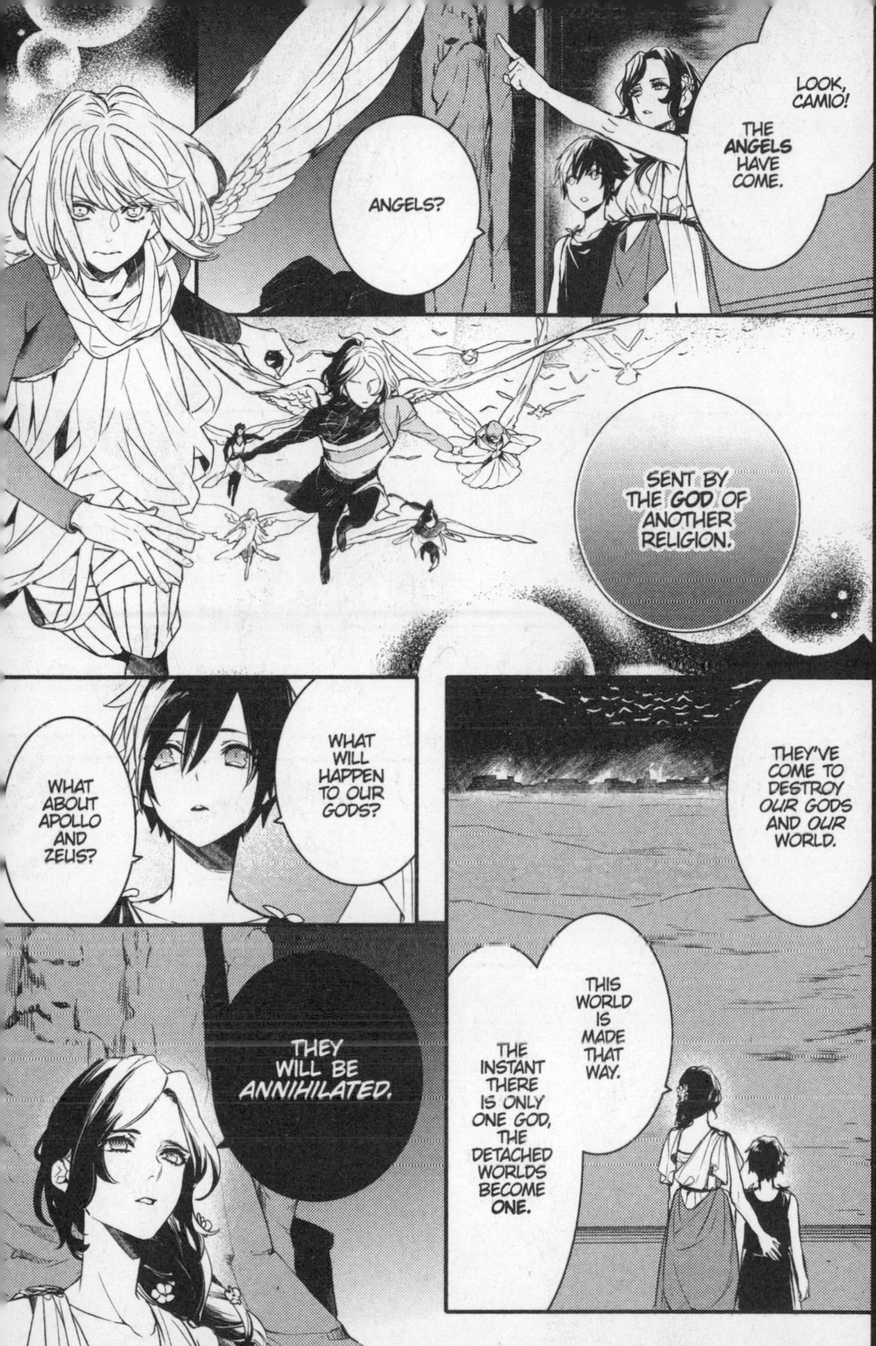
LOOK, CAMIO!
THE ANGELS HAVE COME.
ANGELS?
SENT BY THE GOD OF ANOTHER RELIGION.
THEY'VE COME TO DESTROY OUR GODS AND OUR WORLD.
THIS WORLD IS MADE THAT WAY.
THE INSTANT THERE IS ONLY ONE GOD, THE DETACHED WORLDS BECOME ONE.
WHAT WILL HAPPEN TO OUR GODS?
WHAT ABOUT APOLLO AND ZEUS?
THEY WILL BE ANNIHILATED.

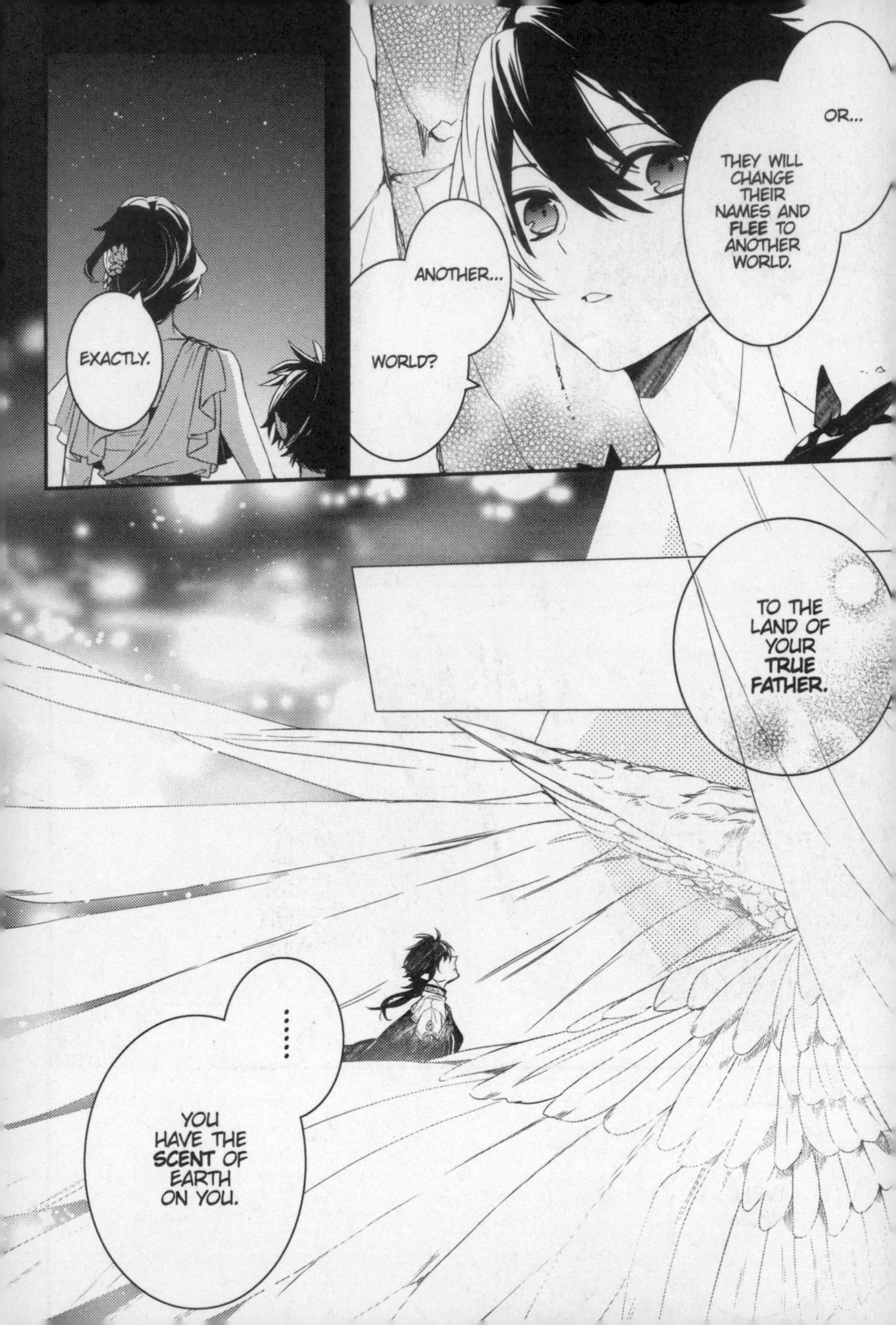
OR...
THEY WILL CHANGE THEIR NAMES AND FLEE TO ANOTHER WORLD.
ANOTHER... WORLD?
EXACTLY.
TO THE LAND OF YOUR TRUE FATHER.
......
YOU HAVE THE SCENT OF EARTH ON YOU.

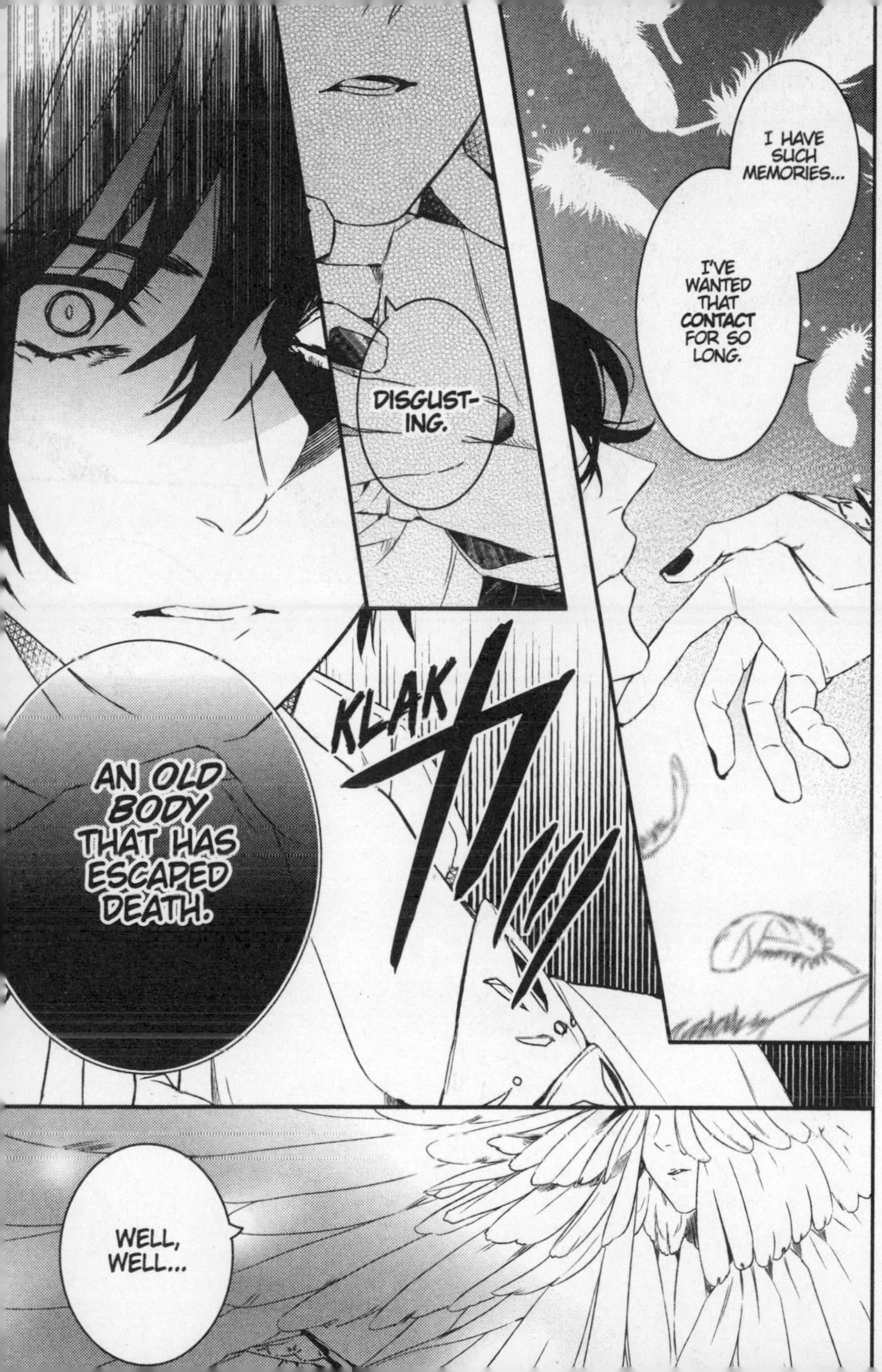
I HAVE SUCH MEMORIES...
I'VE WANTED THAT CONTACT FOR SO LONG.
DISGUST-ING.
KLAK
AN OLD BODY THAT HAS ESCAPED DEATH.
WELL, WELL...

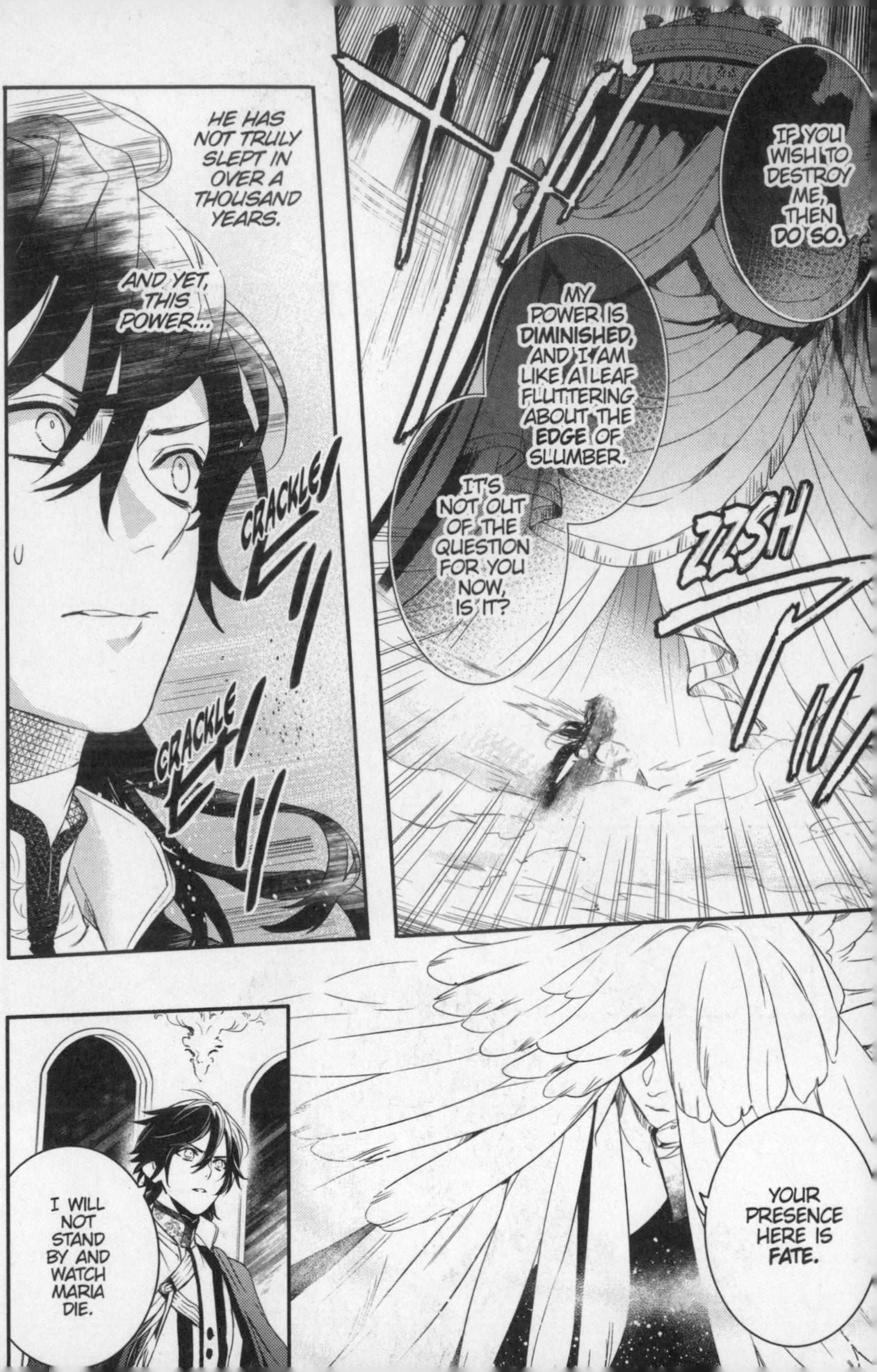
IF YOU WISH TO DESTROY ME, THEN DO SO.
MY POWER IS DIMINISHED, AND I AM LIKE A LEAF FLUTTERING ABOUT THE EDGE OF SLUMBER.
IT'S NOT OUT OF THE QUESTION FOR YOU NOW, IS IT?
ZZSH
HE HAS NOT TRULY SLEPT IN OVER A THOUSAND YEARS.
AND YET, THIS POWER...
CRACKLE
CRACKLE
YOUR PRESENCE HERE IS FATE.
I WILL NOT STAND BY AND WATCH MARIA DIE.

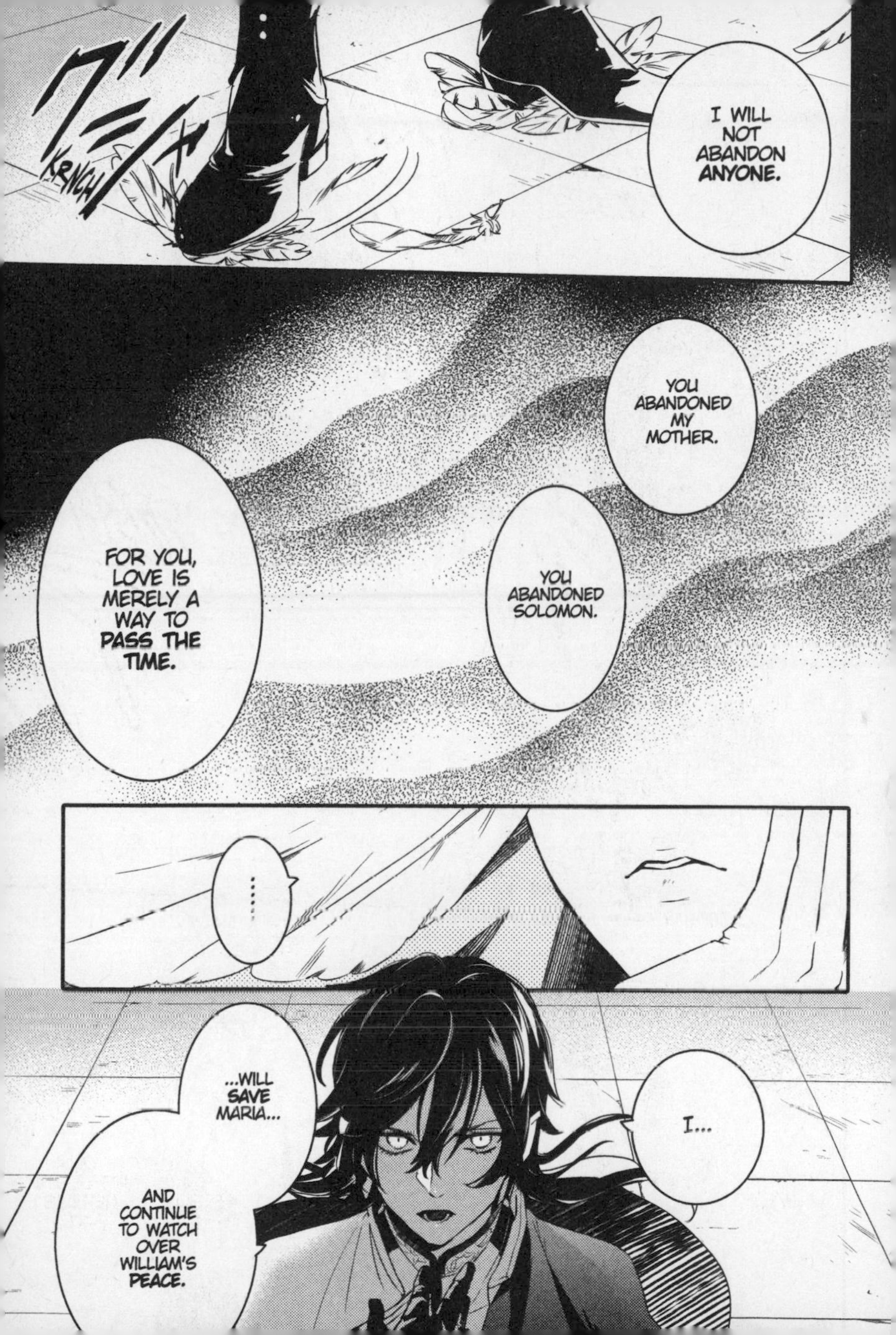
KRNCH
I WILL NOT ABANDON ANYONE.
YOU ABANDONED MY MOTHER.
YOU ABANDONED SOLOMON.
FOR YOU, LOVE IS MERELY A WAY TO PASS THE TIME.
......
I...
...WILL SAVE MARIA...
AND CONTINUE TO WATCH OVER WILLIAM'S PEACE.

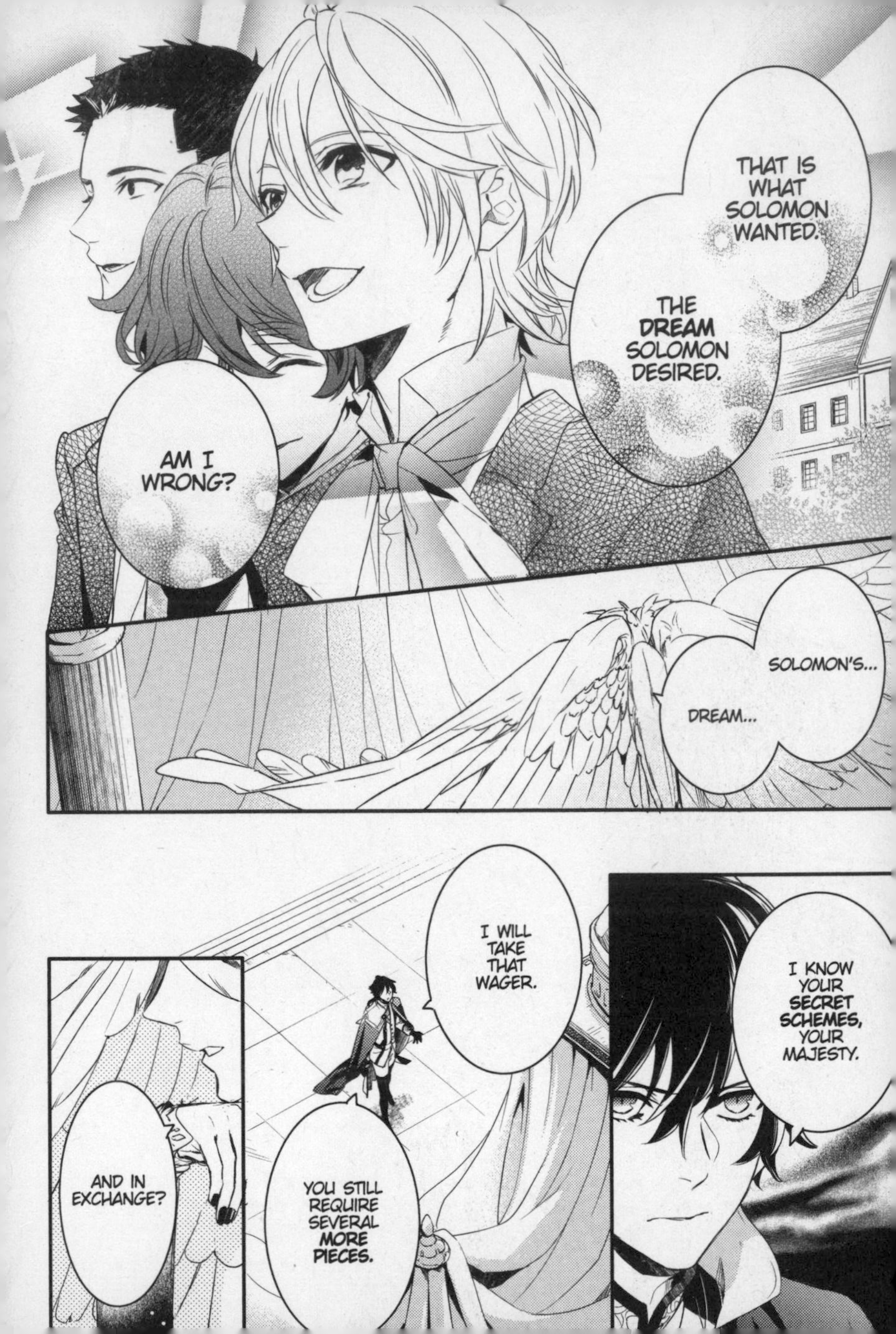
THAT IS WHAT SOLOMON WANTED.
THE DREAM SOLOMON DESIRED.
AM I WRONG?
SOLOMON'S...
DREAM...
I KNOW YOUR SECRET SCHEMES, YOUR MAJESTY.
I WILL TAKE THAT WAGER.
YOU STILL REQUIRE SEVERAL MORE PIECES.
AND IN EXCHANGE?

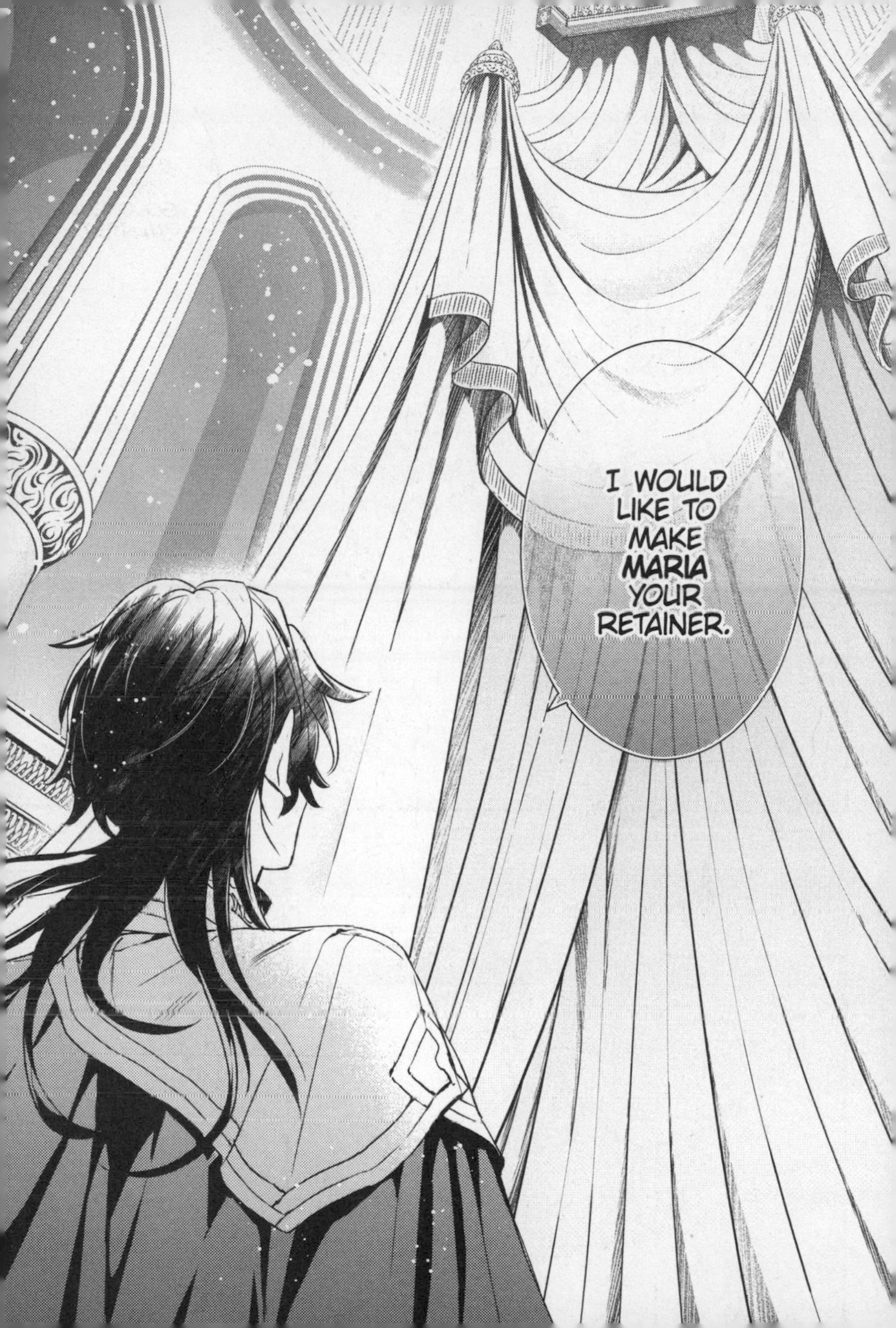
I WOULD LIKE TO MAKE MARIA YOUR RETAINER.

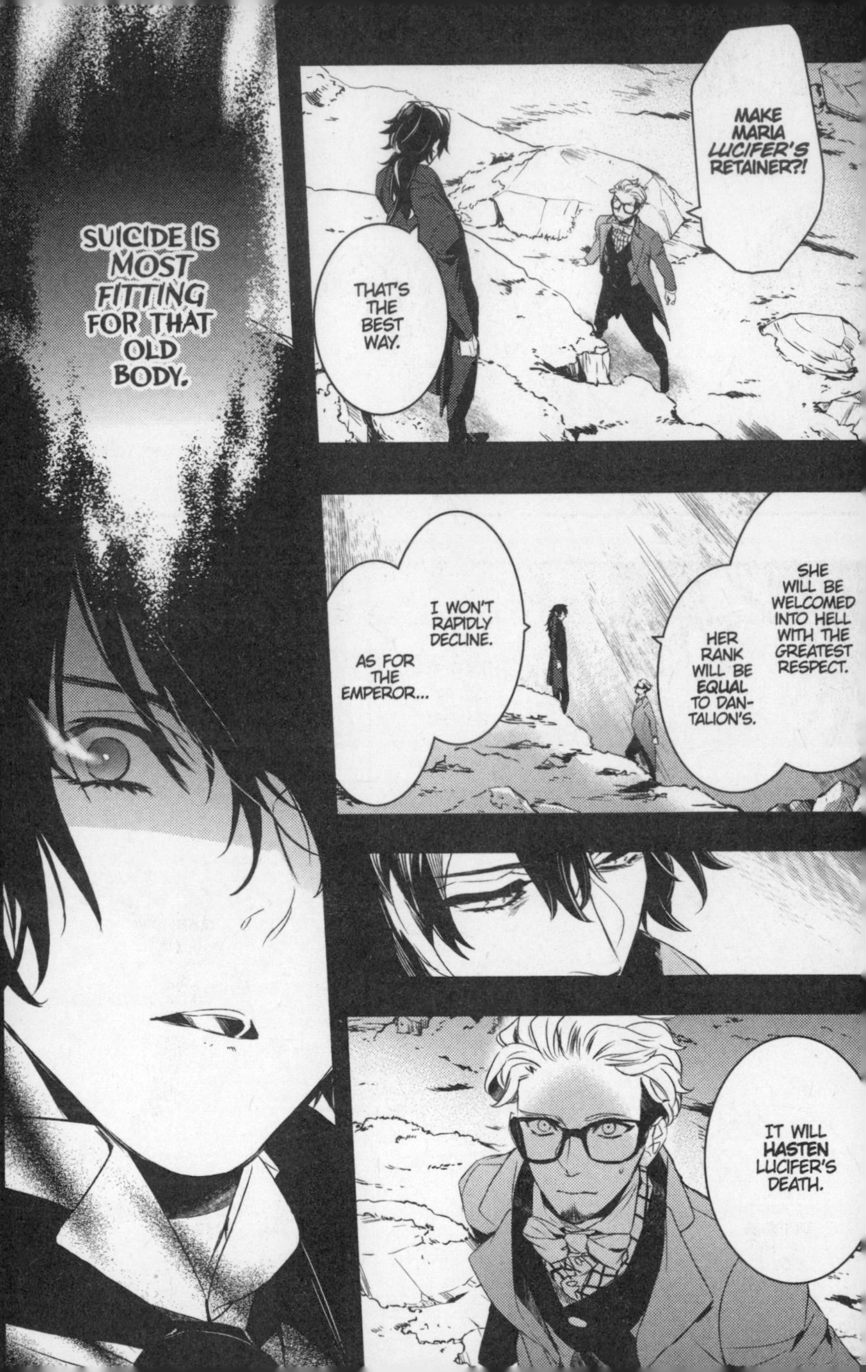
MAKE MARIA LUCIFER'S RETAINER?!
THAT'S THE BEST WAY.
SHE WILL BE WELCOMED INTO HELL WITH THE GREATEST RESPECT.
HER RANK WILL BE EQUAL TO DAN-TALION'S.
I WON'T RAPIDLY DECLINE.
AS FOR THE EMPEROR...
IT WILL HASTEN LUCIFER'S DEATH.
SUICIDE IS MOST FITTING FOR THAT OLD BODY.

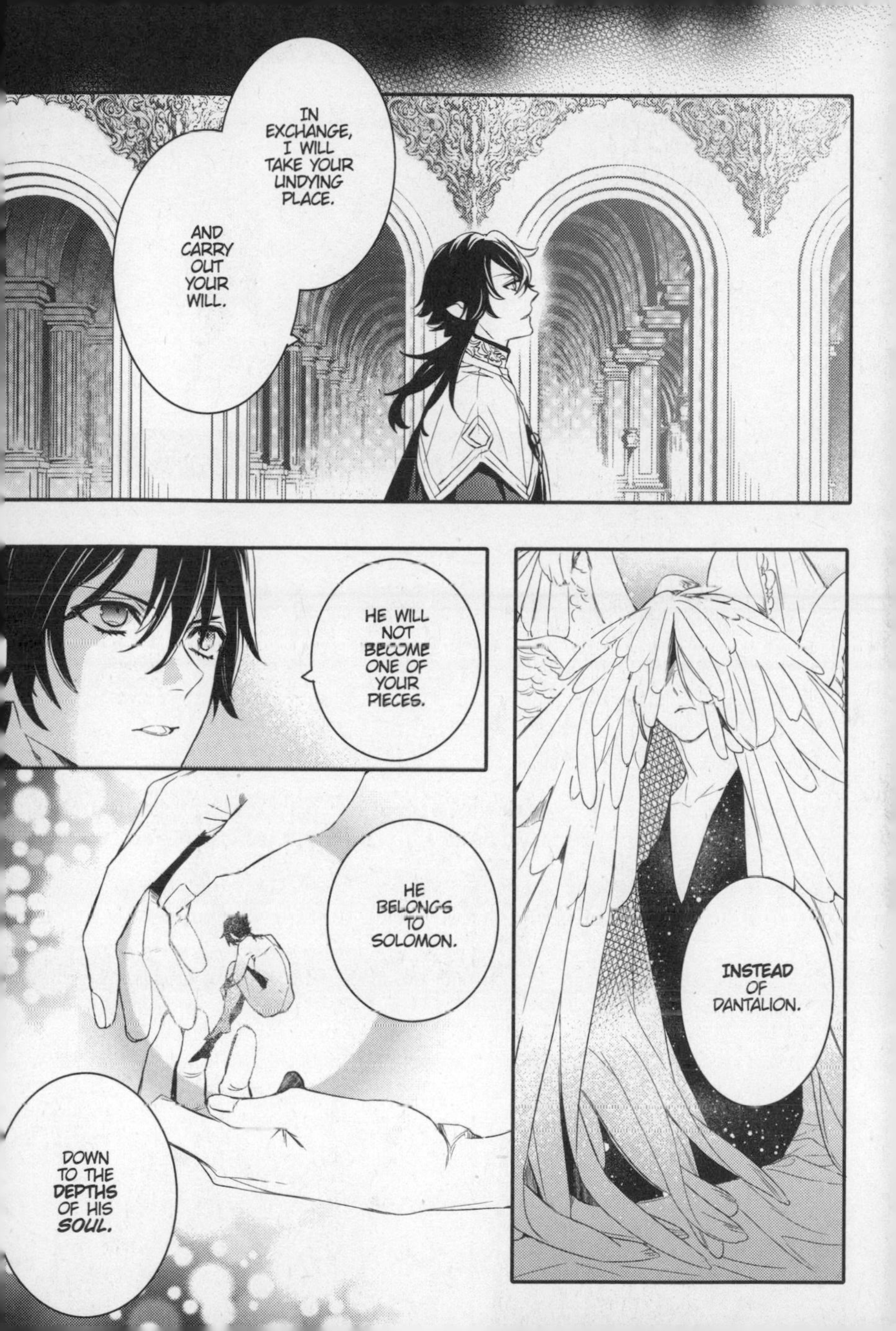
IN EXCHANGE, I WILL TAKE YOUR UNDYING PLACE.
AND CARRY OUT YOUR WILL.
INSTEAD OF DANTALION.
HE WILL NOT BECOME ONE OF YOUR PIECES.
HE BELONGS TO SOLOMON.
DOWN TO THE DEPTHS OF HIS SOUL.

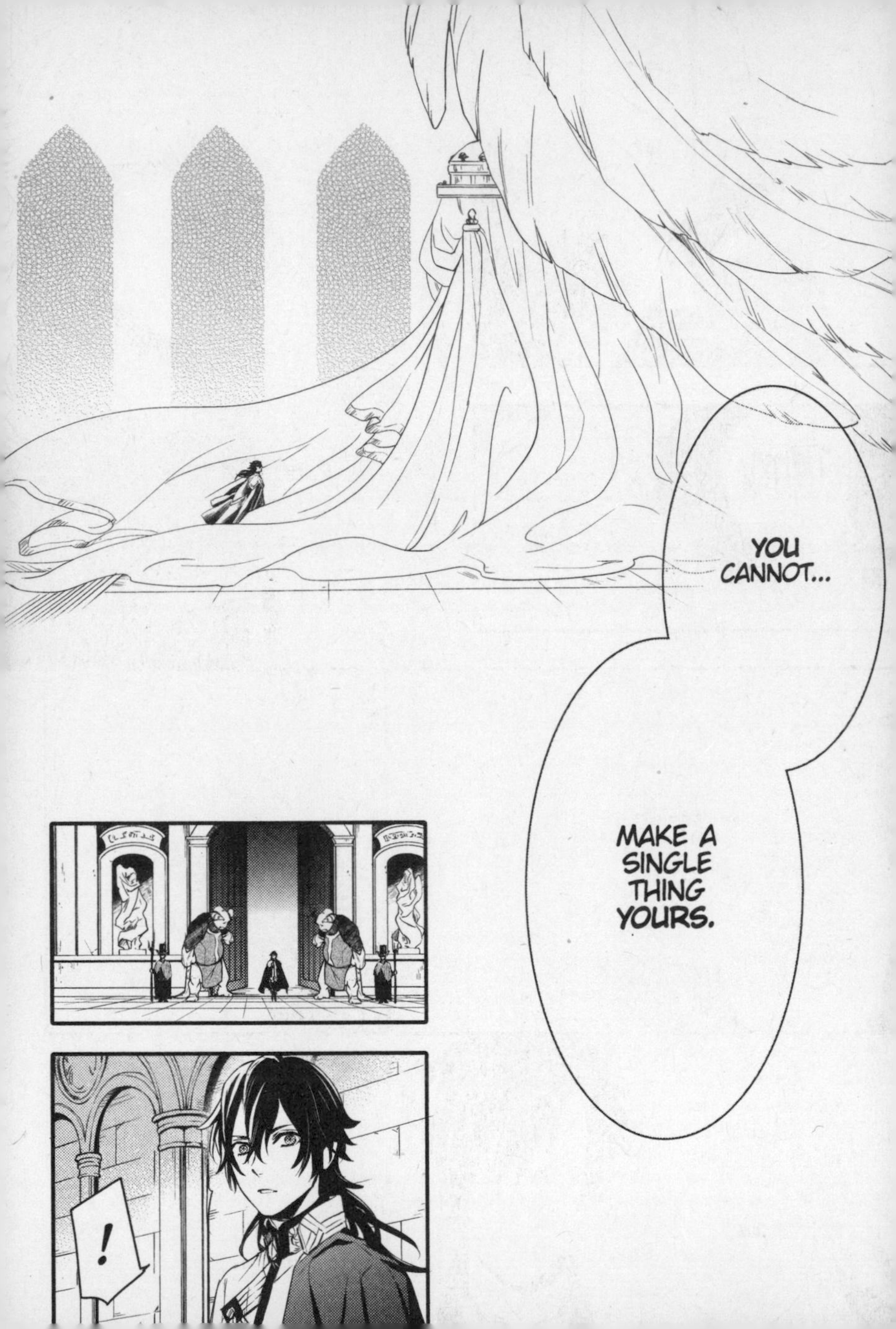
YOU CANNOT...
MAKE A SINGLE THING YOURS.
!

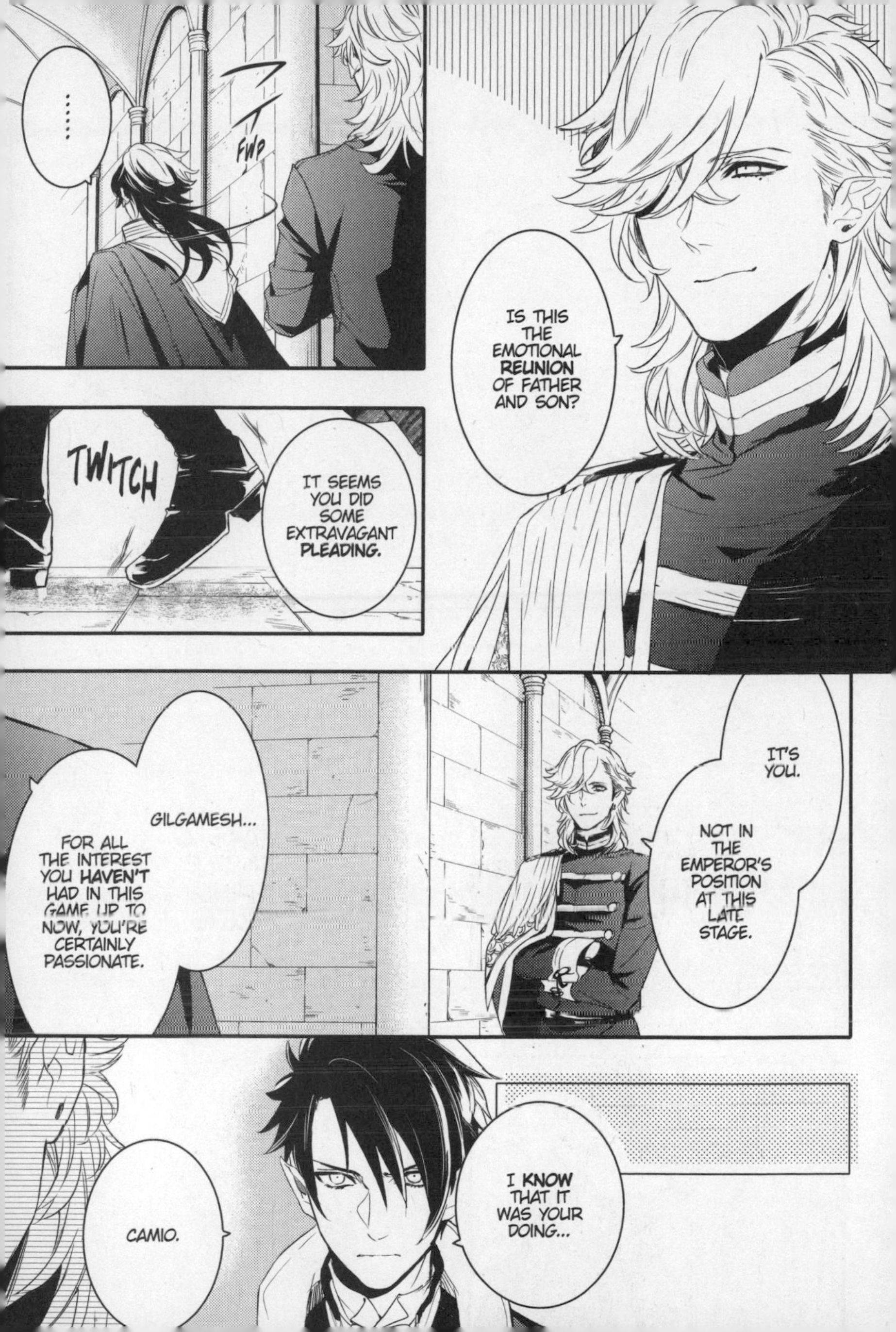
IS THIS THE EMOTIONAL REUNION OF FATHER AND SON?
FWP
......
IT SEEMS YOU DID SOME EXTRAVAGANT PLEADING.
TWITCH
IT'S YOU.
NOT IN THE EMPEROR'S POSITION AT THIS LATE STAGE.
GILGAMESH...
FOR ALL THE INTEREST YOU HAVEN'T HAD IN THIS GAME UP TO NOW, YOU'RE CERTAINLY PASSIONATE.
I KNOW THAT IT WAS YOUR DOING...
CAMIO.

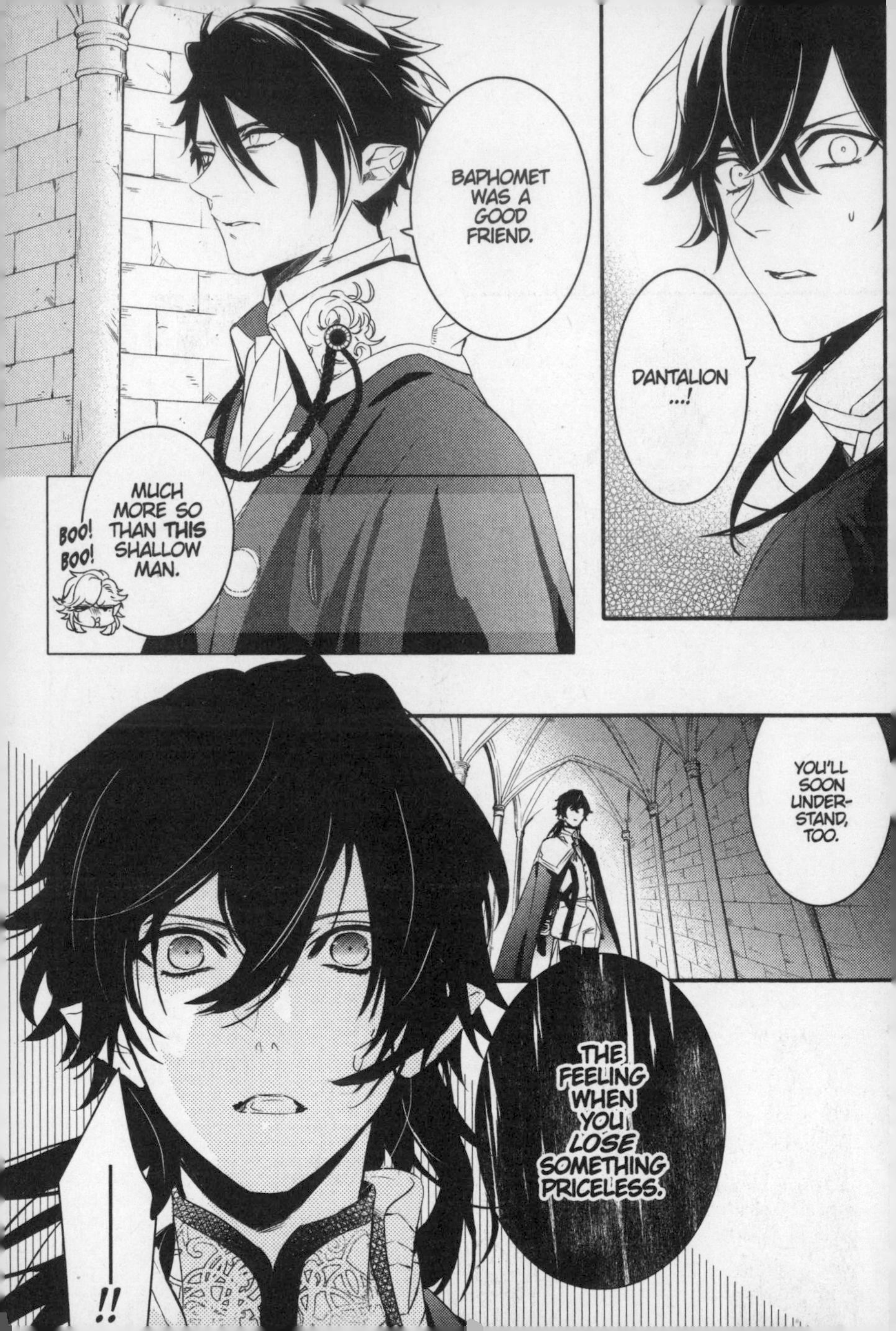
DANTALION ...!
BAPHOMET WAS A GOOD FRIEND.
MUCH MORE SO THAN THIS SHALLOW MAN.
BOO! BOO!
YOU'LL SOON UNDER-STAND, TOO.
THE FEELING WHEN YOU *LOSE* SOMETHING PRICELESS.
——!!

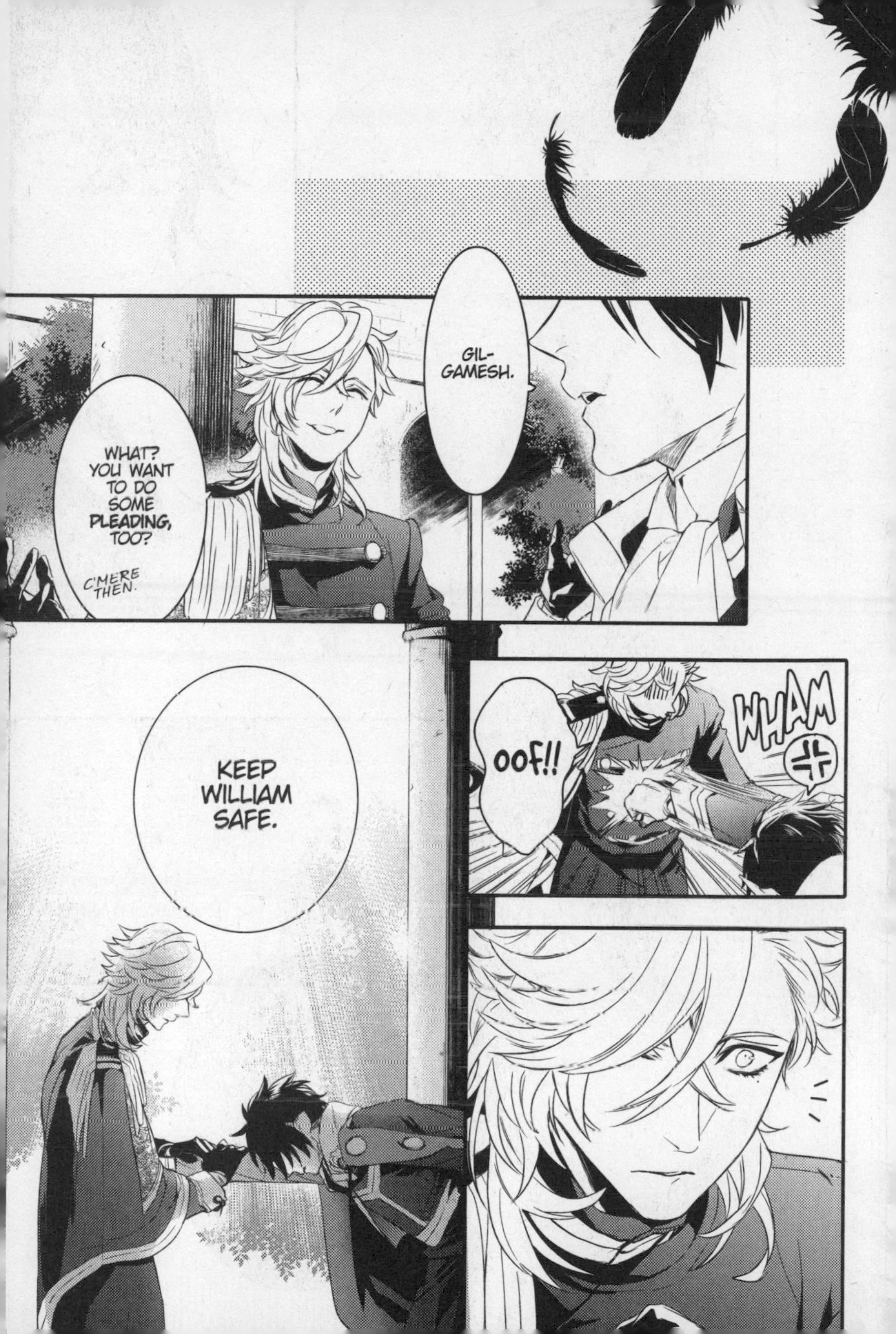
GIL-GAMESH.
WHAT? YOU WANT TO DO SOME PLEADING, TOO?
C'MERE THEN.
WHAM
OOF!!
KEEP WILLIAM SAFE.

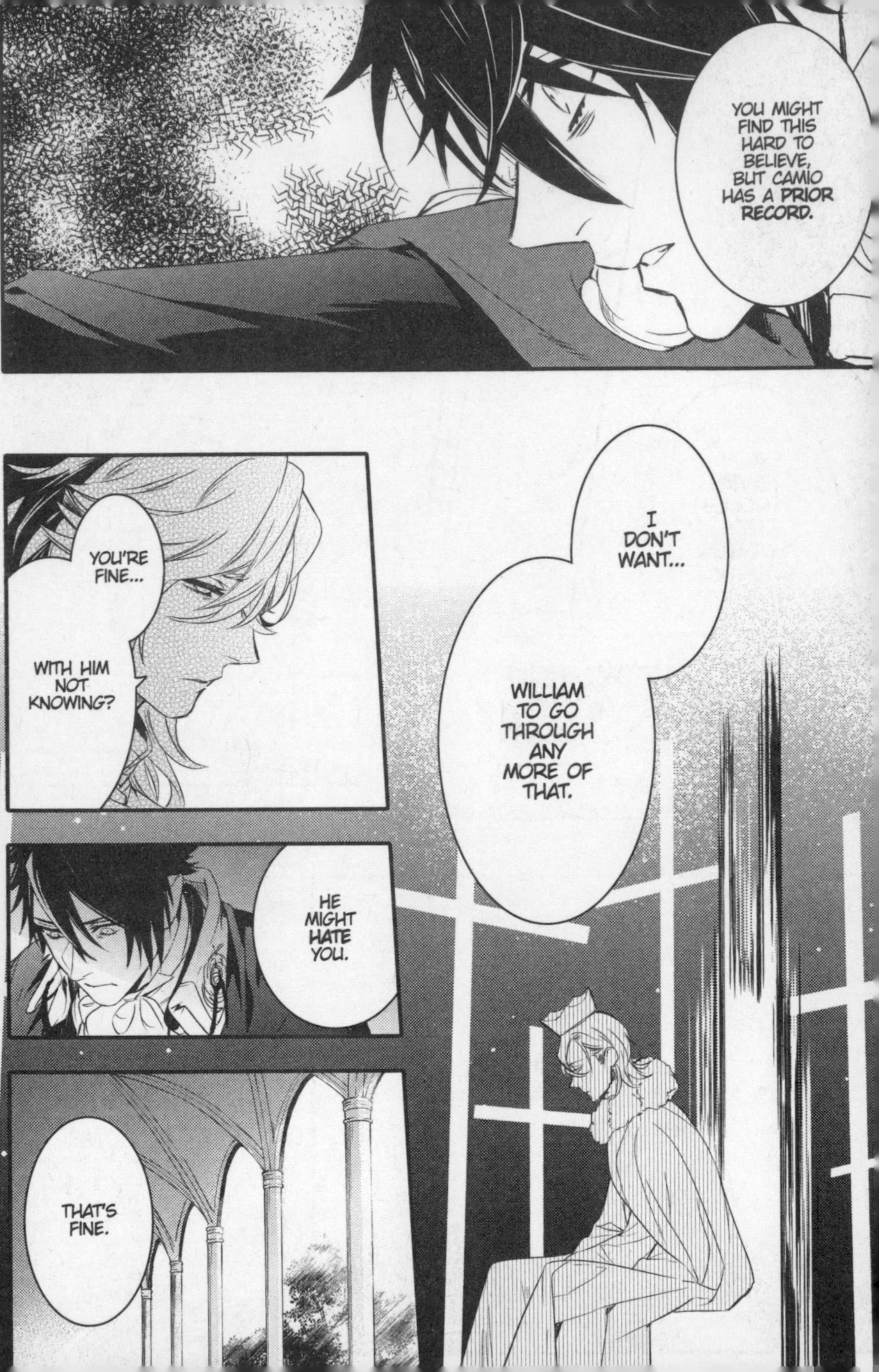
YOU MIGHT FIND THIS HARD TO BELIEVE, BUT CAMIO HAS A PRIOR RECORD.
I DON'T WANT...
WILLIAM TO GO THROUGH ANY MORE OF THAT.
YOU'RE FINE...
WITH HIM NOT KNOWING?
HE MIGHT HATE YOU.
THAT'S FINE.

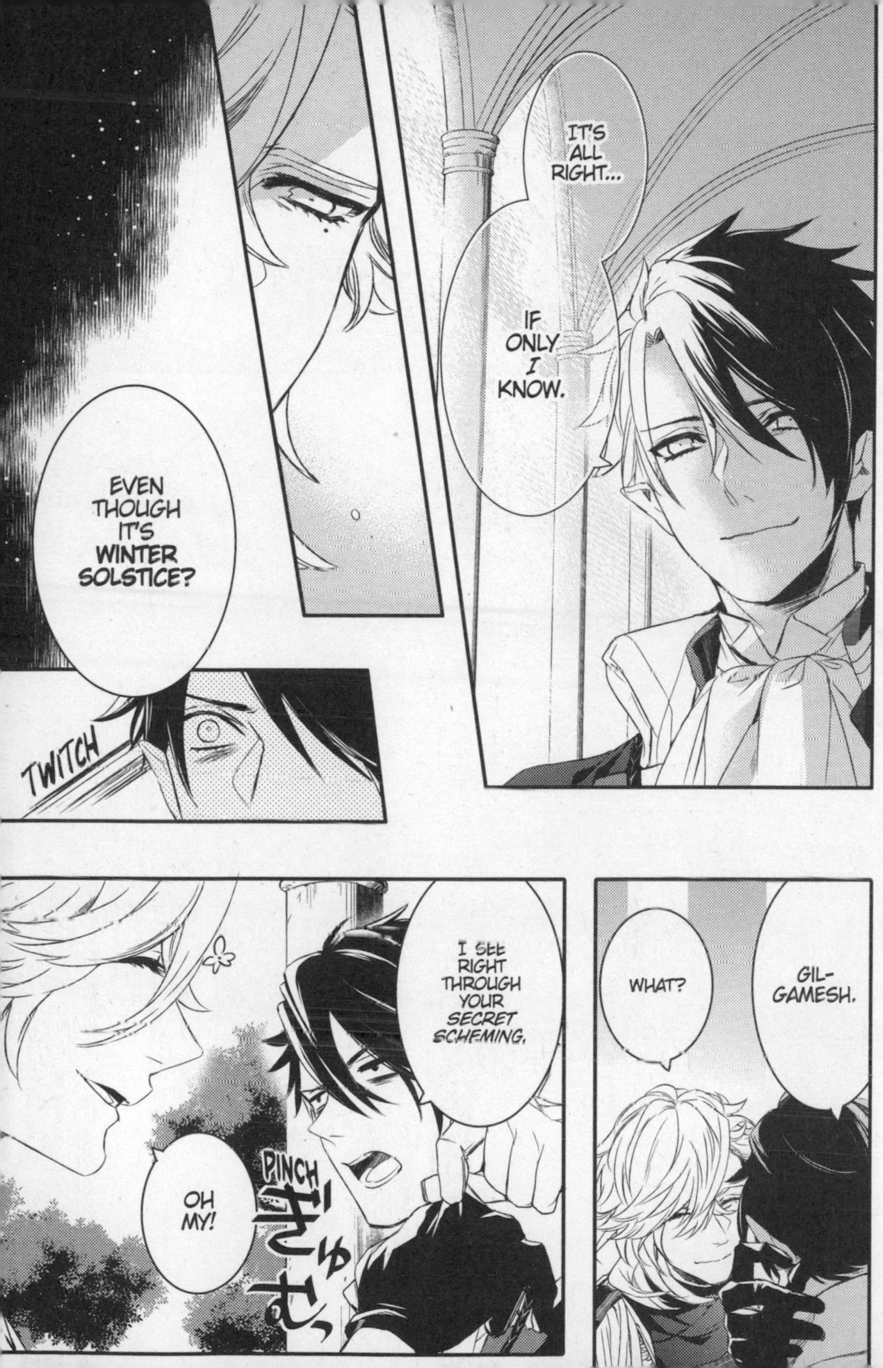
IT'S ALL RIGHT...
IF ONLY I KNOW.
EVEN THOUGH IT'S WINTER SOLSTICE?
TWITCH
GIL-GAMESH.
WHAT?
I SEE RIGHT THROUGH YOUR SECRET SCHEMING.
PINCH
ぎゅむっ
OH MY!

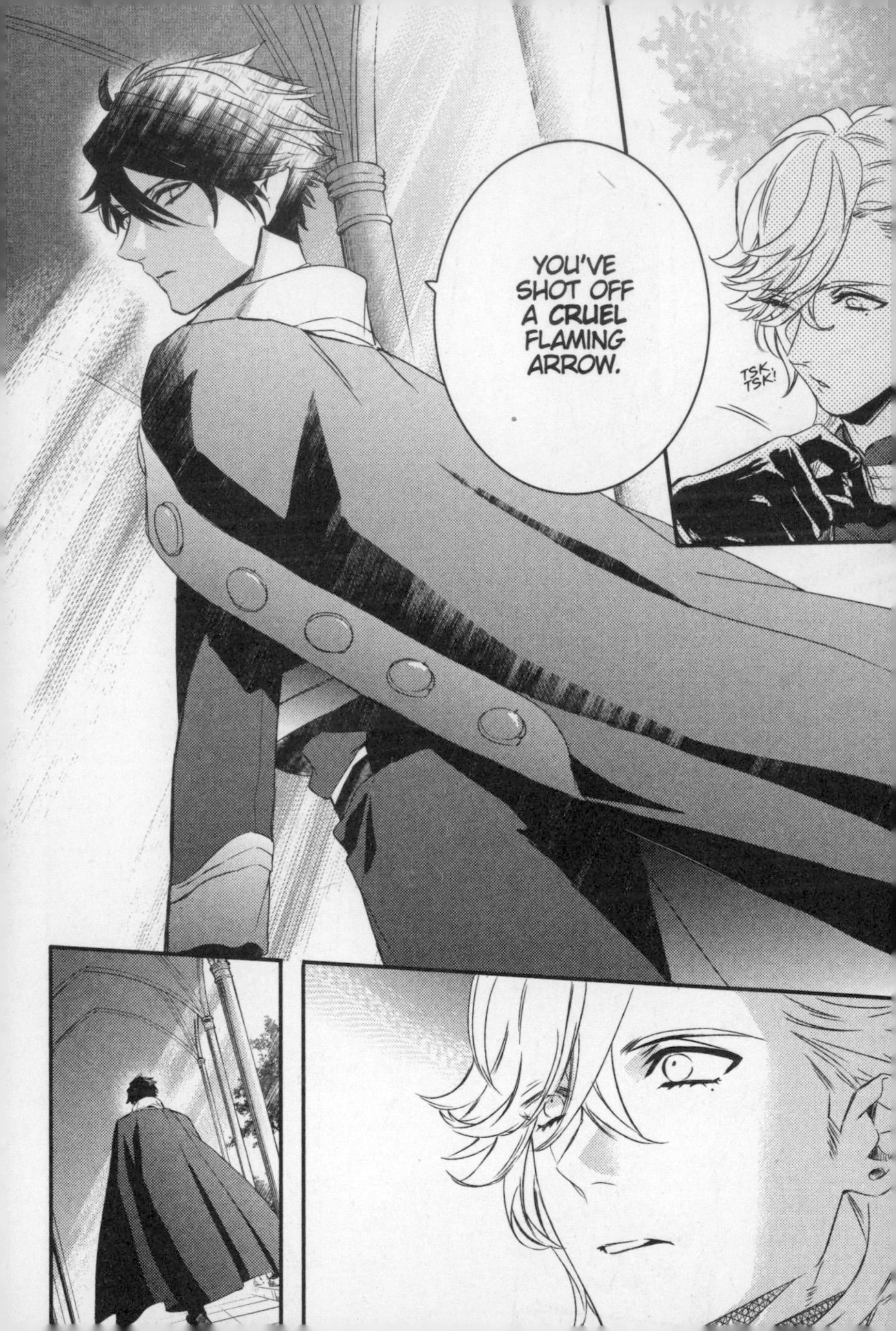
YOU'VE SHOT OFF A CRUEL FLAMING ARROW.
TSK TSK!

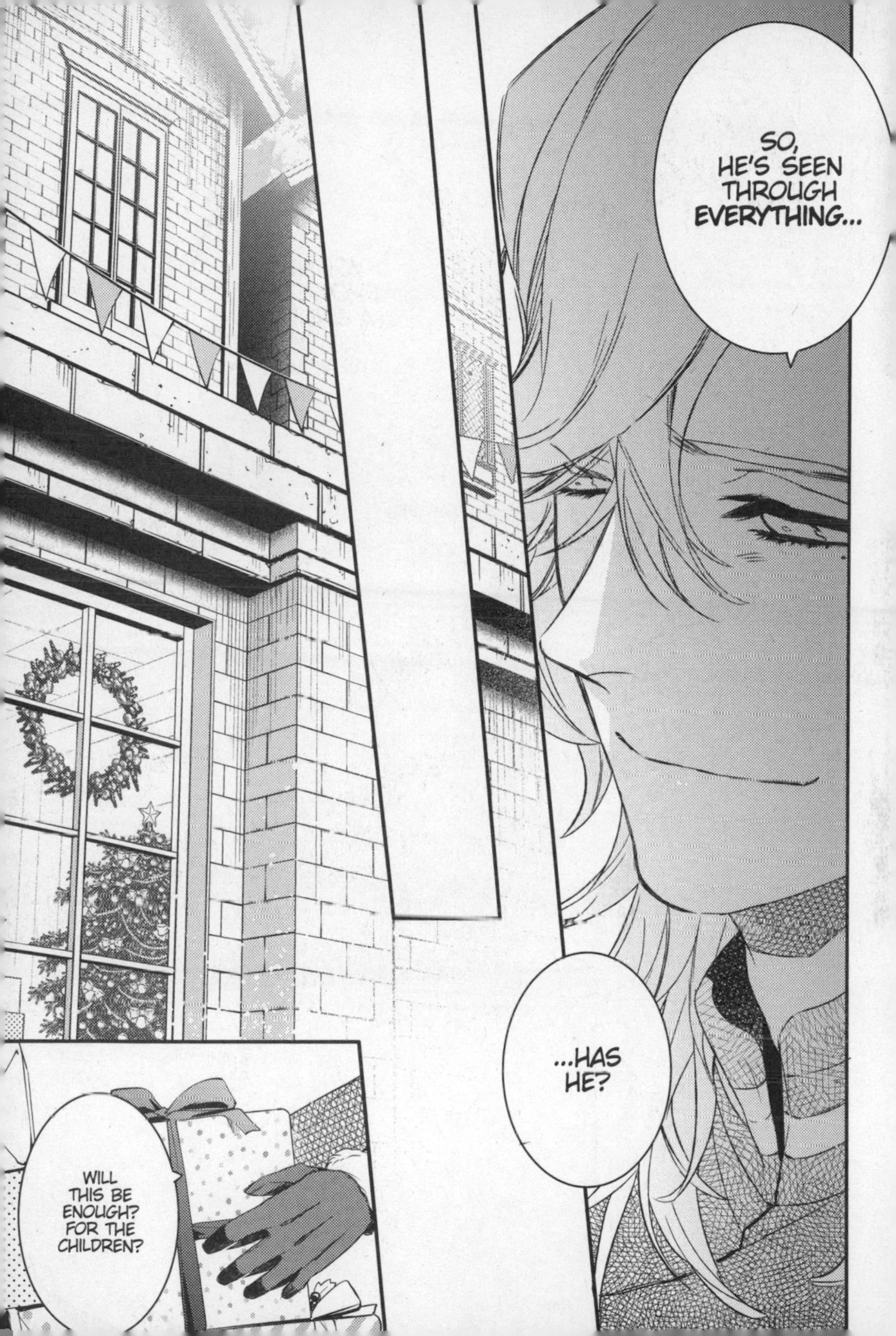
SO, HE'S SEEN THROUGH EVERYTHING...
...HAS HE?
WILL THIS BE ENOUGH? FOR THE CHILDREN?

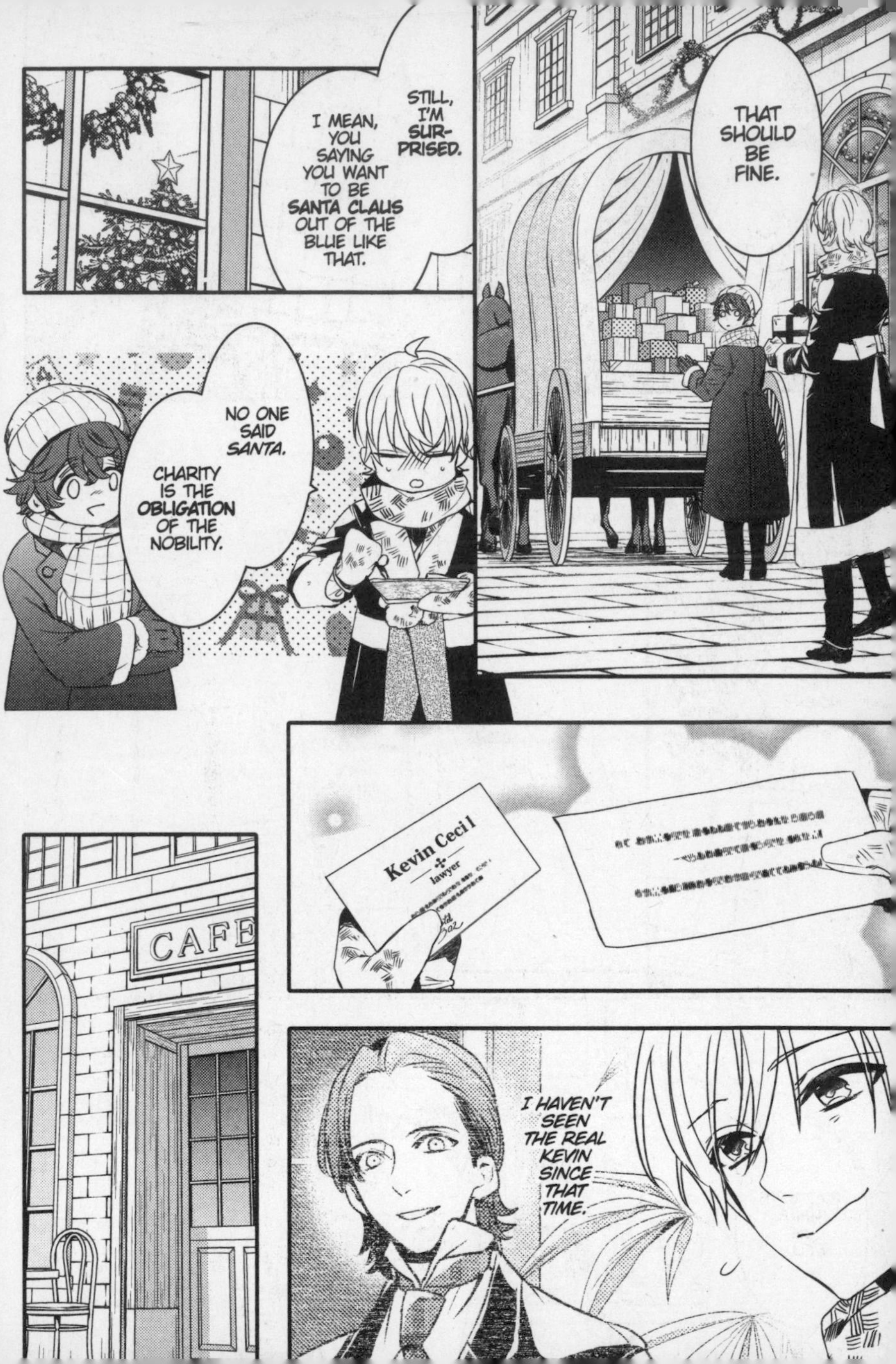
THAT SHOULD BE FINE.
STILL, I'M SUR-PRISED.
I MEAN, YOU SAYING YOU WANT TO BE SANTA CLAUS OUT OF THE BLUE LIKE THAT.
NO ONE SAID SANTA.
CHARITY IS THE OBLIGATION OF THE NOBILITY.
Kevin Cecil
lawyer
I HAVEN'T SEEN THE REAL KEVIN SINCE THAT TIME.
CAFE

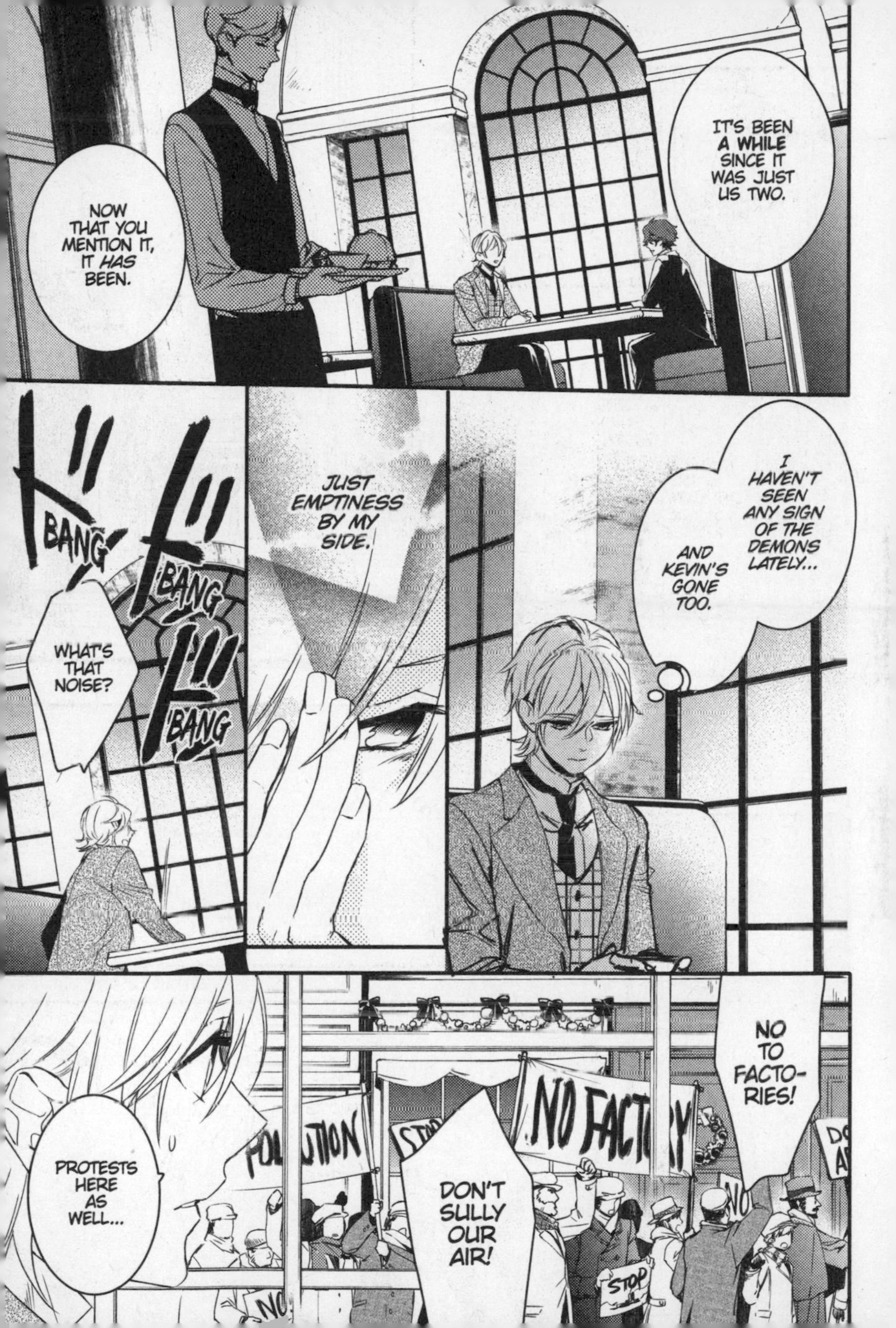
IT'S BEEN A WHILE SINCE IT WAS JUST US TWO.
NOW THAT YOU MENTION IT, IT *HAS* BEEN.
I HAVEN'T SEEN ANY SIGN OF THE DEMONS LATELY...
AND KEVIN'S GONE TOO.
JUST EMPTINESS BY MY SIDE.
BANG
BANG
BANG
BANG
WHAT'S THAT NOISE?
NO TO FACTORIES!
NO FACTORY
DON'T SULLY OUR AIR!
STOP
PROTESTS HERE AS WELL...

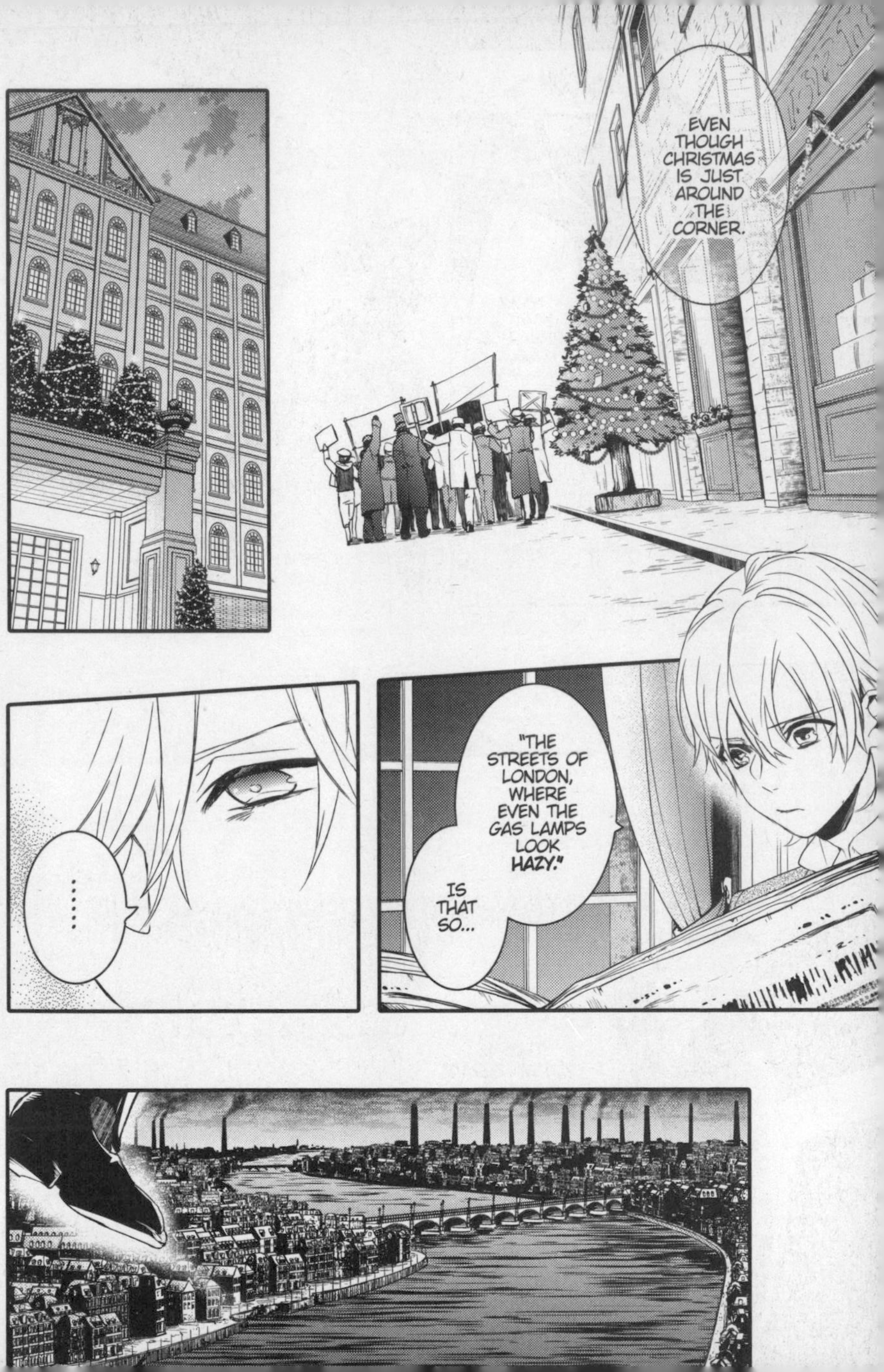
EVEN THOUGH CHRISTMAS IS JUST AROUND THE CORNER.
"THE STREETS OF LONDON, WHERE EVEN THE GAS LAMPS LOOK HAZY."
IS THAT SO...
......

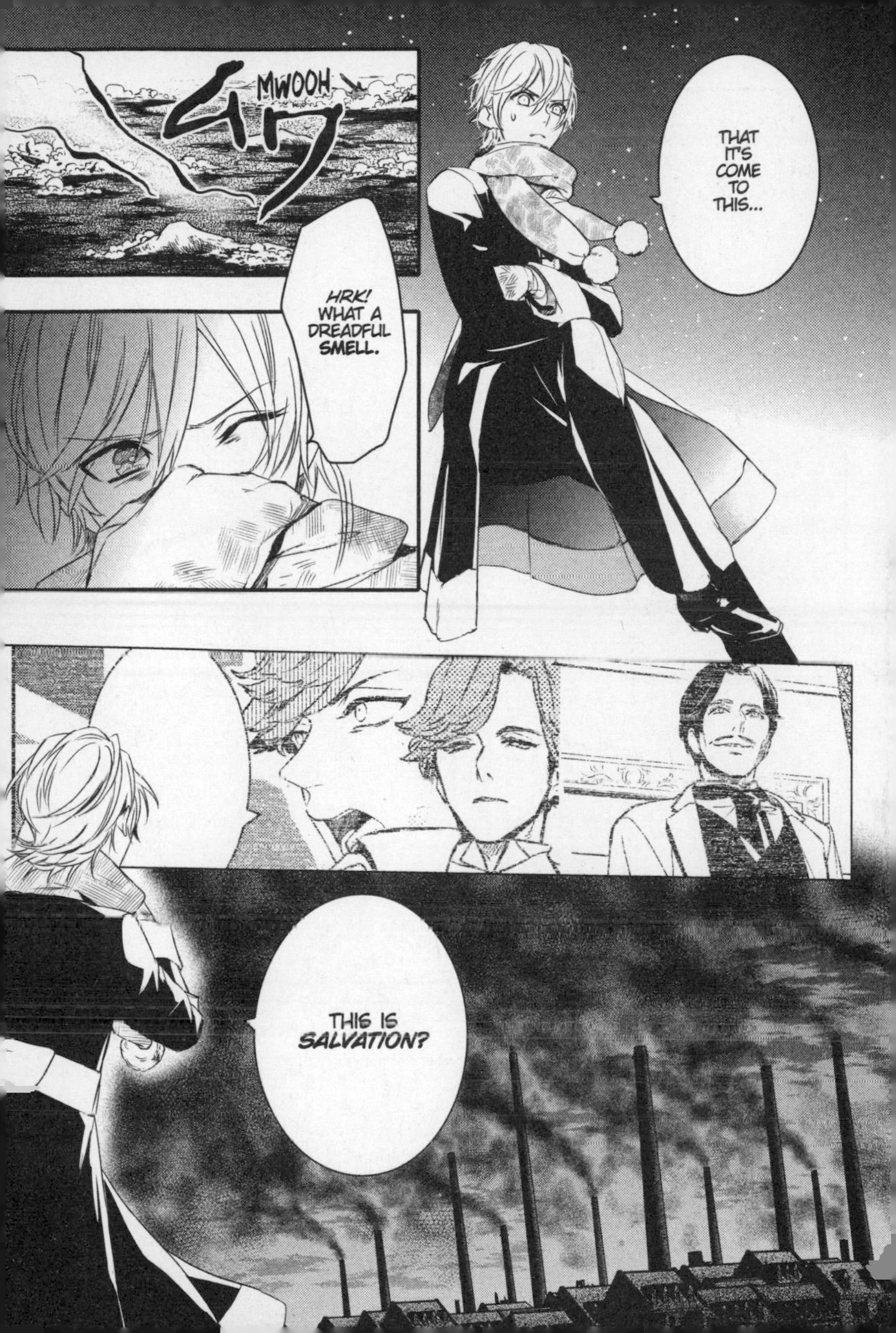
THAT IT'S COME TO THIS...
MWOOH
HRK! WHAT A DREADFUL SMELL.
THIS IS *SALVATION?*

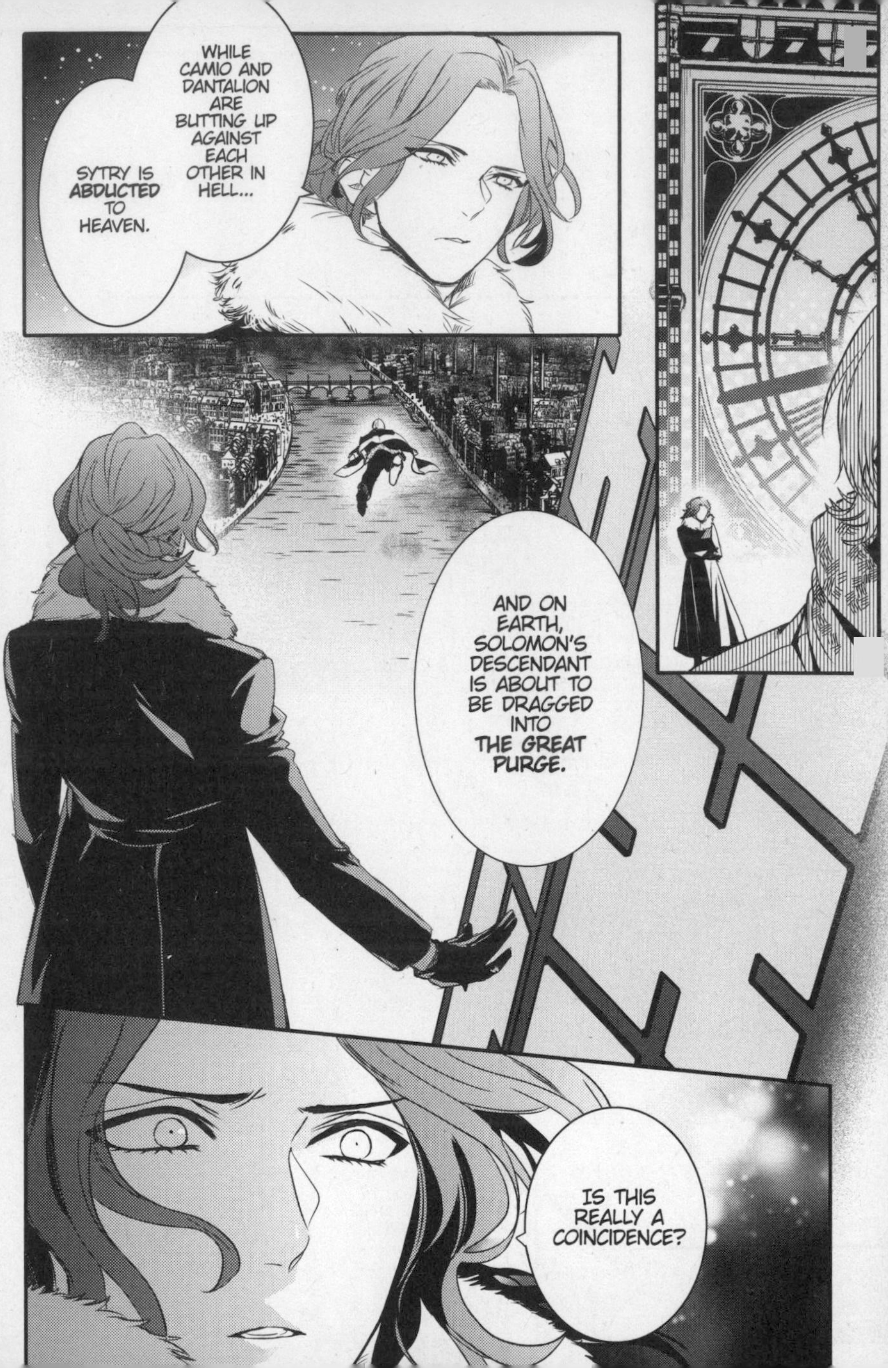
WHILE CAMIO AND DANTALION ARE BUTTING UP AGAINST EACH OTHER IN HELL...
SYTRY IS ABDUCTED TO HEAVEN.
AND ON EARTH, SOLOMON'S DESCENDANT IS ABOUT TO BE DRAGGED INTO THE GREAT PURGE.
IS THIS REALLY A COINCIDENCE?

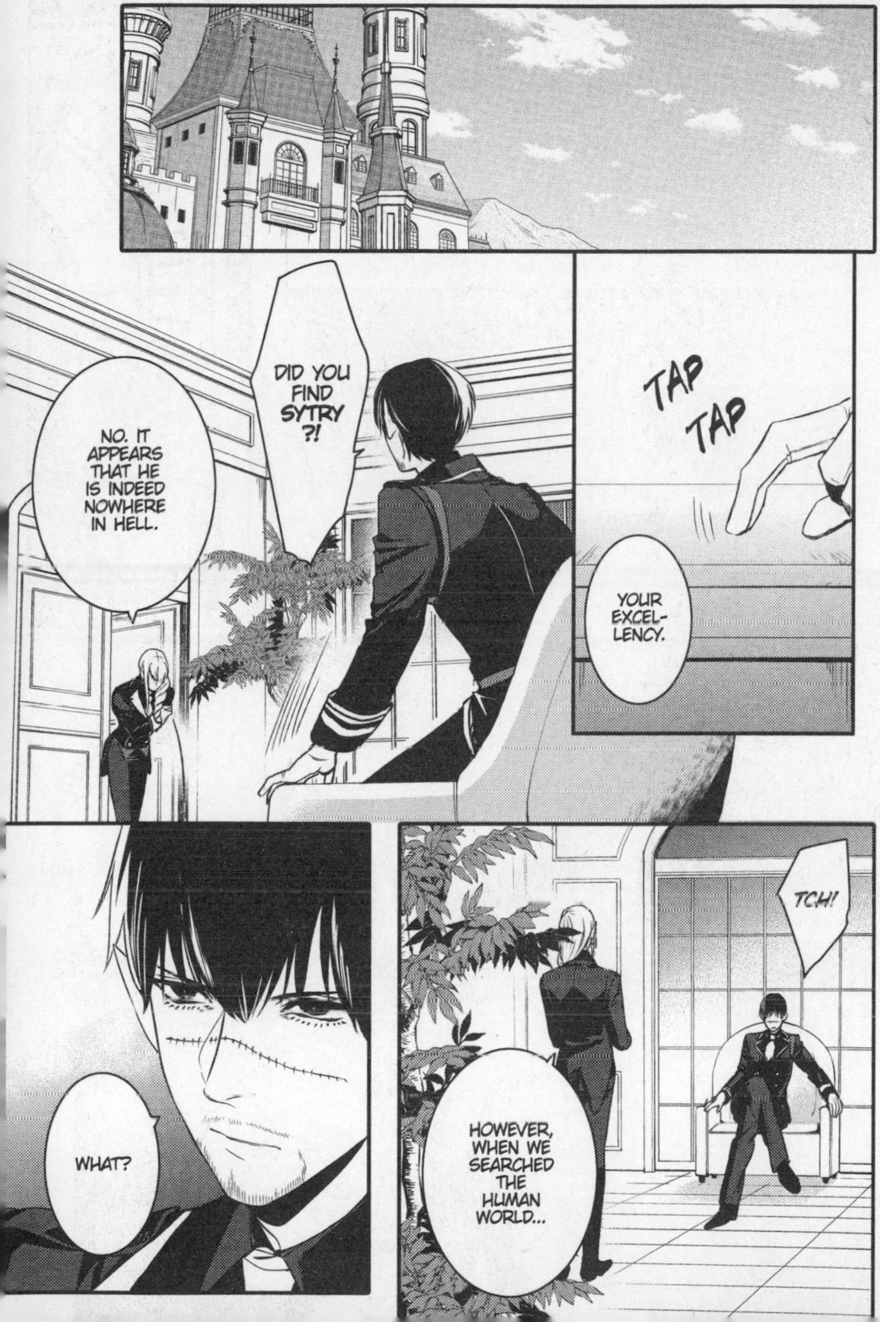
TAP
TAP
YOUR EXCEL-LENCY.
DID YOU FIND SYTRY ?!
NO. IT APPEARS THAT HE IS INDEED NOWHERE IN HELL.
TCH!
HOWEVER, WHEN WE SEARCHED THE HUMAN WORLD...
WHAT?

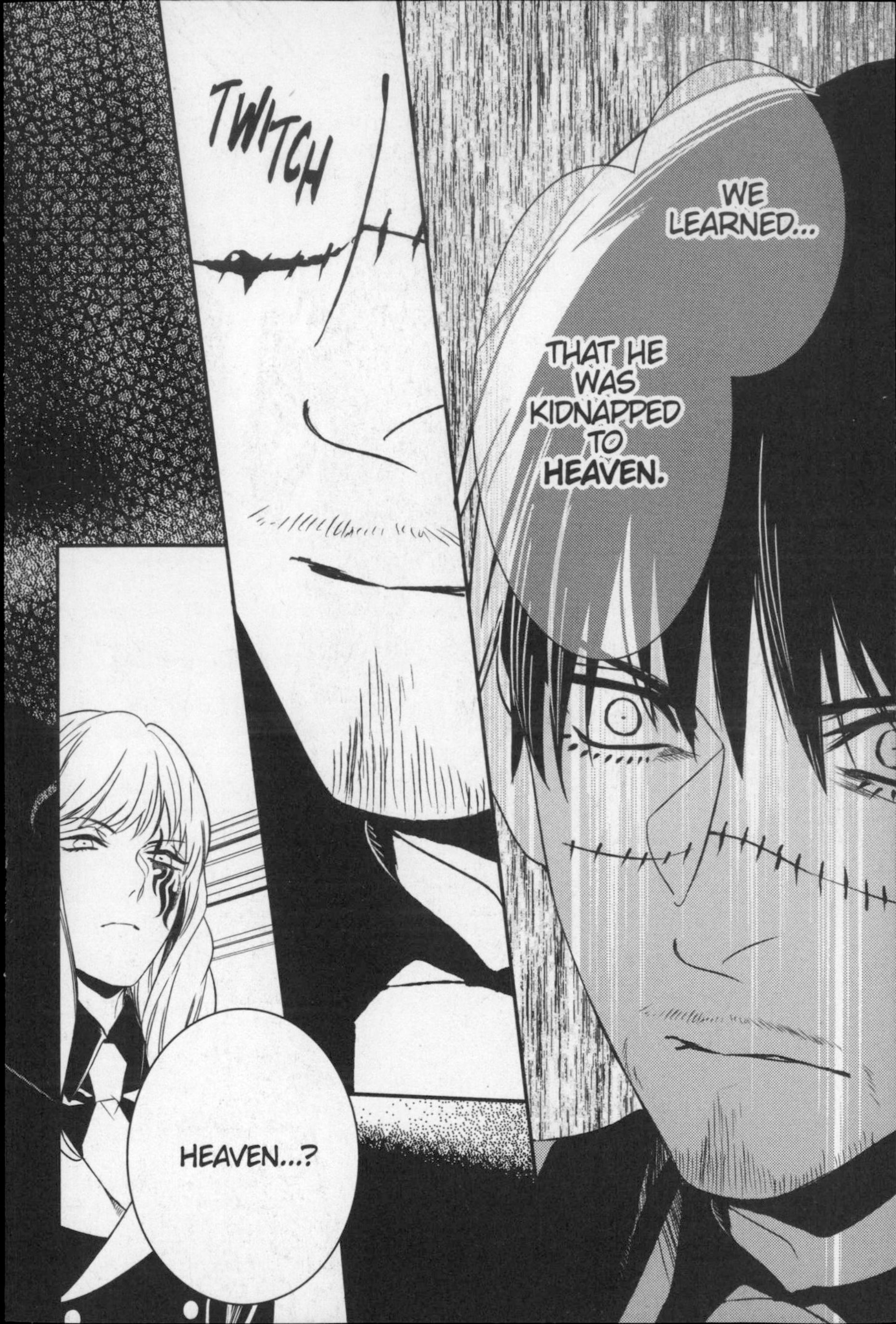
TWITCH
WE LEARNED...
THAT HE WAS KIDNAPPED TO HEAVEN.
HEAVEN...?

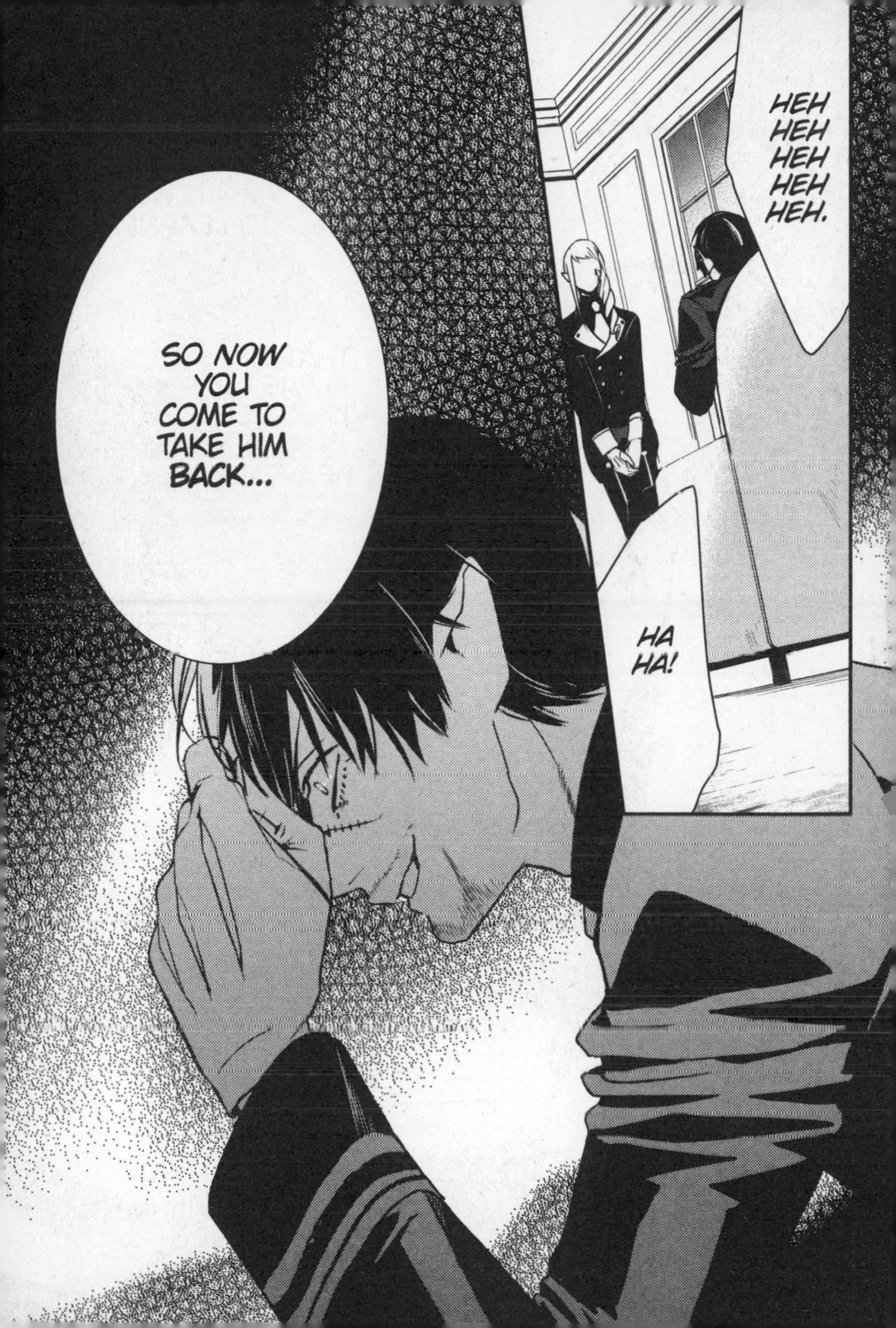
HEH HEH HEH HEH HEH.
HA HA!
SO NOW YOU COME TO TAKE HIM BACK...

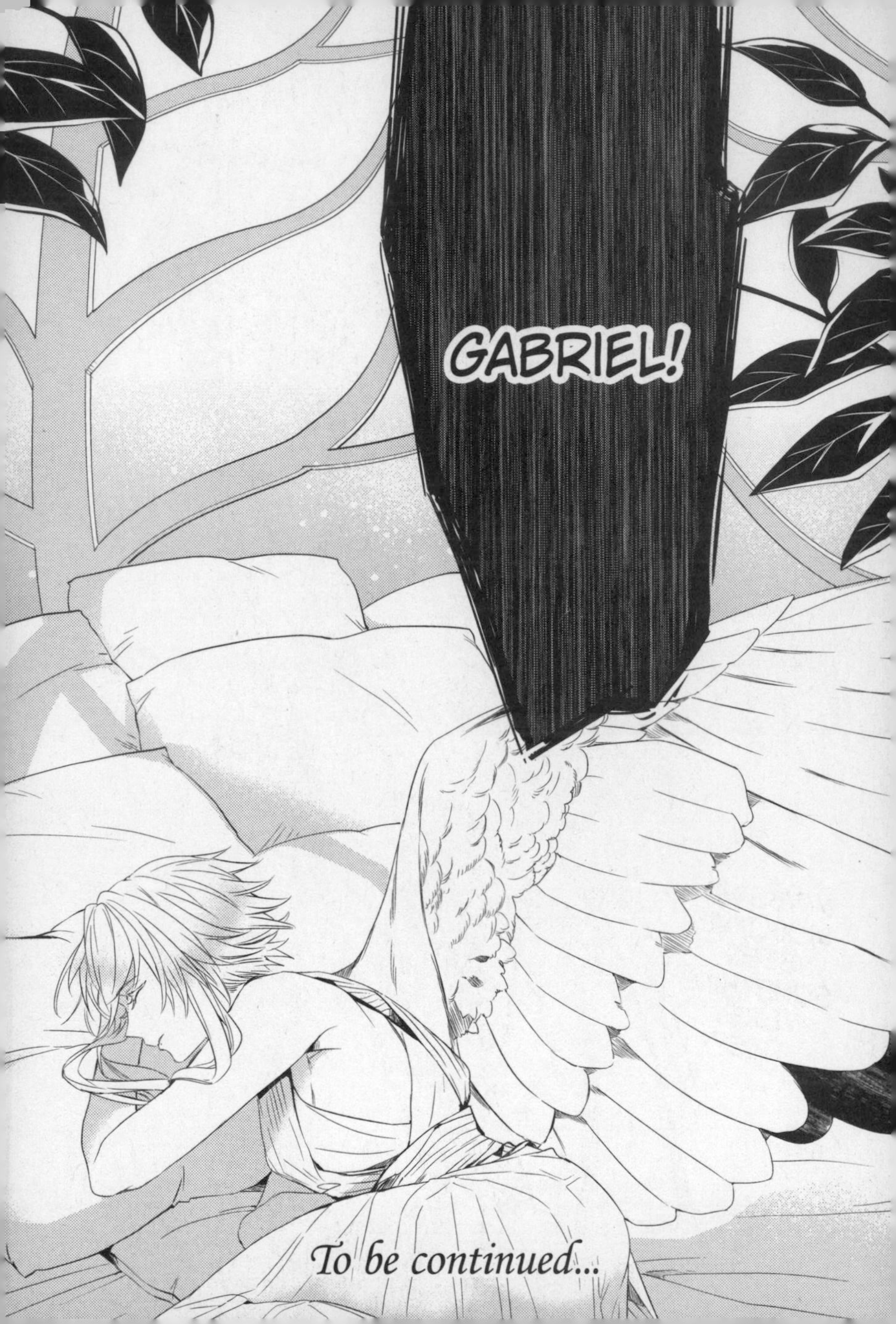
GABRIEL!
To be continued...

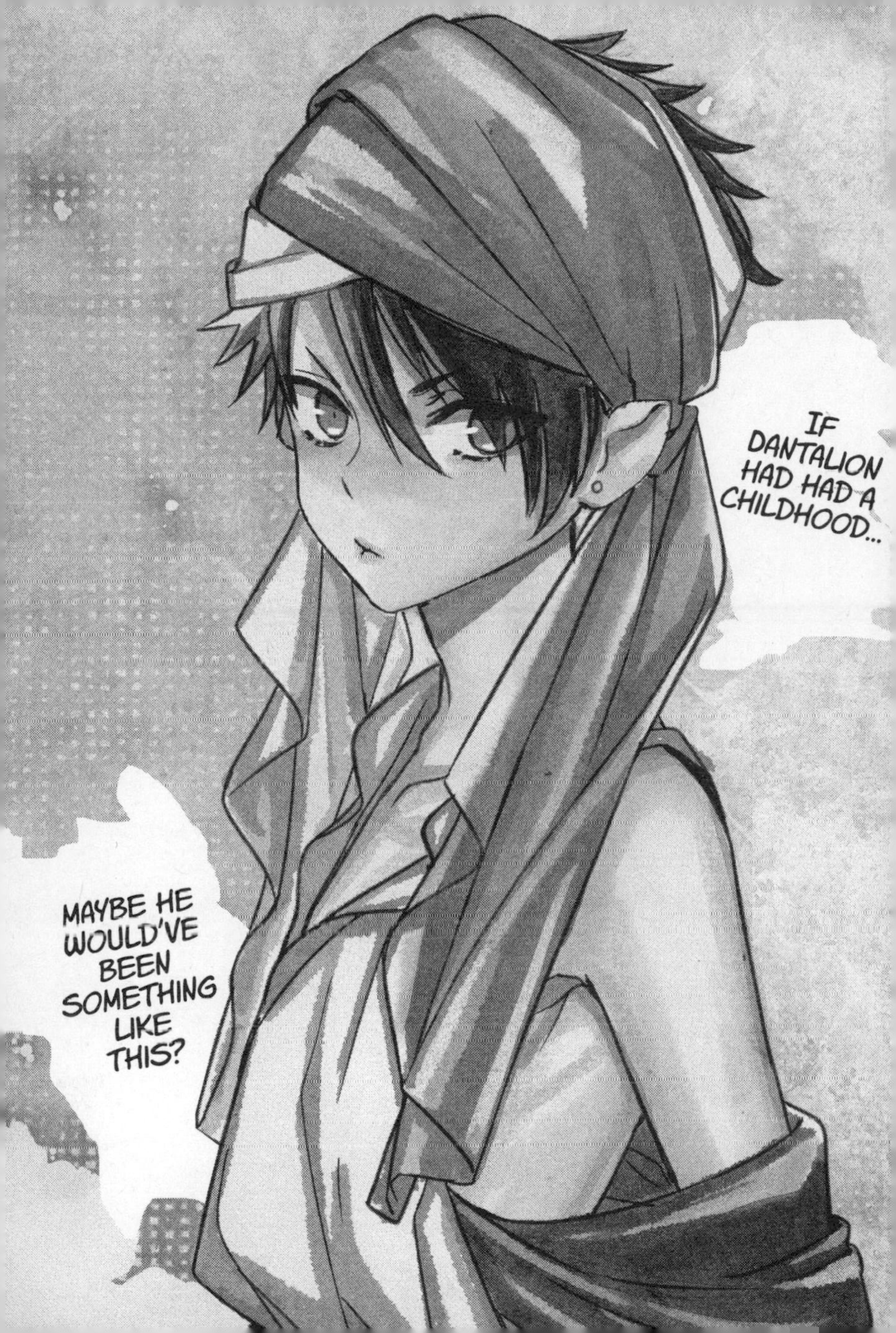
IF DANTALION HAD HAD A CHILDHOOD...
MAYBE HE WOULD'VE BEEN SOMETHING LIKE THIS?

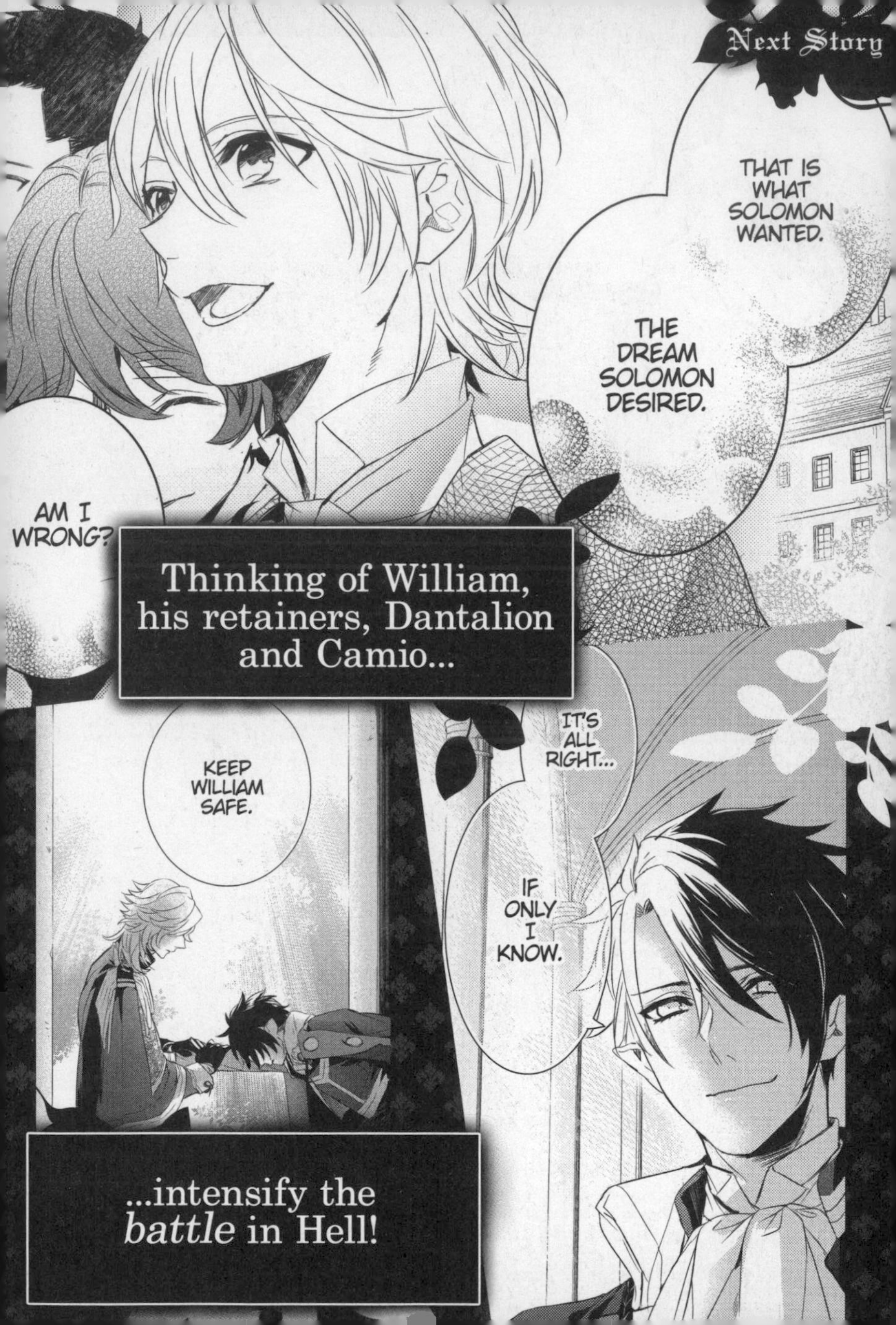
Next Story
THAT IS WHAT SOLOMON WANTED.
THE DREAM SOLOMON DESIRED.
AM I WRONG?
Thinking of William, his retainers, Dantalion and Camio...
IT'S ALL RIGHT...
IF ONLY I KNOW.
KEEP WILLIAM SAFE.
...intensify the *battle* in Hell!

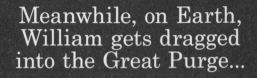

HE
BELONGS
TO
SOLOMON.

Meanwhile, on Earth,
William gets dragged
into the Great Purge...

IS THIS
SALVATION?

And Sytry's whereabouts
are not certain, either!

All the live coals burst into flames?!
The disorder of Volume 13 is
Coming Soon!